Progress in Thin-Layer Chromatography and Related Methods

Progress in Thin-Layer Chromatography and Related Methods

Volume I

A. Niederwieser and G. Pataki
Editors

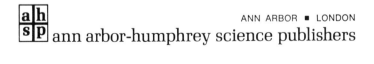
ANN ARBOR ■ LONDON
ann arbor-humphrey science publishers

© 1970 by Ann Arbor – Humphrey Science Publishers, Inc.
Drawer No. 1425, Ann Arbor, Michigan 48106

Library of Congress Catalog Card No. 73-94256
SBN 250-39968-7
Printed in the United States of America

Ann Arbor – Humphrey Science Publishers, Ltd.
5 Great Russell St., London, W. C. 1, England

The Editors

A. Niederwieser, Department of Chemistry, Universitäts-Kinderklinik, Zürich, Switzerland

G. Pataki, Pharmaceutical Department, Sandoz AG, Basel, Switzerland

Contributors to Volume 1

L. S. Bark, Department of Chemistry and Applied Chemistry, Salford University, Salford (Great Britain)

E. Moczar and M. Moczar, Laboratoire de Biochimie du Tissu Conjonctif, Paris (France)

L. J. Morris and B. W. Nichols, Unilever Research Laboratory, Colworth House, Sharnbrook, Bedford (Great Britain)

K. H. Scheit, Max-Planck Institut für experimentelle Medizin, Abteilung Chemie, Göttingen (W. Germany)

N. Seiler and M. Wiechmann, Max-Planck Institut für Hirnforschung, Arbeitsgr. Neurochemie, Frankfurt/M (W. Germany)

F. Snyder, Medical Division, Oak Ridge Associated Universities, Oak Ridge, Tenn. (USA)

E. Zappi, New York Medical College, Department of Microbiology, New York, N.Y. (USA)

Preface

Thin-layer chromatography is now one of the most widely applied methods of separation. A tremendous number of publications in almost all fields of chemistry, biochemistry and the medical sciences demonstrate the advantages of TLC for qualitative and quantitative analysis and for micropreparative purposes. There are several handbooks on this technique in general[1] and also on more specialized subjects.[2] However, it is impossible, particularly for the nonspecialist, to keep step with the present development since the number of publications increases exponentially. It was felt that a series of monographs written by specialists could reflect the continual advances more adequately and would be very useful to everybody interested in TLC. Because different chromatographic techniques are used simultaneously as well as in connection with many other physicochemical methods, it was decided that the series also should include the combination of TLC with other analytical techniques, *e.g.*, with radioactive techniques, gas chromatography, and reflectance spectroscopy.

The first volume of this international series contains seven contributions. Two of them (by L. S. Bark and F. Snyder) deal with the general problems of the R_M-function and its use in structural analysis, and of thin-layer radiochromatography. The other five chapters describe specialized subjects, such as the separation of lipids by Argentation-TLC (by L. J. Morris and B. W. Nichols), TLC of DANS-amines (by

---

1. Stahl, E., Ed., *Thin-Layer Chromatography* (New York: Academic Press, 1965); Randerath, K., *Thin-Layer Chromatography* (New York: Academic Press, 1965); Bobbitt, J. M., *Thin-Layer Chromatography* (New York: Reinhold, 1963); Truter, E. V., *Thin-Film Chromatography* (London: Cleaver-Hume, 1963); Kirchner, J. G., *Thin-Layer Chromatography* (New York: Interscience, 1967).

2. Neher, R., *Steroid Chromatography* (Amsterdam: Elsevier, 1964); Pataki, G., *Techniques of Thin-Layer Chromatography in Amino Acid and Peptide Chemistry* (Ann Arbor, Michigan: Ann Arbor Science Publishers, Inc., 1968).

N. Seiler and M. Wiechmann), TLC of iodoamino acids (by R. Zappi), the use of TLC in structural elucidation of glycoproteins (by E. Moczar and M. Moczar), and the separation of oligonucleotides (by K. H. Scheit).

All the authors, working, in general, at the forefront of their specialized field, were able to treat their subjects critically and authoritatively. The editors did not fix rigid rules, so some of the chapters are review-like while other authors treat the literature less comprehensively, and prefer to describe important techniques in detail.

The editors hope that this first volume as well as the following volumes of this series will be an aid for chemists, biochemists, biologists, clinical chemists and medical scientists in keeping step with the techniques of TLC and that it will help in the practical performance of their work.

Basle/Zürich, November 1969
A. Niederwieser
G. Pataki

Contents

TLC-Nomenclature xii

Chapter 1 1
L. S. BARK
*The R_M Function and Its Use in the Structural Analysis
of Organic Compounds*
    General Problems 1
    Determination of $\Delta R_{M(g)}$-Values 12
      Steroids 17
      Acids and Esters 25
      Phenols 28
      Amines 37
      Steric Factors 39
    The Use of ΔR_M-Values for Structural Elucidation 41
    Changes Brought about by Modification
      of Structure ($\Delta R_{M(r)}$-values) 43
    Conclusion 47
    References 48

Chapter 2 53
F. SNYDER
Thin-Layer Radiochromatography and Related Procedures
    Description of Techniques 53
      Elution Analysis 53
      Strip Scanning 55
      Autoradiography 57
      Zone Analysis: Area Scraping and Zonal Profile Scans
        by Liquid Scintillation Radioassay 58
      Beta Camera 60
      Combustion Analysis 61
    Radiation Safety Applied to Radiochromatographic Procedures 61
    Radiation Decomposition 62
    Radiopurity Determination 62
    Biochemical and Chemical Alterations
      Measured by TLC Radiochromatography 63
    The Use of Labeled Internal Standards
      in Studies of Chromatographic Resolution 63
    Mass Measurements by Radiometric Procedures 63
      Liquid Scintillation Quenching 63
      The Use of Labeled Derivatives 66

On-Line Computer Monitoring of
    Radiochromatographic Measurements 66
Specific Applications of Radiochromatography
    to Compounds of Biological Interest 67
Gas-Liquid Radiochromatography 67
    Combustion Techniques 67
    Noncombustion Techniques 68
References 69

Chapter 3 75
L. J. MORRIS and B. W. NICHOLS
Argentation Thin-Layer Chromatography of Lipids
    Introduction 75
    Fatty Acids 77
    Diglycerides and Triglycerides 82
    Phospholipids and Glycolipids 84
    References 88

Chapter 4 95
N. SEILER and M. WIECHMANN
TLC Analysis of Amines as Their DANS-Derivatives
    Reaction of Dansyl Chloride with Amines,
        Phenols, and Other Compounds 98
      Reactivity of Different Functional Groups 98
      Reaction Conditions 103
        Labeling of Amines and Phenols
          in the Nanomole Scale 104
        Synthesis of DANS-Derivatives in Preparative Scale 107
        Preparation of 1-Dimethylamino-naphthalene-
          5-sulphonyl Chloride 108
      Some Side Reactions 109
    TLC Separation of DANS-Amides 111
      General Considerations 111
      Generally Applicable Separating Systems 112
      Catechol Derivatives 117
      Aliphatic Diamines 118
      Choline 119
      Amino Sugars 120
      Rf-Values of DANS-Derivatives 127
    Quantitative Determination of DANS-Derivatives 127
      Fluorescence Characteristics of DANS-Derivatives 127
      Elution Method 128
      Direct Fluorometric Evaluation 131
      Microdetection of Amines in Tissues 135
      Estimation of Enzyme Activities 137
    Conclusion 138
    References 139

Chapter 5 147
E. ZAPPI
*Identification of Circulating Phenolic Iodoamino Acids by
Thin-Layer Chromatography*
    Chromatography on Silica Gel 150
    Chromatography on Cellulose 154

Other Techniques   157
Detection   157
Quantitative Determination   161
Extraction Procedures   163
References   164

Chapter 6   169

E. MOCZAR and M. MOCZAR
Thin-Layer Chromatography in Studies of Carbohydrate
Side Chains of Gylcoproteins

Analysis of the Monosaccharide Components   170
  Neutral Sugars   170
    Hydrolysis of Glycoproteins   170
    Hydrolysis of Glycopeptides   171
    Application of the Samples for TLC   171
    Chromatography on Inorganic Layers   171
    Chromatography on Cellulose Layers   174
    Chromatography on Thin-Layers of Organic Polymers   175
  Hexosamines   175
    Hydrolysis of Glycoproteins and of Glycopeptides   175
    Separation by TLC   175

Quantitative Determination of Neutral and Amino Sugars   176
  Densitometric Determination
        of Neutral Sugars and Osamines   177
  Spectrophotometric and Volumetric
        Determination after Elution   181
    Elution of the Spots   181
    Elution of the Nondetected Sugars   181

Separation of Sugars and Their Derivatives Formed
      by Partial Hydrolysis of Heteropolysaccharides   181
  Partial Hydrolysis with Mineral Acids   182
      Detection of the Aspartamido-Glucosaminic Linkage   182
  Partial Hydrolysis by Ion-Exchange Resin
        and Chromatography   182
    Hydrolysis   183
    Chromatography of Partial Hydrolysates   183
    Detection of Oligosaccharides   183
    Scope and Limitation of the Method   184
  Acetolysis of the Polysaccharides
        and TLC of the Products   184
    Acetolysis   185
    TLC of Acylated Sugar Derivatives   186
    Separation of the Deacylated Oligosaccharides   188

TLC of Methylated Sugars   189
  Methylation   189
  Hydrolysis of Methylated Polysaccharides   189
  Chromatography of Partially Methylated Sugars   189
  Detection of Partially Methylated Sugars   191
  Scope and Limitation of the Method   191
Conclusion   191
References   191

Chapter 7 197
K. H. SCHEIT

Layer Chromatography of Oligonucleotides
    Thin-Layer Chromatography
      of Oligonucleotides on Cellulose 198
    Silica Gel TLC of Deoxyoligonucleotide Triesters 198
    Preparative Layer Chromatography
      of Deoxyoligonucleotide Triesters 202
      Synthesis of Deoxythymidylyl-(3'-5')-3'-O-acetyl-
        4-thiodeoxythymidine-trichloroethylester 202
      Synthesis of 5'-O-Trityldeoxythymidylyl-
        (3'-5')-deoxythymidylyl-(3'-5')-3'-O-acetyl-
        4-thiodeoxythymidine-(bis)-trichloroethylester 203
    Silica Gel TLC of Oligonucleotides 204
    Preparative Layer Chromatography of
      Nucleotides and Oligonucleotides 212
    References 213

Appendix 215
    Conversion of Rf-Values to R_M-Values
    Rf-R_M Conversion Table 216
    References 218

Index 219

TLC-Nomenclature
Used in This Volume

The nomenclature used in TLC differs widely from author to author. Several expressions may give rise to misunderstandings, for example "development" which stands for "chromatography" as well as for "detection." Such expressions should be avoided completely. Other terms used in literature are not correct from the standpoint of physicochemistry: "mobile phase" is sometimes used for the liquid in the chromatographic chamber but should be restricted for the liquid moving within the chromatographic layer. Due to the existing nonequilibrium between the layer material and the solvent as well as the gas phase in the chamber, the composition of the mobile phase usually does not correspond to the composition of the solvent in the chamber and changes locally and temporarily on the chromatogram. Similarly, the composition of the surface of the chromatographic layer material, the "stationary phase" in the chromatographic sense, usually is not known. It seems to be more adequate to use terms like layer material, adsorbent, impregnated adsorbent, etc. To avoid any misunderstanding we list in the following some expressions used in this volume.

Term	Definition
adsorbent	a powder of at least about 50 m²/g specific surface area. In adsorption chromatography the adsorbent surface forms the stationary phase by interaction with the mobile phase and the gas phase in the chamber.
adsorption chromatography	chromatography on an adsorbent.

Term	Definition
to apply	to apply the test solution to the chromatographic layer.
bed	a layer or column of (porous) material containing the stationary phase, the interstices being filled with mobile phase.
chamber	the vessel in which chromatography takes place, usually a closed trough-chamber of a relatively large volume (see also sandwich-chamber).
chamber saturation	equilibration of the gas phase in the chamber with the solvent. By convention, chamber saturation is achieved by lining the walls of the trough-chamber with filter paper being in contact with the solvent. The time needed for saturation is reduced from about 1 hour to about 5 minutes by vigorously shaking the closed chamber for about 10 seconds. Chamber saturation prevents an appreciable evaporation of mobile phase from the chromatogram, but leads to an impregnation of the nonwetted part of the adsorbent layer with solvent vapors.
chromatogram	thin-layer during and after chromatography, or its reproduction.
to chromatograph	to make a chromatogram; to undergo chromatography.
chromatographic system	the whole physicochemical state under which chromatography occurs: adsorbent, solvent, chamber saturation, temperature, relative air humidity, technique (ascendent, horizontal, descendent), etc.
chromatographic technique	special arrangement used for chromatography, *e.g.*, descending solvent flow, multiple chromatography, running through technique, etc.
chromatography	multiple physiochemical equilibrium distribution of dissolved or vaporized substances between a stationary and a mobile phase, for the purpose of separation or characterization.
detection	visualization of chromatographed substances.
diluent	volatile liquid used for spreading a nonvolatile liquid stationary phase on a solid support.
elution	extraction of substances from layer material after chromatography.

Term	Definition
flow direction	direction of migration of the solvent in the layer.
front	the *visible* boundary between solvent wetted layer and "dry" layer material. It should be emphasized that the "dry"-appearing layer material may contain appreciable amounts (about 30% w/w) of solvent or solvent components if a trough chamber is used with chamber saturation.
GC, gas chromatography	chromatography using a gas as the mobile phase.
GLC, gas-liquid chromatography	chromatography using a gas as mobile phase and a liquid as stationary phase.
hRf	100 × Rf-value.
immersion line	line of application of the solvent to the layer.
impregnation	loading of the layer material with a solid or liquid (impregnant) to effect a change in the chromatographic properties of the layer.
iteration chromatography	multiple chromatography in the same direction using the same solvent.
layer	uniform sheet of porous material containing the stationary phase.
length of run	distance between starting point and solvent front.
to migrate	traveling of the sample or of the solvent front in flow direction.
mobile phase	liquid transporting the sample through the chromatographic bed (*e.g.*, layer), being in interaction with the stationary phase and the gas phase in the chamber. Therefore not a priori identical with the solvent.
multiple chromatography	chromatography repeated several times using the same or different solvents.
partition chromatography	chromatography on a layer material impregnated with a liquid which is not completely miscible but equilibrated with the solvent.
precoated sheets (plates)	commercially available thin-layer plates or sheets ready for chromatography.

Term	Definition
resolution	the degree of separation of two substances, measurable, *e.g.*, as $R = d/(w_1 + w_2)$, where d is the distance of the peak maxima, and w_1 and w_2 are the peak widths (at half height) of substance 1 and 2. Resolution is practically complete if $R \geqq 1.5$.
reversed phase chromatography	chromatography on a solid support impregnated (*e.g.*, using a volatile diluent) with a nonpolar and nonvolatile liquid as stationary phase. Chromatography is effected by a polar solvent equilibrated with the nonpolar liquid.
Rf-value	distance starting point to center of substance spot divided by the distance starting point to solvent front.
R_M-value	$\log\left(\dfrac{1}{Rf} - 1\right)$. Conversion table Rf − R_M see Appendix.
to run, run	to chromatograph, chromatography.
sample	substance(s) to be chromatographed.
sandwich-chamber	thin-layer plate covered by a cover plate at a distance of up to about 2 mm. Several devices are commercially available.
solvent	one- or multi-component liquid employed for chromatography, forming the mobile phase by interaction with the stationary phase and the gas phase in the chamber. Not a priori identical with the mobile phase.
start, starting point	point of application of the substance to be chromatographed, usually at a distance of 10 mm from the immersion line.
stationary phase	the surface region of an adsorbent or a stationary liquid dispersed on an inert support, being in interaction with the mobile phase.
TLC, thin-layer chromatography	liquid-solid or liquid-liquid chromatography on a layer up to 2 mm thick in a chamber containing a gas phase.
two-dimensional TLC	successive runs in directions orthogonal to each other.

The Editors

Chapter 1

The R_M Function and Its Use in the Structural Analysis of Organic Compounds

by L. S. Bark

The special fundamentals necessary for the employment of Martin's relation in TLC have also been reviewed elsewhere. It must be emphasized that it is absolutely necessary, at least in TLC, to check the chromatographic system for its applicability for structural analysis: many solvents used in TLC separate partially into their components on the chromatogram. Rf-values and R_M-values (see Appendix) measured in the usual way are often meaningless in these cases (M. Brenner, A. Niederwieser, G. Pataki, and R. Weber in *Thin-Layer Chromatography*, 1st ed. Ed. by E. Stahl, pp. 75 *et seq.*, 1962; A. Niederwieser, M. Brenner, Experientia **21**, 50, 105, 1965).

GENERAL PROBLEMS

Paper chromatography and thin-layer chromatography have been successfully used for some years as methods of separating individual organic substances from mixtures of related compounds. It is possible, if the material has been chromatographed previously under the same conditions, to use the separation obtained to establish qualitative evidence of the identity of the separated substances. Such evidence is generally based on the Rf-values, or on the color reactions of the substances corresponding to those of a standard substance or mixture. It is also possible to obtain a quantitative measure of the separated substances by comparison of spot color density, etc., with the corresponding parameter obtained for known amounts of standard materials. Using a different mass scale, it is possible to use the separation techniques for the isolation of sufficient quantities of a pure material to enable one to apply the techniques of mass spectrometry and related physical methods to the material and so obtain information concerning some of the groups present in the compound and, if sufficient analysis can be made, it is possible to obtain some structural or conformational analysis of the material.

It is not always necessary, however, to resort to other physical techniques for the structural analysis of some organic materials. Theoretically it is possible to utilize the techniques of chromatography and the results obtained directly from chromatography. It is with this idea that we are concerned at present.

The role of chromatography in structural analysis is based simply on the idea that the chromatographic behavior of a molecule in a particular chromatographic system is the result of a thermodynamically fundamental property of the molecule, and that if we slightly modify either the molecule by a suitable chemical reaction or the chromatographic system, then the resulting changes in chromatographic behavior are caused and determined by the structure of the molecule(s) concerned.

The theoretical basis for the study of the relationship between the structure of molecules and their chromatographic behavior is that initiated by Martin[1,2,3] who proposed a theoretical relationship between the chemical potential (μ) of a molecule and its partition coefficient (α) when the substance was chromatographed by partition chromatography. The partition coefficient was related to the Rf-value of the substance and subsequently to the R_M-value (as defined by Bate-Smith and Westall[4]).

For any consideration of the scope and limitations of the various methods proposed for the structural analysis of compounds, based on a study of their R_M-values obtained under various conditions, it is thus necessary to examine how this theoretical background was devised, what approximations and assumptions were made, and to assess in a critical manner how acceptable these ideas and assumptions are in the light of present day knowledge.

For an ideal solution, *i.e.*, one which obeys Raoult's Law:

$$\mu_A^S = \mu_A^{So} + RTlnN_A^S \tag{1}$$

where

μ_A^S equals the actual chemical potential of compound A

μ_A^{So} equals the chemical potential of compound A in some defined standard state

N_A^S equals the mole fraction of A in the phase S

R and T are the gas constant and the temperature (in °K) of the system.

If, as in much of chromatography, we have a two phase system where the two phases are in equilibrium, then if the two phases are denoted by superscripts S and L, when equilibrium is established, the chemical potentials of all components common to the two systems are the same.

Thus:

$$\mu_A^L - \mu_A^S = 0 = \mu_A^{Lo} - \mu_A^{So} + RTlnN_A^L - RTlnN_A^S$$

if

$$\Delta\mu_A = \mu_A^{Lo} - \mu_A^{So} = RTln\left[\frac{N_A^L}{N_A^S}\right]$$

where

$\Delta\mu_A$ equals the free energy necessary to transport 1 mole of A from phase S to phase L

since

N_A^L/N_A^S equals the partition coefficient (α) of the component A in the two phases L and S

then

$$\Delta\mu_A = RTln\alpha. \tag{2}$$

The molecule A will consist not only of one group but also of groups such as methylene (>CH$_2$), hydroxyl (-OH), amino (-NH$_2$), etc.
So

$$\Delta\mu_A = \Sigma m\Delta\mu_{CH_2} + n\Delta\mu_{OH} + o\Delta\mu_{NH_2} + \ldots \qquad (3)$$

where m, n, o, etc. signify the number of each specified group in the molecule.

Thus we can say that, assuming that there is no interaction between any groups within the molecule, the change in free energy necessary to transport the molecule A from one phase to the other is the sum of the free energies necessary to transport each of the individual groups from one phase to the other.

It follows, then, that if we have two molecules A and B, which differ by only one group—say, a methylene group—then the difference in the free energies necessary to transport A or B from one phase to the other will be the free energy necessary to transport one methylene group from one phase to the other.

The addition of any group—say, group X to the molecule A to form the compound B—alters the chemical potential and hence the logarithm of the partition coefficient of the compound between the two phases considered by a value, which depends only on the natures of X and of the phases used. In any chromatographic system, this alteration should be constant and independent of the molecular weight of the parent molecule and of the chemical nature of the parent molecule. Expressing this in mathematical terms:

if

$$B = A + X$$

then

$$\Delta\mu_B = \Delta\mu_A + \Delta\mu_X$$

and

$$\ln\alpha_B = \frac{\Delta\mu_A}{RT} + \frac{\Delta\mu_X}{RT}$$

thus

$$\ln\alpha_B - \ln\alpha_A = \frac{\Delta\mu_X}{RT}$$

rearranging terms:

$$\ln\frac{\alpha_B}{\alpha_A} = \frac{\Delta\mu_X}{RT} \, . \qquad (4)$$

Thus, the relationship between the partition coefficients of two substances differing only by a group X is determined solely by the nature of the phases employed.

The relationship between the partition coefficient of a solute and its chromatographic parameters arises from a consideration of partition chromatography as used originally in column chromatography and then applied to paper chromatography. The most widely used term is the Rf-value, which is always defined as the ratio of the migration distance of the solute from the point of application to the distance traveled by the solvent (measured from the same point). This Rf term is related to the partition coefficient by the following equation:

$$\alpha = \frac{A_L}{A_S}\left(\frac{1}{Rf} - 1\right) \tag{5}$$

where A_L and A_S are defined as the cross-sectional areas of the mobile phase and the stationary phase respectively and which are assumed to be uniform for the whole of the migration distances under consideration. Consden, Gordon, and Martin tested this equation experimentally, using a paper chromatographic system, by using a given water content for the paper. From this, and from a knowledge of the weights of the dry paper and the wet chromatogram, they were able to deduce the phase ratio (A_L/A_S). The water content of the paper was chosen so that for one of the compounds studied the values of the partition coefficient obtained by direct measurement and calculated from the above equation were in agreement. This established the relationship between the partition coefficient and the Rf-value of a solute when they are both determined under the same experimental conditions.

This relationship has been systematically investigated by several workers in column chromatography, paper chromatography, and in thin-layer chromatography, and varying results have been obtained. These are discussed later. Earlier workers, such as Mulvany,[5] who tested the equation on a series of sugars, and Benson,[6] who investigated a series of carboxylic acids, attempted the verification of the equation without determining the actual A_L/A_S ratio, but they assumed certain values. Bate-Smith and Westall[4] examined the Martin postulates with respect to paper partition chromatography. They showed that a wide variety of natural polyphenolic compounds of the flavone type obeyed Martin's theory very closely indeed. They suggested that the A_L/A_S may be regarded as having a constant value K_1 for any given system. Thus Equation 5 becomes

$$\alpha = K_1\left(\frac{1}{Rf} - 1\right)$$

and

$$\ln\alpha = \ln K_1\left(\frac{1}{Rf} - 1\right).$$

From Equation 2, since

$$\Delta\mu_A = RT\ln\alpha$$

$$\ln\alpha = \ln K_1 \left(\frac{1}{Rf} - 1\right) = \frac{\Delta\mu_A}{RT}. \qquad (6)$$

The term $\ln K_1 \left(\dfrac{1}{Rf} - 1\right)$ is more directly related to the partition coefficient and the chemical potential of a particular solute, than is the simple term Rf. They introduced a term R_M^* such that

$$R_M = \log_{10} \left(\frac{1}{Rf} - 1\right). \qquad (7)$$

Rearranging Equations 6 and 7 we have

$$\log_{10}e \cdot \log_{10}\alpha_A = \log_{10}K_1 \cdot \log_{10}e \cdot R_{M(A)}$$

$$= \log_{10}e \cdot \frac{\Delta\mu_A}{RT}.$$

In any given system, if T is kept constant, it follows since R, K_1, and $\log_{10}e$ are constant or are assumed to be constant:

$$\log_{10}\alpha = K_2 + R_{M(A)} = \frac{\Delta\mu_A}{RT} + K_2.$$

Thus, from Equation 4 and by rearranging terms we have

$$\log_{10}e \cdot (R_{M(A)} - R_{M(B)}) = \frac{\Delta\mu_x}{RT}.$$

Thus, ΔR_M for the introduction of a group X into a molecule A to give a molecule B, is constant for a given system.

Since the free energy of the whole molecule is considered to be the sum of the partial free energies of the single functional groups constituting the molecule, we can see that the R_M-value for the whole molecule is the sum of the partial ΔR_M-values for the constituent functional groups, and from Equation 3:

$$R_{M(A)} = K + m\Delta R_{M(CH_2)} + n\Delta R_{M(OH)} + o\Delta R_{M(NH_2)} + \ldots \qquad (8)$$

This is the basic equation for the structural analysis of organic compounds by the measurement of their chromatographic parameters. The value of K depends on the chromatographic system used and may be termed the fundamental, ground, or system constant.

Since the original equations were derived for partition chromatography but are independent of the mechanism of chromatography, provided the distribution isotherm is linear, the basic equation should apply equally as well to any other distribution system.

*Rf to R_M conversion table, see Appendix.

The problems associated with using ΔR_M-values are naturally dependent upon obtaining accurate, precise, and reproducible Rf-values, and on the validity of one of the main assumptions inherent in the derivation of the equation relating R_M and Rf, namely, that the ratio of A_L/A_S is a constant over the range of chromatographic conditions studied. It is accepted practice in chromatography to report Rf-values to ±0.02 or in some special cases ±0.01 Rf units. By implication, then, any two experimental values which differ by 0.04 or less Rf units, or in the special cases by 0.02 or less Rf units, are regarded as being the same value. It can readily be seen that only certain ranges of Rf-values can be useful when considering analysis involving R_M-values. Consider three compounds—A, B, and C—whose Rf-values are accepted as

$$Rf_A = 0.10 \qquad Rf_B = 0.50 \qquad Rf_C = 0.90$$

Thus, assuming that the experimental conditions are sufficiently standardized so that values are accepted with a tolerance of ±0.02 units, the R_M-values for the three substances can be considered between the following ranges:

Compound	A		B		C	
	Rf	R_M	Rf	R_M	Rf	R_M
Upper	0.12	0.865	0.48	0.035	0.88	−0.865
Lower	0.08	1.061	0.52	−0.035	0.92	−1.061
Difference		0.196		0.070		0.196

These variations are significant. They are brought about by the logarithmic relationship between R_M and Rf and by the fact that the reciprocal of Rf is used in the calculation of R_M. Some measure of the significance of this variation in R_M at upper and lower 10% of the Rf range is brought better into perspective if one considers that a difference of 0.10 Rf units in the Rf-values 0.45 and 0.55 produces a ΔR_M of only 0.174 R_M units. This is less than that of 0.196 at the Rf-values of 0.10 and 0.90 for Rf-values considered to be experimentally identical.

Implicit in the Rf/R_M relationship is the assumption made by Bate-Smith and Westall that the A_L/A_S ratio remains constant. From Equation 5 it can be seen that under ideal solution conditions the R_M of the substance will vary if the A_L/A_S ratio varies, and hence the total effect on the R_M-value can be quite significant. It is thus necessary to examine how tenable this assumption is in practice.

In liquid-liquid column chromatography, the assumed constancy of the phase volumes and hence the ratio of the cross-sectional areas of the phases is dependent upon the evenness of the packing of the column. In paper chromatography and thin-layer chromatography the system can suffer from a lack of a lateral restraining boundary. In the original work on this problem,[4] the weight of the mobile phase used was determined and from this the cross-sectional area A_L was calculated; an assumed water content was used to calculate A_L/A_S. There are of course errors inherent in this assumption, and Consden, Gordon, and Martin pointed out that the Rf-values were apparently dependent on the distance of the starting line from the point at which the solvent entered the paper, measured from the solvent reservoir. This implies that the stationary phase may vary with the amount of solvent used.

In a much more detailed study by Giddings, Stewart and Ruoff[7] it was shown that movement of the solvent (*n*-butanol) through paper was a true diffusion phenomenon and obeyed diffusion equations. There exists a gradient, in the weight of solvent per unit length of paper, which is not strictly linear. This work substantiated previous work involving aqueous solvents.[8] In this latter work it was shown that there is apparently little or no correlation between the density or surface tension of a solvent and its rate of rise and migration through the paper. As would be expected, there was a moderate correlation with the viscosity. They found that with liquids containing the same number of carbon atoms, the rate of rise at a specific height falls off in the following order: hydrocarbons, ethers, esters, alkyl halides, ketones, carboxylic acids and alcohols. It may well be that this is due to the tendency of some of the solvents to form hydrogen bonds with the cellulose units of the paper. Bush[9] attributes the swelling of cellulose to a similar cause and reports that although aqueous solvents may swell cellulose much more than water alone, the overall effects are somewhat obscure. He remarks that the volume of the stationary phase increases more than does the volume of the interstices. We may thus infer that this will alter the ratio of the volumes of the two phases, since the solvent may be regarded as filling the interstices and providing a covering over the stationary phase.

With impregnated papers, various workers[10, 11] have reported that the method of impregnation can cause considerable changes in the Rf-values by altering the phase ratio. Green and Marcinkiewicz[12] consider that impregnated papers, prepared by dipping them in a solution of the stationary phase in a volatile organic diluent and then allowing the solvent to evaporate while the papers were suspended in air, are not suitable for the determination of Rf-values and subsequently R_M-values, with the accuracy required for testing the Martin equation, and hence for use in the structural analysis of compounds. They consider that there is a significant gradient of stationary phase produced by gravity in the direction that the paper is hung for drying. They thus advocate the use of "tankless chromatography." The production of papers by their recommended method is a tedious process and is scarcely used by other

workers. However, Green and Marcinkiewicz have recognized this and
suggest that more conventional methods can be used provided that the
Rf-values of certain key compounds or standards have been obtained
under "tankless" conditions. It is then, in their opinion, admissible to
use these values along with those of unknown compounds of similar Rf
range, and hence to obtain structural relationships. Without giving any
reasons, they impose two restrictions on the use of Rf-values so obtained:

1. The Rf-values must lie between 0.20 and 0.80.
2. The running time should not exceed 5 hours.

They stress, however, that the Rf-values obtained by conventional chromatographic methods are usually different from those obtained under
"tankless" conditions, and that they cannot be directly compared with
each other. They suggest that if the conventional chromatography is
carried out as practically ideally as possible, then it is permissible to
compare ΔR_M values from each type of system.

Copius-Peereboom[13] investigated the properties of the chromatographic system, paraffin oil–acetic acid–water, as applied to the analysis
of sterols. The variation of the cross-sectional areas occupied by the
stationary and the mobile phases was studied. After development, the
chromatogram was cut into successive zones, each representing about
15% of the solvent traverse. The quantity of acetic acid was determined
by titration; the amount of water was calculated by assuming similar
solvent gradients for water and acetic acid. The paraffin content was
determined gravimetrically. The data given indicated that the amount
of paraffin oil in each zone is not the same; that there is a slight increase
along the chromatogram. The amount of mobile phase, on the other
hand, greatly decreased in the higher zones of the chromatogram. There
was apparently a steep decrease in the amount of mobile phase about
halfway up toward the solvent front. Copius-Peereboom states that this
is probably caused by a weakening of the ascending capillary forces.
As a result of both effects, the A_L/A_S ratio apparently decreased linearly
from start to solvent front. A similar decrease had been found by other
workers using petroleum–acetic acid–water,[14] and undecane–acetic
acid–water.[15]

Reversed phase thin-layer chromatography using cellulose as a support for a series of impregnants has been reported by many workers. In
cases where the layers were prepared by slurrying a mixture of the impregnant in a volatile diluent with the chromatographic grade cellulose
powder and allowing the diluent to evaporate while the plate was horizontal, the probability of gravity producing a gradient on the plate is
zero. The amount of impregnant and the amount of solvent have been
determined. Bark and Duncan[16] investigated the distribution of a re-

versed phase of tri-n-butyl phosphate and a series of solvents of various concentrations of hydrochloric acid.

Bark and Halstead[17] investigated the distribution of a reversed phase of a long chain amine on cellulose when various concentrations of hydrochloric acid were used as solvents. In all cases the impregnated cellulose layers were divided into bands parallel to the solvent front. The bands were removed, weighed, washed free of impregnant, and reweighed. The solvent in each band was determined gravimetrically. The A_L/A_S ratio for a given band was calculated from the measured volumes of stationary phase and mobile phase. The amount of acid extracted by the stationary phase was calculated, and the actual volume of the stationary phase, as a result of this extraction, was calculated.

The phase ratios along the plate were not constant and varied with the molarity of the acid used. The distributions of the reversed phases were reasonably constant; the greatest variation in any one plate was less than 5%. Although the profiles obtained for the two dissimilar reversed phases were somewhat different, each was reasonably linear at bands corresponding to Rf-values of 0.15 to 0.80. The variations may well be caused by some hydrogen bonding between the acid solvent and the cellulose support which had previously been regarded as inert or inactive. A significant contribution to the work on phase ratios is that of Daly,[18] who studied the chromatography of phenols on reversed phases of formamide and methylated formamide impregnated onto cellulose. Hexane was used as the solvent, and Daly investigated the ratio *in situ* by using ^{14}C-labeled formamides to investigate the distribution of the impregnant as the chromatography proceeded. On another set of plates he investigated the solvent distribution by using hexane marked with ^{14}C-labeled cyclohexane. His results show that for this system, where the solvent cannot form hydrogen bonds with either the "inert" cellulose or the impregnant, for a given loading of any particular amide, the phase ratio was remarkably constant over the range equivalent to Rf-values of 0.1 to 0.9 units.

There are thus cogent experimental reasons for restricting the use of ΔR_M-values to those obtained from Rf-values in the range of 0.1 to 0.9 units, even when the system is as nearly ideal as possible. In other systems it may be necessary to compare ΔR_M-values with those from standard compounds, which chromatograph into the same regions of the plate as do the compounds under consideration. Since it is often necessary to utilize the results obtained by one set of workers using various experimental conditions, and to compare them with results obtained by other workers, it is perhaps important at this stage to consider what assumptions have been made and what significance should be given to each one.

There are two points which are fundamental to the production of meaningful Rf-values:

1. The concentrations of solute employed throughout should be such that the solution approximates the ideal.
2. The two phases do not alter in composition over the chromatographic run, they have a constant cross-sectional ratio, and there is an equilibrium distribution of the solute between the phases at all times.

These two assumptions alone indicate that several experimental parameters must be carefully controlled, *e.g.,* variations in the temperature of the system not only will alter the distribution isotherm but also may cause alteration of the composition of the solvent system especially in a multi-component system. Also, it may cause the establishment of steady-state conditions in contradistinction to equilibrium conditions.

Multi-component systems are particularly affected by change in temperature. Bark and Graham[19] working with phenoxyacetic acids chromatographed on cellulose, using a monophasic *n*-butanol–ammonium hydroxide solvent at temperatures of $20\pm1\,^{\circ}C$, found that on increasing the temperature to about $23\,^{\circ}C$ the *n*-butanol separated, causing a severe alteration in the composition of the solvent and consequent variation in the Rf- and R_M-values. Rubin and co-workers[20] found that the Phenyl Cellosolve-heptane system appears to reverse its phase with rise in temperature, and consequently R_M-values may be very unreliable close to the critical temperature.

The major, and indeed the most critical, assumptions in the basic equation (Equation 8) are that the introduction of a substituent group into a molecule has no effect on any group already in the molecule, and that the same group has the same effect however arranged in the molecule. Martin has pointed out that there are very severe limitations regarding this assumption, and various workers have indicated that the word "group" must be more closely defined before any theoretical interpretation can be attempted. Bush[21] in his consideration of this point suggests that for any given type of solvent system, the effect of a substituent in a *given position and orientation* is highly characteristic, in terms of ΔR_M-values, when compared with other positions and orientations. He suggests that the word "group" should not be taken to mean just primary or secondary hydroxyl, carbonyl, amino, etc., but should also be defined by position.

Martin has suggested that one of the main reasons for the apparent failure of the simple treatment lies in stereochemical factors as well as in the various electronic interactions that can occur when a group is introduced into a molecule.

In many compounds are groups which can be regarded as the main chromatographically functional group. This group, or these groups, will to a large extent dominate the chromatographic behavior of the molecule, and it is the electronic or steric effects on these groups which will be manifested as possible deviations from the simple approximation. Wherever there is a group that takes part in pronounced or obvious electronic interaction with one or another of the phases, it is this group that will be affected radically by changes in the electron density of the molecule.

So far we have mentioned only the constitutional effects which alter the R_M of a compound, but it is always to be emphasized that the R_M of a compound should really be defined with respect to a particular chromatographic system, since the partition coefficient of a solute must be related to the nature of the phases. The relationship between the partition coefficients and the phase composition has been the subject of several papers.[22-25] Soczewinski and co-workers[26-28] have commented on the parallelism between partition chromatographic parameters and the solubility of the solute in one of the phases. These studies have generally been aimed at obtaining some idea of the mechanism of the chromatographic process, so that the nature of the chromatographically functional group can be ascertained. If the solute and solvent interact in one system—say by hydrogen bonding—but do not interact in another solvent system under consideration, then there will be difficulty in applying the Martin additivity theory to a consideration of the molecular parameters, which determine the R_M-values. In an investigation[28] involving three alkaloids (brucine, cinchonine, and codeine) chromatographed in solvent systems of the type *m*-xylene–*n*-pentanol–buffer solution and tetralin–cyclohexanone–buffer solution, it was reported that in spite of the strong molecular interactions involved, there was a great amount of similarity between the R_M versus composition and log C_s (where C_s = solubility in moles per liter) versus composition relationships. Some correlation was reported between the solubility of some naphthols in nonpolar and weakly polar solvents such as hydrocarbons and chlorinated hydrocarbons, and the R_M-values in the corresponding solvent systems.

The importance of selecting the appropriate solvent systems for the purpose of obtaining ΔR_M-values cannot be overemphasized. Since the ΔR_M-value of the constituent group of a solute in two solvent systems is proportional to the free energy necessary for the transfer of the particular group from one phase to the other, it follows that the more the natures of the two systems are different, then the larger will be the difference in the energy required, or the larger will be the difference in the R_M-values. In partition chromatography, the greater the immiscibility of the two phases, then the greater the difference in the R_M-values. In the cases where adsorption plays an important role, the emphasis will be on the relative strengths of the interaction of the chromatographed substance with the adsorbent, or if this is common to both systems, the difference in the two R_M-values will depend on the relative ease of interaction of the solute with the mobile phases. Obviously, if the interaction between the solute and the adsorbent is small, the free energy required for the transfer of the solute to the mobile phase will also be small, and the difference in R_M-values of the molecule will be determined mainly by the relative natures of the mobile phases.

It may be seen from the foregoing work that changes in the R_M of a compound can thus be brought about by changes in the constituent groups and by changes in the solvent system. It is proposed that the system used by Bush[9] be followed: to distinguish these changes by using the term $\Delta R_{M(g)}$ to denote the change in R_M brought about by the addition of a single group into the molecule, and by using the term $\Delta R_{M(s)}$ for the change in R_M of a particular molecule when it is chromatographed in two different systems, either two partition systems or two adsorption systems. In some of the work using ΔR_M-values for structural analysis, it is common to observe the effect of reacting a compound to cause substitution of one group in the original compound by another group, *e.g.*, oxidation of, say, a primary alcohol to an acid. The change in the R_M-values of the *two* compounds is often significant, and because of this Bush proposed to use a term $\Delta R_{M(r)}$. (This is the change in R_M brought about by chemical modification.)

Thus the R_M terms in use will be:

(1) R_M — being proportional to the fundamental constant and the sum of the $\Delta R_{M(g)}$ for all the particular groups which constitute a molecule

(2) $\Delta R_{M(g)}$ — the difference in the R_M-values of the substances, differing only by the addition of one group to one compound and chromatographed under identical conditions

(3) $\Delta R_{M(s)}$ — the difference in the R_M-values of a compound when chromatographed in two systems

(4) $\Delta R_{M(r)}$ — the difference in the R_M-values of two compounds, brought about by the chemical modification of one group in the molecule. The two compounds are chromatographed under identical conditions.

DETERMINATION OF $\Delta R_{M(g)}$-VALUES

As previously indicated (Equation 8) the R_M-value of a compound is related to the $\Delta R_{M(g)}$-values of its constituent groups by the relationship

$$R_{M(A)} = K + m\Delta R_{M(CH_2)} + n\Delta R_{M(OH)} + 2 \ldots$$

where

$\Delta R_{M(CH_2)} \equiv \Delta R_{M(g)}$ for the methylene group

and

$\Delta R_{M(OH)} \equiv \Delta R_{M(g)}$ for the hydroxyl group.

This fundamental constant K is a composite factor that includes the system constant, which depends upon the natures of the phases used, or the "inert" support (in the case of partition chromatography by reversed phase systems).

It is not possible to calculate either group constants or the fundamental constant from first principles; they can only be determined experimentally. This is not easy. For the determination of group constants there are not many series of compounds which differ only by the sequential introduction of a similar group. The exception is homologous series, which differ by the addition of a methylene group—CH_2. Although there are other series, one problem encountered by the introduction of more polar groups is that it soon becomes necessary to change the polarity of the chromatographic system.

The determination of the fundamental constant by experimental methods requires that one choose a fairly simple compound. Prochazka,[29] in a discussion of the meaning of the fundamental constant, quotes as an example the case of adipic acid:

$$R_M = K + 4\Delta R_{M(CH_2)} + 2\Delta R_{M(COOH)}$$

If the R_M-value of adipic acid is measured in a chosen system, and from its value we subtract $2 \times \Delta R_{M(g)}$ for the carboxyl group, and $4 \times \Delta R_{M(g)}$ for the methylene group, then the value for the constant K is obtained. As Prochazka indicated, the method of calculating K suggests a somewhat paradoxical situation, namely, if we deprive the "substance" of all its groups, atoms, and structural features, the "substance" remaining has an R_M-value equal to K. This illustrates the real meaning of the constant because it indicates the R_M property of the chromatographic system, and not that of the "substance."

Having a knowledge of fundamental constant theoretically should allow one to deduce the structure of a compound by a method proposed by Schauer and Burlirsch.[30] They indicate that the structure of a compound with an unknown functional group can be calculated if all the group constants are known in a series of (n + 1) solvent systems. Although they quote some examples in their paper, in practice this method is very tedious to use. Not only do the group constants have to be determined, but care must be taken to ensure that in the molecules used to ascertain a group constant, the group has relatively the same position in all molecules. For example, the position of the amino group in a series of amino acids has a relatively large influence on the final R_M of the compound. An acid containing an α-amino group has a higher R_M-value than the corresponding acid with an ω-amino group.

In their work, Schauer and Burlirsch quote fundamental constants of the order of 0.57 for a system using Whatman No. 1 paper with a phenol–water solvent, and for Whatman No. 4 paper using a n-butanol–acetic acid–water solvent, they quote a fundamental constant of 0.26.

The value of K is not zero, because the ratio of the phases of the system is not unity; in general there is always more mobile phase than stationary phase. Indeed, A_L/A_S ratios of 7:8 are common.[16]

In view of the fact that it is not always easy to determine the fundamental constant, many workers have not used this as the basis of their calculations but have considered the Rf- or R_M-value of the parent member of the homologous series or other series of compounds. Thus, for example, in a series of aliphatic alcohols, the basic member is methyl alcohol and the R_M of a compound (n-$CH_3 \cdot (CH_2)_n \cdot OH$) would be regarded as $\Sigma R_{M(CH_3OH)} + n\Delta R_{M(CH_2)}$; a series of dicarboxylic acids, however, would use malonic acid and not oxalic acid as the parent member of the series.

We must further define the term group constant. It is not enough to state that for all methylene groups or all hydroxyl groups there is a group constant. If this were the case, then according to Equation 8 there should be no difference in the R_M-values of two isomeric substances, and hence it should be impossible to separate isomers in any system. Fortunately for the many people using chromatography to separate isomers, this is not the case. It would appear necessary then to extend the ΔR_M concept to include some positional effects; the nature of the group must be considered to have a somewhat different chromatographic function dependent on its neighboring groups. If we consider the hydroxyl grouping, it is clear that we must at once differentiate between phenolic hydroxyl and aliphatic hydroxyl. In the latter there will be a difference in the chromatographic behavior of the hydroxyl corresponding to whether it is a primary, secondary, or tertiary alcohol. When the chemistry of the hydroxyl groups in the vast array of steroids, polyhydroxy alcohols, etc. is considered, it becomes apparent that the property of the hydroxyl group varies depending upon whether it be an isolated group, axial or equatorial, or whether it be vicinal to another hydroxyl group or to any other chemically and hence chromatographically functional group. Thus we are extending the concept to include various types of interactions in the molecule. Various opinions have been expressed concerning the correctness of extending the theory to this breadth, but the majority viewpoint seems to be somewhat pragmatic; if by so extending the theory we make it more useful, then this is sufficient and valid reason.

Some authors, notably Marcinkiewicz and co-workers[31] have extended the theory to include ΔR_M-values for atoms, *e.g.*, they measure $\Delta R_{M(C)}$ for the carbon atom, $\Delta R_{M(H)}$ for the hydrogen atom. They have moreover[32] extended the parameters to include chain branching and the presence of a double bond.

Under the assumption that Martin's theory is valid, and that we take the intent of Equation 8, then it should be the case that the various chromatographic parameters can be used in the same equation; that is, they can be added algebraically.

Before considering the now extended version, it is advantageous to examine some of the earlier work of various authors to see how the necessity for the extension arose and also to obtain some information regarding the types of systems which have been systematically examined. In their original work, Bate-Smith and Westall[4] plotted the R_M-values obtained by chromatographing, among others, a series of hydroxy acids (benzoic acid, *p*-hydroxy benzoic acid, protacatechuic acid, and gallic acid; 0, 1, 2, 3 hydroxy groups) in *m*-cresol–acetic acid, and a series of flavones (galangin, kaempferol, quercetin, and quercetagetin; 3, 4, 5, 6 hydroxy groups) in *m*-cresol–acetic acids and obtained two parallel lines. This they regarded as indicating that the $\Delta R_{M(OH)}$ was additive in each series, and the parallel nature of the lines indicated that it was the same in both series. They reported similar trends for a series of compounds whose hydroxyl groups had been subjected to glycosidation with glucose. In this series the R_M-values were proportional to the number of glucose units added. They did report several instances of departure from regularity, and attributed these to constitutional factors and especially to ortho or vicinal arrangement of substituent groups.

Long, Quayle, and Stedman[23] observed an approximately linear relationship between the R_M-values and the number of methylene groups in the molecule for both mono- and dicarboxylic acids. In an attempt to show the validity of the equation, Bush[9] plotted curves of R_M versus number of carbon atoms in the chain for homologous series such as carbinol dinitrobenzoates and carbonyl dinitrophenyl-hydrazones chromatographed in a solvent of heptane–methanol. These values were calculated from various sources of results, and it is noteworthy that although experimental conditions were not standardized throughout, the graphs showed that in both series the $\Delta R_{M(CH_2)}$ was approximately the same $(-0.25, -0.23)$. The plots indicate that the first member of the series did not always fit in with the linearity of the others. He also plotted the R_M-values for a series of fatty acid dinitrophenylhydrazides,[34,35] which had been chromatographed in the reversed phase system tetralin–90% methanol. For the range C_5–C_{21} a linear relationship was obtained with a $\Delta R_{M(CH_2)}$ of approximately $+0.12$. There were definite and serious deviations from linearity for the range C_1–C_3 or C_4. He suggested that this is due to the conformational rigidity and the size of the tetralin molecule. The linearity is obtained only when the aliphatic chain of the homologs becomes sufficiently larger than the solvent molecules, allowing random interactions to predominate over sterically orientated reactions.

Howe[36] chromatographed 111 carboxylic acids including mono-, di-, tri-, and tetra-carboxylic acids. He used two monophasic solvents, *n*-propanol saturated with ammonia and *n*-propanol saturated with sulfurous acid. In both solvents the majority of his series showed a close approximation to linearity up to compounds containing eight carbon atoms; above this carbon number, both the straight chain and the hydroxy-monocarboxylic acids rapidly approached a limiting value of Rf. This was similar to the results for such compounds previously reported[37] in similar alkaline solvents. He reported that although the lines representing the series showed a general similarity of slope, they were not strictly parallel to one another, and he thus was unable to give a precise $\Delta R_{M(CH_2)}$ in all the series. Even over the strictly linear parts of his curves, the ΔR_M-values varied on different lines. While Green and McHale[38] attribute Howe's findings on the lack of constancy of $\Delta R_{M(CH_2)}$ partly to experimental deviations in the several cases where the Rf-values were greater than 0.80, there is no doubt that the simple evaluation of $\Delta R_{M(CH_2)}$ from a series of compounds cannot always be achieved. Green and McHale[38] consider that deviations are attributable to a molecular interaction of the CH_2 group, and that deviation from linearity can be taken to indicate this.

While this might be so, many of the supposed interactions are not evident from any source other than these chromatographic deviations. Franc and Jokl,[39] as a result of a study concerned with the chromatography of aromatic isomers of homologs of phenol, dihydroxy benzenes, and pyrocatechols, concluded that Martin's theory of additivity as simply expressed was not valid. Bark and Graham[40] chromatographed a series of nuclear-substituted nitrophenols in a series of chromatographic systems using various substrates (cellulose, alumina-impregnated cellulose, alumina-impregnated glass fiber) and a single nonpolar solvent (anhydrous cyclohexane). From the results obtained, they concluded that because of the ease of delocalization of electronic effects in these nuclear systems, it was not possible to assign group parameters. In a series of studies of the effect of substituent groupings on the chromatographic behavior of phenoxyacetic acids, Bark and Graham[41-44] suggested that the Rf-value and hence the R_M-value of an acid was due to four main factors: (a) the behavior of the fundamental chromatographically functional group—the acid grouping, (b) the nature and number of the substituent groups, (c) the relative positions of the fundamental group and the substituent group or groups, and (d) the relative positions of the substituent groups. The mechanism of the chromatography was probably a mixture of partition and adsorption, the solvent was *n*-butyl alcohol saturated with water or 1.5M ammonia, and the separations were attributed to variations in the strengths of the hydrogen bonds formed between the carboxylic acid grouping or the halogeno substituents and the water–butanol and cellulose. Although a relatively large number of acids were studied, and to a first approximation their R_M-values depended on the number of substituents, it was not possible to deduce a simple $\Delta R_{M(CH_2)}$-value or $\Delta R_{M(Cl)}$-value for the series. This they considered to be due, in part, to the mechanism of the distribution of the solute, the acids being in their opinion distributed between the phases both by partition and adsorption. However, Brenner *et al.*[45] have found that the $\Delta R_{M(CH_2)}$ is a constant in thin-layer chromatography.

The value reported by these latter workers is exceedingly low compared to that of other functional groups. It has already been indicated that the application of the Martin additivity principle has been attempted by many workers for a large number of compounds. It is desirable at this point to consider, in some detail, some of the groups of compounds to which the most work has been directed. It is beyond the intention of this short review to give all the work which has been done in any particular field, and to this end the work discussed here will have been investigated mainly with the Martin theory in mind.

Steroids

The greater volume of published work deals with the various classes of steroids, and it is from this work that many of the significant advances have come. The steroids offer what is probably one of the best skeletal structures on which to substitute or modify definite chemical groupings, because they are essentially structures in which electron delocalization is not readily accomplished. This means that the influence of a group, in chromatographic terms, will not be apparent in any alteration of the chemical potential of a group placed in a nonvicinal position, or placed by the conformation of the molecule at a distance greater than the van der Waals distance from the new substituent.

The ΔR_M approach for the steroids was first intensively analyzed as a technique for characterization and conformational analysis of steroids by Bush[9] in 1961 in what must be regarded as the definitive work in this particular field. It had been used previously by others, for example, Macek and Vejdelek[46] in 1955. They determined the number of α-diol groupings in the steroid molecule by comparing the Rf/R_M-values obtained when the steroids were chromatographed in two systems, both essentially formamide-impregnated paper with chloroform as the solvent; in one system, a small amount of boric acid was incorporated into the formamide phase. As expected those steroids with α-diol groups formed the well established boro-complex, became more polar, and hence had lower Rf-values in the "boric acid" system. The increment in ΔR_M was approximately 0.3–0.4 for one α-diol grouping and 0.8–1.2 for two α-diol groupings.

The use of boric acid in such systems was also investigated by Brooks and co-workers.[47] They found that when investigating the chromatographic behavior of some steroidal 11:12 diols, the addition of boric acid to the solvents markedly affected the migration of derivatives containing the 11α, 12α- and 11β, 12β-diol groups. They studied derivatives of tigogenin, and tigogenone with oxygen containing substituents at the 11- position, and some sapogenins with substituents in the 12- position. Their values indicated a ΔR_M characteristic of each polar group. The order of the ΔR_M-values matched the relative chemical properties of the group, and they noted that reduction of the activity of a group, caused by interaction between adjacent polar groups, altered the ΔR_M-values. This was especially so in the case of the equatorial hydroxyl groups. They obtained satisfactorily reproducible ΔR_M-values, calculated for the 11α, 11β-hydroxyl groupings and for the 11- and 12-oxo-groups. These values were calculated from their own results and from those of other workers. They used their findings to discuss the possibility of hydrogen bonding at the 11- position, involving hydroxy- or keto- groups, and linked their work on chromatography with work using infrared spectroscopy. They considered various solvents and listed a series of ΔR_M-values for the groups in each of the solvents.

This was in some respects the beginning of the extension of the simple ΔR_M-value to include ΔR_M-values for group type, solvent change, and modification of the molecule by reaction. Bush's work put the problem into perspective. He calculated each type of ΔR_M-value for many compounds, using his and other peoples' results, and his resultant collection of many hundreds of ΔR_M-values is an essential part of any worker's library. A few examples will indicate some of the scope of this work. (Progesterone has been chosen as the example to illustrate the ΔR_M-values available and how they vary.)

For ease of comparison, the first values are given from one solvent system (Tables I–IV): light petroleum–toluene–methanol–water (50: 50:70:30).[10] The parent compound of the series is pregn-4-ene-3,20-dione (progesterone) (P).

These examples are of necessity just a few of the many examples quoted by Bush; although he quotes many examples using his values, it

Table I

$\Delta R_{M(g)}$- Values for different substituents of the progesterone series
obtained from above solvent on paper at 34°C

Substituent	6βOH(a)	11αOH(e)	11βOH(a)	11-keto	14αOH(t)
$\Delta R_{M(g)}$	0.95	1.35	0.91	0.64	0.95

Substituent	15α(OH)(é)	15β-OH(a')	16α-OH	17α(OH)(t)	21·OH(p)
$\Delta R_{M(g)}$	1.47	1.32	1.42	0.75	0.67

Solvent:[10] light petrol–toluene–methanol–water (50:50:70:30).
a = axial, á = quasi-axial, e = equatorial, é = quasi-equatorial, p = primary,
t = tertiary.

Table II

Variation in $\Delta R_{M(g)}$-values for some members of the progesterone series

	$\Delta R_{M(g)}$ of substituent		
Substance	*11α-OH*	*11β-OH*	*11-keto*
P (progesterone)	1.35	0.91	0.64
P-6β-ol	1.71	—	0.75
P-17α-ol	1.58	1.07	0.60
P-17α-21-diol	1.65	1.07	0.70
P-21-ol	1.58	0.93	0.75

(For chromatographic system, see Table I.)

Table III

Variation in $\Delta R_{M(r)}$-values for some members of the progesterone series

Substance	*11-keto to 11β-OH(a)*	*11-keto to 11α-OH(e)*	*21-OH to 21-acetate*
P (progesterone)	0.27	0.41	
P-17α-ol	0.47	0.98	
P-17,21-diol	0.37	0.95	−0.73
P-21-ol	0.18	0.83	−0.88

(For chromatographic system used, see Table I.)

is still only possible to obtain an approximate R_M-value for a particular steroid, and conversely from a knowledge of the R_M-value to obtain some idea of the structural conformation of the substance. To further one's knowledge of the substance, chromatographic study must be part of an investigation.

Many other workers have investigated the chromatographic behavior of steroids, both on paper and on thin-layers of various adsorbents.

Table IV

Variation in ΔR_M-values for changes in solvent
(All the values are approximate)

| Substituent | Solvents | | | |
	(a)	(b)	(c)	(d)
6β-OH	1.1	1.2	1.3	1.6
11-keto	0.72	0.61	0.81	0.82
11α-OH	1.6	1.6	1.8	1.6
11β-OH	1.0	1.0	1.2	1.0
15α-OH	1.6	1.55	1.85	—

solvents: (a) As in Table I
(b) Light petrol–toluene–methanol–water (66:33:85:15)
(c) Light petrol–benzene–methanol–water (66:33:80:20)
(d) Benzene–methanol–water (100:50:50).

Monder,[48] using silica gel plates and various solvent systems such as ethyl acetate saturated with water or methylene dichloride–ethyl acetate–aqueous formic acid has systematically applied the ΔR_M concept to derivatives of corticosteroids to illustrate an approach to the characterization of steroids containing the 17α-ketol side chain. He has studied the 21-dehydro steroids and the 17β-carboxyl steroids (the etienic acids). He lists a range of $\Delta R_{M(s)}$-values for the derivatives of the 17β-ketol steroids, and from these it is possible to calculate $\Delta R_{M(g)}$, $\Delta R_{M(s)}$ and $\Delta R_{M(r)}$ values; a selection of these are given in Tables V(a) and V(b).

From a statistical consideration of his results Monder showed that the standard variation was usually less than the scatter of results. Thus, again it is shown that any single ΔR_M results should be regarded only as indications of possible structure and must be used in conjunction with other values and other evidence.

Also using thin-layer chromatography for the chromatographic study of some saturated 21-deoxy-C_{21}-steroids, Lisboa[49] applied single and multiple one-dimensional chromatography to separate and characterize these compounds. He used a series of eight solvent systems and investigated over 50 21-deoxy-pregnane steroids on Silica Gel G. He, like Monder, investigated the effect of the R_M-values of oxidation of the steroid under controlled conditions. The oxidations were accomplished with periodic acid[50] or with cupric acetate. The solvents used by Lisboa were similar to those used by other workers[51, 52] for the separation of this type of steroid. A series of solvent systems is necessary, not only to obtain $\Delta R_{M(s)}$-values, but also because no one solvent is able to differentiate all the steroids considered. Indeed their resolution is only possible with the application of single and multiple one-dimensional chromatography.

Table V(a)

ΔR_M of 17α-Deoxy-ketol steroids according to Monder[48]*

Substance	$\Delta R_{M(A)}$				$\Delta R_{M(B)}$				$\Delta R_{M(C)}$			
Solvent	1	2	3	4	1	2	3	4	1	2	3	4
Corticosterone	0.31	0.27	0.49	0.39	0.17	0.18	0.04	0.02	0.35	0.46	0.49	0.41
11-Dehydro-corticosterone	0.42	0.28	0.50	0.40	0.28	0.25	0.00	0.00	0.33	0.50	0.50	0.40
3β, 11β, 21-Trihydroxy-allopregnan-20-one	0.34	0.20	0.34	0.22	0.09	0.20	0.00	0.00	0.43	0.40	0.37	0.22
3β, 21-Dihydroxy-gallo-pregnane-11,20-dione	0.24	0.22	0.28	0.24	0.18	0.17	0.00	0.00	0.42	0.38	0.28	0.24
Mean	0.31	0.23	0.40	0.31	0.18	0.20	0.01	0.00	0.38	0.43	0.41	0.32
$\pm$ Standard deviation	0.07	0.04	0.11	0.09	0.08	0.03	0.03	0.01	0.05	0.05	0.10	0.10

$\Delta R_{M(A)} = R_M$ (untreated steroid)–R_M (steroid-21-aldehyde)
$\Delta R_{M(B)} = R_M$ (steroid-21-aldehyde)–R_M (steroid etienic acid)
$\Delta R_{M(C)} = R_M$ (untreated steroid)–(steroid etienic acid).

Solvents:
1. Ethyl acetate saturated with water
2. Methylene chloride–ethyl acetate–88% aq. formic acid (19:19:2)
3. Chloroform–acetone–acetic acid (10:10:1)
4. Chloroform–acetone–acetic acid (12:8:1).

*Courtesy of *Biochemical Journal*.

Table V(b)

ΔR_M of 17α-Hydroxy-ketol steroids according to Monder[48]*

Substance	$\Delta R_{M(A)}$				$\Delta R_{M(B)}$				$\Delta R_{M(C)}$			
Solvent	1	2	3	4	1	2	3	4	1	2	3	4
Cortisol	0.23	0.25	0.44	0.37	−1.13	−0.16	−0.64	−0.54	−0.88	0.11	−0.24	−0.16
Cortisone	0.20	0.21	0.38	0.37	−1.30	−0.11	−0.62	−0.58	−1.06	0.08	−0.32	−0.29
11-Deoxy cortisol	0.27	0.17	0.39	0.31	−1.12	−0.01	−0.54	−0.51	−0.92	0.13	−0.27	−0.20
Δ' Cortisone	0.16	0.23	0.25	0.26	−1.31	−0.10	−0.68	−0.51	−1.15	0.13	−0.44	−0.25
Δ' Cortisol	0.17	0.21	0.25	0.24	−1.24	−0.11	−0.57	−0.40	−1.04	0.10	−0.31	−0.17
Mean	0.20	0.21	0.34	0.31	−1.22	−0.12	−0.61	−0.53	−1.01	0.11	−0.32	−0.21

$\Delta R_{M(A)}$ = R_M (untreated steroid) − R_M (steroid-21-aldehyde)
$\Delta R_{M(B)}$ = R_M (steroid-21-aldehyde) − R_M (steroid etienic acid)
$\Delta R_{M(C)}$ = R_M (untreated steroid) − R_M (steroid etienic acid).

Solvents:

1. Ethyl acetate saturated with water
2. Methylene chloride–ethyl acetate–88% aq. formic acid (19:19:2)
3. Chloroform–acetone–acetic acid (10:10:1)
4. Chloroform–acetone–acetic acid (12:8:1).

*Courtesy of Biochemical Journal.

Lisboa's and Monder's work confirm Bush's work, that when a functional group is introduced into a steroid molecule, or when the substituents in a steroid skeleton are altered by a chemical transformation, then a series of definite alterations in the R_M-values of the substances is caused by these modifications. Lisboa listed the $\Delta R_{M(OH)}$-values for hydroxyl groups at a series of carbon positions (C-3, C-5, C-6, C-12, C-17, C-20) and $\Delta R_{M(O)}$-values for keto groups at C-6, C-11, C-12, and C-20, for a great number of the steroids investigated. For cases where no interacting groups are present, there are no serious deviations of the $\Delta R_{M(g)}$-values for the above groups and positions, calculated from different steroids. However, in some cases, deviations did occur. For example, the $\Delta R_{M(6-OH)}$-values for this series were somewhat greater than those he had previously reported[53] for the Δ^4-3-oxo-steroids in both the androstane and the pregnane series. The contribution of a keto group at C-6, C-11, and C-20 was similar in all the systems used and was greater than those calculated for a 12-oxo-group (See Table VI). Again the effect of the mutual interference of vicinal groups was noted.

Table VI

$\Delta R_{M(g)}$-Values for keto groups at C-6, C-11, C-12, C-20
of progesterone derivatives on cellulose paper according to Lisboa[49]*

		Solvent							
Group	Skeleton	1	2	3	4	5	6	7	8
6-oxo-	5β-P-3, 20-one	0.43	0.20	0.28	0.23	0.06	0.21	−0.02	0.06
11-oxo-	3α-ol-5β-P-20-one	0.56	0.18	—	—	0.12	0.24	—	0.13
	3β-ol-5α-P-20-one	0.48	0.12	0.28	0.23	—	0.07	0.09	0.05
	5α-P-3, 20-one	0.51	0.18	0.22	0.22	0.07	0.18	−0.02	0.09
	5β-P-3, 20-one	0.55	0.20	0.30	0.23	0.04	0.25	0.00	0.06
12-oxo-	5β-P-3, 20-one	0.19	0.06	0.14	0.09	−0.02	0.11	−0.09	0.00
20-oxo-	5α-P-3β-ol	0.27	0.20	0.06	0.11	0.11	0.11	0.00	0.14
	5β-P-3α-ol	0.48	0.27	—	—	0.11	0.14	—	0.24
	5β-P-3α-6α-ol	0.19	0.18	0.24	0.20	0.26	0.23	0.00	0.14
	5β-P-3-one	0.48	0.18	0.23	0.22	0.13	0.14	0.14	0.25

Solvent:

  1. Cyclohexane–ethyl acetate (50:50)
  2. Cyclohexane–ethyl acetate–ethanol (45:45:10)
  3. *n*-Hexane–ethyl acetate–acetic acid (20:75:5)
  4. *n*-Hexane–ethyl acetate–ethanol–acetic acid (13.5:73:4.5:20)
  5. Benzene–ethanol (80:20)
  6. Benzene–ethanol (90:10)
  7. Chloroform–ethanol (90:10)
  8. Chloroform–ethanol (95:5).

*Courtesy of *Steroids*.

Although a very detailed consideration of the results shown indicates that great care must be taken not to oversimplify the possible alterations, the results do show general agreements. For a particular solvent, however, it is not always possible to estimate the $\Delta R_{M(g)}$ with the desired precision.

Lisboa has calculated $\Delta R_{M(r)}$-values for the transformations of keto groups to hydroxyl groups at various positions for these steroids, and he gives a series of tables relating approximately 20 group inter-conversions. Using his values he showed that it is possible to obtain the probable Rf-value for the characterization of an "unknown" steroid; he considered the steroid 5α-pregnane-3,17-dione, which on being chromatographed in cyclohexane–ethyl acetate (50:50) solvent, has an actual Rf-value of 0.53. He calculated the probable Rf-value, assuming that the compound had been obtained either from 5α-pregnane–3β,20α-diol (compound A) by oxidation with periodate or from the steroid 5α-pregnane-3β, 20β diol (compound B), by a similar reaction. His calculations are given below.

(a) from A:

Rf of (A) in cyclohexane–ethyl acetate	=	0.27
R_M of "parent" compound A	=	+0.432
$\Delta R_{M(r)}$ 5α(H)-3β-ol $\rightarrow$ 5α(H)-3-one	=	−0.275
$\Delta R_{M(r)}$ 20α-ol $\rightarrow$ 20-one	=	−0.146
calculated R_M for 3,17-dione	=	+0.011

This corresponds to Rf = 0.49.

(b) from B:

Rf of B in cyclohexane–ethyl acetate	=	0.31
R_M of "parent" compound B	=	0.348
$\Delta R_{M(r)}$ 5α(H)-3β-ol $\rightarrow$ 5α(H)-3-one	=	−0.275
$\Delta R_{M(r)}$ 20β-ol $\rightarrow$ 20-one	=	−0.080
		−0.007

This corresponds to Rf = 0.51.

Thus the calculated Rf-values (0.49, 0.51) are in close proximity to the actual 0.53. However, the divergence is such that again it is imperative to use several solvents, together with the identification of some of the functional groups by formation of derivatives and application of specific color reactions, before a definite characterization of a steroid can be achieved.

Much work has now accumulated many results for different steroids on a variety of systems using both paper chromatography and thin-layer chromatography. Neher[54] has extended the work of Bush[9] in some respects, and Lisboa[55, 56] has reported the R_M-values of approximately

250 steroids, many naturally occurring, some synthetic. Doorenbos and Sharma[57] have indicated solvent systems which they claim can be used for the study of the widest range of steroids, from the simple cholestane and androstane series to complex heterocyclic steroids. Even with all the literature, results and values available, one of the great problems is the lack of systematization of the results. Although a great deal of worthy "qualitative" work has been done, much of it has been reported without indication of the precise conditions used and has generally been aimed at showing how slight variations in chromatographic behavior indicate group interaction in the steroid. This is perhaps inevitable, since probably the main *raison d'etre* of chromatography, up to the present time, has been the relatively easy separation of mixtures of known substances.

Acids and Esters

Using generally smaller molecules of much less complexity does not necessarily result in a simplification of the factors. Although there are fewer positional factors to be noted if the compound is a straight chain compound, no better relationships between R_M- and ΔR_M-values have been found than have been obtained for the steroids. Some of the most significant work on aliphatic systems is on acids and acid esters. Reichl[58] chromatographed a series of organic acids under standardized conditions and obtained a series of constants for the various constituent parts of the molecule. His values indicate that the differences in Rf obtained from the Rf measured, and that calculated from the R_M—itself calculated from the ΔR_M-values—was generally less than encountered in experimental error, except in one or two examples.

For a series of dicarboxylic acids, hydroxy acids, and a few amino acids chromatographed on Whatman No. 1 paper by a descending technique using as solvent a mixture of equal volumes of *n*-amyl alcohol and 5M formic acid, he quoted the following values:

Table VII

ΔR_M-Values

	$\Delta R_{M(g)}$
System (or ground) constant (K)	+0.97
For each C atom	+0.12
Chain branching	+0.25
Primary hydroxyl group	−0.73
Secondary hydroxyl group	−0.50
Tertiary hydroxyl group	−0.58
Carboxylic acid group	−0.63
α-Amino group	−1.65
α-Keto group	−0.39

Consideration of one or two examples indicates how close to reality are these terms:

(a) Lactic acid $CH_3 \cdot CH(OH) \cdot COOH$

$$R_M = K + 3\Delta R_{M(C)} + \Delta R_{M(COOH)} + \Delta R_{M(sec. OH)}$$
$$= 0.97 + 0.36 - 0.63 - 0.50$$
$$= 0.20$$

Rf = 0.61. Value found by experiment: Rf = 0.62.

(b) Aspartic acid $COOH \cdot CH_2CH(NH_2) COOH$

$$R_M = K + 4\Delta R_{M(C)} + 2\ R_{M(COOH)} + 1\ R_{M(\alpha.NH_2)}$$
$$= 0.97 + 0.48 - 1.26 - 1.65$$
$$= -1.46$$

Rf = 0.03. Value found by experiment: Rf = 0.03.

For a similar series of acids, chromatographed by ascending chromatography on Schleicher-Schüll 2043b paper in ethyl acetate–acetic acid–water (3:1:1), the chromatographic parameter had altered. The system or ground constant had increased to 1.02, the value for each C atom to 0.21, etc.

Such close agreement with the postulated values seemed to prove the validity of the Martin additivity principle. Reichl extended his work[59] to indicate how some classification of the acids could be obtained from a direct consideration of the R_M-values obtained. (In his work he expressed his results as $R_M = \log\ (Rf[1\text{-}Rf])$ because this function increases as the Rf-value increases. In this review, Reichl's values in his later work[59] will be referred to as $-R_M$-values.) He examined 36 acids in two pairs of solvents and plotted his results as a two-dimensional graph of the $-R_M$-values in one solvent against those found in the other. He found that by drawing parallel lines across his graph he could separate the acids into groups dependent upon the number of carboxy groupings present. This treatment was generally correct, but it is interesting to note that maleic acid and phthalic acid were anomalous in both sets of solvents. He ascribed this abnormality to the interaction of adjacent carboxyl groups and termed this an "ortho effect."

Although Howe[36] in his investigations used similar systems, he did not notice such anomalous behavior. He plotted the R_M-values for the acids in *n*-propanol–ammonia against the $\Delta R_{M(s)}$ obtained on considering the R_M-values of the acids obtained in the two solvents, *n*-propanol–ammonia and *n*-propanol–sulfurous acid. He was able to divide the mono-, di-, tri-, and tetracarboxylic acids into distinct parts of the graph by a series of parallel lines, in a manner similar to that of Reichl, and was able to predict, from the R_M-values of a substance, the number of acidic groups therein. He also reported that he was able to obtain, to a first approximation, an indication of other groups such as alkyl, aryl, amino, hydroxy, and bromo which may be present, and to some extent, the manner in which they are arranged. However, he was not able to give precise $\Delta R_{M(g)}$-values. Although in *n*-propanol–ammonia a plot of R_M against the number of carbon atoms was linear for unsubstituted dicarboxylic acids from C_2 to C_{10} with a $\Delta R_{M(CH_2)}$ of approximately 0.25 units for unsubstituted monocarboxylic acids, the graph was only linear from C_2 to C_8, and from C_{10} to C_{13} there was no change in the $\Delta R_{M(CH_2)}$; for C_2–C_8 the $\Delta R_{M(CH_2)}$ was approximately 0.10 units. Howe concluded that without a very large increase in the number of Rf-values obtained it was premature to attempt calculations of R_M-values from ΔR_M-values.

While Howe's work has been criticized because some of his R_M-values were obtained from Rf-values outside the limits (0.1 and 0.9), even within these limits for some "long chain" compounds there is an apparent deviation from the expected value. It is the present author's opinion[60] that this deviation is inevitable when one considers the chromatography of molecules having a long alkane chain attached to a very chromatographically active functional group such as the carboxyl group. This can form hydrogen bonds very strongly with a polar substrate, in this case cellulose or cellulose–water. Up to a certain size of alkane chain, one can regard the molecule as a rigid rod-like unit, with the alkane chain held in the mobile layer. At this stage any increase in the number of methylene groups adds a definite increase in the proportion of the molecule in the moving phase; this is reflected in the steady increase of the chemical potential, and the additive increase in the $\Delta R_{M(g)}$-value. Above a certain length of alkane chain, spiraling of the chain occurs, and it is possible that some of the alkane chain can lie along the interface and not be effectively in the mobile phase. The probability of this will increase as the chain length increases, and hence there will be a tendency for the Rf- and hence R_M-values to approach a limiting value. The limiting value for an homologous series will vary depending on the substrate and the mobile phase. Chain branching will tend to confer rigidity onto the molecule, and therefore the number of carbon atoms needed before any spiraling takes place will be much increased. In cases where there are two functional groups, one at each end of the molecule, it is then considered that the molecule will be folded or bent, and the rigidity will be consequently increased. The α-hydroxy monocarboxylic- and the unsubstituted monocarboxylic acids would thus be expected to show the deviation before the dicarboxylic acids or the ω-amino carboxylic acids. This theory is well supported by Howe's observations. The "first member" anomaly apparent on some of Howe's findings probably exists because the first methylene group is substituted into a unique molecular environment; the second methylene is not. This is the member from which the start should be made.

Phenols

A large array of work has been done attempting to relate the chromatographic behavior of phenols with their molecular structure. The work divides itself into at least two fairly distinct sections, one concerned with phenols having relatively small-sized nuclear substituents, and the other concerned with phenols having relatively large-sized substituents. Those concerned with the latter section, Marcinkiewicz, Green, and McHale[31] chromatographed over 70 phenolic type substances (phenols, indanols, alkoxy and aryloxy phenols, chromanols and coumarins) in a stationary phase of ethyl oleate and a solvent of 25% v/v aqueous ethanol. They later extended their work to cover more substances and various reversed phase systems, generally involving cellulose paper impregnated with olive oil and mobile phases of aqueous ethanol. They first calculated $\Delta R_{M(CH_2)}$-values from two series of compounds, (1) p-ethylphenol to p-n-amyl phenol and (2) from p-ethoxyphenol to p-n-heptyloxyphenol. The values were +0.462 and +0.448, respectively, giving a mean value of +0.455. The maximum deviation in either series was only 0.032. However, some of the Rf-values used were outside the range generally agreed upon as being acceptable; for example, Rf for p-ethoxyphenol was 0.88 and Rf for p-n-heptyloxyphenol was 0.04. In calculating $\Delta R_{M(CH_2)}$ it was indicated that the values obtained from p-cresol could not be used, since the methylene group here is attached directly to an aromatic ring and is thus under the electronic influence of that ring. This CH_2 is regarded as being constitutively different from a homologous CH_2 group. Marcinkiewicz, Green, and McHale calculated the $\Delta R_{M(ring\,attached\,CH_2)}$-value by comparing phenol with its mono-, di-, and tri-methylated derivatives but restricted their calculations to those phenols that did not contain substituents ortho to the hydroxy group. Thus the series is essentially: phenol, 3-, 4-, 3, 4-, 3, 5-, and 3,4,5-methyl phenols. The value obtained was 0.305 ± 0.018, which value is significantly different from the value of $\Delta R_{M(CH_2)}$ in an aliphatic chain.

The ΔR_M-value was not restricted to groups but extended to other structural parameters. For example, having noted that the presence of a double bond in a molecule altered the Rf-value, they compared a series of pairs of compounds differing only by the presence or absence of a double bond; for example, p-n-butyl phenol and p-n-crotyl phenol, or p-cyclopentyl phenol and p-cyclopent-2-enyl-phenol. The values were not constant, but this is to be expected since the position of the double bond, with respect to the aromatic ring, varies, and its electronic influence on the ring will of necessity vary depending on the number and nature of the groups between it and the ring. This postulation is supported by the values obtained for compounds such as p-pent-4-enyloxy-phenol, where the double bond of the side chain is separated from the aromatic ring by the ether oxygen. Bark[44] had previously indicated in work on phenoxyacetic acids that the ether oxygen acts as an electronic buffer and prevents electronic effects passing to and from the nucleus and the side chain.

The work of Marcinkiewicz and his colleagues is perhaps most significant in that they extended the additivity principle to include atomic ΔR_M parameters. They indicated that they arrived at this when it became necessary to relate the R_M-values of compounds containing fused aromatic rings, naphthols, phenanthrols, anthrols, etc. to some other parameters than, say, $\Delta R_{M(phenol)} + \Delta R_{M(CH_2)}$. Since they concluded that all the ΔR_M-values (for, say, $-CH_2$; $-CH_2$ ring attached; $-CH_2$ ring attached and ortho to hydroxy) stem from the differing constitutive relationships of the carbon and hydrogen atoms in these compounds, compared to those existing in the homologous series, it should be possible to consider carbon and hydrogen atoms separately. It should be feasible to assign to each a ΔR_M-value that is determined by both the normal additive quantity and also by a structural factor, depending on the relation of the atom to the rest of the molecule. They pertinently state that although theoretically it is possible to do this, in practice, in all but the simplest molecules there would be so many parameters that the task of assigning ΔR_M-values, calculated from such parameters, would be far too complex. Thus they simplified the process by emulating the method of Reichl[58] and assigned the same ΔR_M-value to carbon atoms, whatever their position or structural relationship in a molecule. They then ascribed all other variations in the ΔR_M-values of groups containing only carbon and hydrogen, to the variations in the ΔR_M contributions of structurally different hydrogen atoms. They point out that this immediately reduces the experimental requirements and also makes the calculation much more manageable. The ΔR_M-values were then determined for all the types of hydrogen atoms; regardless of whether these are in an alkane side chain, in a primary aromatic nucleus, or in a fused ring they can all be regarded as being α, β, γ, δ, etc. to the aromatic nucleus.

Marcinkiewicz *et al.* extended the concept to $\Delta R_{M(oxygen)}$ with respect to the nature of the group to which the oxygen is attached. Thus, they were able to assign (for the chromatographic system, ethyl oleate–25% aqueous ethanol) the following ΔR_M parameters for carbon, hydrogen and oxygen (Table VIII).

In this work and in later reported work,[61] Green and co-workers considered the effect of such electronic disturbance as hyperconjugation and

Table VIII

$\Delta R_{M(g)}$-Values for some substituents

Substituent	$\Delta R_{M(g)}$
Each carbon atom	+0.263
Aromatic hydrogen	+0.010
α hydrogen	+0.014
β hydrogen	+0.048
γ hydrogen	+0.084
δ hydrogen	+0.096
ϵ hydrogen	+0.096
O in $-OCH_2R$	−0.844
O in $-OCHR_2$	−1.076
O in $-OCR_3$	−1.445
O in $-OCH_3$	−0.558
O in $-OC_6H_5$	−0.242

It is considered that the electronic displacement effect is negligible for hydrogen atoms further away from the aromatic ring than the δ-position. Thus, if we wish to calculate the R_M-value for a particular compound, we can start with a parent member of the series (phenol) and algebraically add the various parameters. They quote as one of their many examples the calculation of the R_M-value for p-pent-4-enyloxy-phenol:

$$R_M = R_{M(phenol)} + 9\Delta R_{M(\delta\text{-hydrogen})} + 5\Delta R_{M(C)}$$
$$+ \Delta R_{M(O\ in\ -OCH_2R)} - \Delta R_{M(aromatic\ hydrogen)}$$
$$= -1.063 + 0.864 + 1.315 - 0.844 - 0.010$$
$$= +0.262\ (Rf = 0.345).$$

The experimental value found was 0.269 (Rf = 0.35).

have shown that the $\Delta R_{M(aromatic\ H)}$ is a variable factor, always low in value but varying from positive to negative value, depending on the system used. This variation in parameters for hydrogen is not confined to aromatic systems. It is suggested that in certain systems the $\Delta R_{M(olefinic\ H)}$ may not have the same value as $\Delta R_{M(paraffinic\ H)}$ because of the variation in the acceptor properties of the respective hydrogen atoms.

Using a series of compounds containing hydroxy groups they arrived at ΔR_M-values for such parameters as CHO, "isoprene units," $-NO_2$, chain branching, etc. The latter was necessary because it was found that branched compounds ran faster in reversed phase systems than did unbranched compounds of similar molecular formulas. Empirically they concluded that in a considerably diverse group of substituted phenols, if there were (n) branchings in the substituent chain attached to the benzene nucleus, then there were (n − 1) branch parameters to be used in the calculation of the R_M-value. No attempt was made at any theoretical explanation of the nature and the origin of the branch parameter. Consideration of the "spiraling" of alkane chains may satisfactorily account for the deviations from the normal; for the long chain acids as found by Howe (see page 27) it is likely that a similar effect may be operative here. Green and McHale[61] postulate that "changes in molar volume and accessibility of hydrogen atoms towards solvent molecules may contribute to the effect" (*sic*) branching parameter. Nevertheless, no theoretical explanation was given by Green *et al.*; however, as used in calculating R_M-values, the procedure was generally admissible. They showed successful correlations between calculated and experimental R_M-values for many of their phenolic compounds with branched side chains. Considering that some of the compounds they used for illustrating the validity of their work are structurally very complex—such as ubiquinones, and vitamins K_1 and K_2—it must be accepted that whatever the cause of the ΔR_M-branching parameter, it is a necessary factor to be included in the calculation of R_M-values. In an attempt to examine the parameter in more stringent conditions, Green[61] attempted to use it and other parameters in calculating the R_M-value of squalene (a C_{30} isoprenoid hydrocarbon). This example is also of interest in that they used it to illustrate the possibility of having to use different ΔR_M-values for ethylenic and paraffinic hydrogen atoms, and also because although the hydrocarbon is not aromatic, the parameters used may be obtained from aromatic systems. (The values were obtained by chromatographing hydrocarbons and tocyl ethers[32] in a reversed-phase system of liquid paraffin–95% aqueous ethanol.) The values quoted for parameters are:

K (ground or system constant) $= -0.573$
$\Delta R_{M(C)} = +0.053$
$\Delta R_{M(H)} = 0.030$
$\Delta R_{M(branching)} = -0.354$
$\Delta R_{M(double\ bond)} = -0.113$.

Squalene is $C_{30}H_{50}$, with six double bonds and six branch units. Thus, assuming that the olefinic hydrogen atoms have a ΔR_M-value different from the paraffinic hydrogen atoms, they quote:

1. $R_M(squalene) = K + 30\Delta R_{M(C)} + 62\Delta R_{M(H)}$
$+ 5\Delta R_{M(branch)} + 6\Delta R_{M(double\ bond)}$
$= -0.573 + 1.590 + 1.860 - 1.670 - 0.678$
$= 0.529$ (Rf $= 0.225$).

2. Assuming that all the hydrogens are equal and ignoring the double bonds:

$R_M(squalene) = K + 30\Delta R_{M(C)} + 50\Delta R_{M(H)} + 5\Delta R_{M(branch)}$
$= -0.573 + 1.590 + 1.500 - 1.670$
$= +0.766$ (Rf $= 0.14$).

Since the R_M-value found in the system is 0.477 ($\equiv$ Rf = 0.245), it seems that Green *et al.* are justified in this example in using the branching parameter and also in considering that the olefinic hydrogen is somewhat different from the paraffinic hydrogen.

Various workers have investigated phenols substituted with relatively small size groups, with varying numbers and types of substituents. Franc and Jokl[39] made a study of phenol, resorcinol, pyrocatechol, and some of their alkylated substituents, in an attempt to obtain evidence of the validity of the additivity principle. They found that although Equation 8 was generally valid, deviations occurred. They attempted to relate the deviations to the dipole moment of the solute. This is done by effectively adding yet another constant (for a particular solute) to the equation. However, since they studied only a few phenols in a small number of systems, their findings cannot be realistically applied without further study.

Bark and co-workers[40, 62-74] have investigated over 200 nuclear substituted phenols, mainly alkylated, halogenated, nitrated, and related phenols with a mixture of the aforementioned groupings. These have been investigated in experimental conditions specifically chosen to give experimental values of R_M which can be used for the purpose of molecular structural studies. A wide range of chromatographic supports have been used, from cellulose papers, alumina-impregnated papers, glass fiber papers, and thin-layers of cellulose, polyamides and alumina, each impregnated with various stationary reversed phases. These stationary phases have varied in polarity and have included cyclohexane, benzene, dioxane, ethyl oleate, ethyl acetate, methanol, ethanol, formamide, and substituted formamides. Many have been used in admixture to give monophasic systems of various polarities.

This work was done not only to investigate the relationship between molecular structure and chromatographic behavior, but also to obtain evidence for the mechanism of the chromatography of these compounds. This latter is necessary because without evidence of whether the distribution of the solutes is caused by adsorption, partition, or a mixture of the two phenomena and of how the steric and electronic effects of substituents play a vital role in deciding which mechanism predominates, it is not likely that any cogent explanation of any apparent deviations from the simple Martin equation will come about. It was necessary in some of this work to examine the problems associated with the impregnation of layers, since it is obvious that very low loadings of polar layers such as cellulose or alumina with, say, ethyl oleate or dioxane, will force the layer material to play a part in the distribution; thus both types of distribution phenomena (adsorption and partition) will be observed. On the other hand, high loadings of the impregnant can result in the mobile phase displacing some of the impregnant from the supposed stationary phase and hence a nonlinear profile of the phases ratio is inevitable. This will cause apparent deviations from the Martin relationship, since the system parameter K of Equation 8 will not be a constant value over the length of the chromatographic run. From the examples of calculations involving K, already given, it can be seen that this is often a major factor in determining the R_M-value of a compound; *e.g.*, in Green's calculation for squalene the K value (-0.573) is appreciably larger than the branching parameter (-0.354) and several times larger than $\Delta R_{M(CH_2)}$ (0.113), so that any alteration in this factor will have obvious and probably different effects on the R_M-values of solutes at different points on any run where progressive displacement of the impregnant occurs. As previously mentioned, the *in situ* investigation of the A_L/A_S ratio was done for one solvent-impregnant series, in order to establish optimum loadings.[18]

In the work using ethyl oleate as the stationary phase on cellulose, and solvents of aqueous ethanol[65] to chromatograph a series of alkyl-, and alkoxy-phenols, it became apparent that the ortho-effect was of major importance. Plots of the R_M-values of the phenols against the number of carbon atoms in the side chain were linear if the phenols were classified into the following groups: poly-alkyl phenols containing no ortho groups, alkyl phenols containing one substituent ortho to the phenolic hydroxy group, and alkyl phenols containing two groups ortho to the phenolic hydroxy grouping. It must be emphasized that deviations from linearity occur. Some of these are in accordance with the theory postulated by Bark.[60] If we consider the values obtained for phenols substituted with *n*-alkyl groups in the 4-positions, then strict linearity is observed only to *n*-amyl phenol with a $\Delta R_{M(CH_2)}$ of $+0.350$ (for solvent 37.5% v/v aqueous ethanol); 4-*n*-nonyl-phenol shows a marked deviation from the expected value. If we consider the values obtained using branched chains, the deviations are even more noticeable; the deviation for the series 4-*n*-butyl, 4-*sec*-butyl, 4-*tert*-butyl increases with the effective decrease in chain length. The deviation may be explained in terms of steric factors and by electronic factors. It is supposed that the hydrocarbon part of the molecule will lie flat in the interface of the two phases, with the phenolic grouping acting as the major point of solvation by the oxonium mobile solvent phase. Solvation of the phenolic group by hydrogen bonding will remove the molecule from the stationary phase, and this "liberated" molecule will be carried in the direction of the solvent flow. The increase in the number of methylene groups in an *n*-alkane chain extends the molecular axis in the direction of the solvent flow. Because each molecule is regarded as being solvated at the phenolic group only, the force needed to move the more compact molecule into the eluent phase and temporarily away from the effective sphere of action of the

mobile phase is probably less than that needed to remove the more extensive molecule. In other words, the probability of a molecule, moving
by thermal and diffusive agitation in the mobile phase being placed in the
vicinity of the stationary phase, is lower for compact molecules than it
is for long, extensive molecules. This should apply no matter what the
solvent and layer material, or the mechanism of distribution include.

The problem of ortho substituents and the electronic effects of such
groups as halogeno-, nitro-, amino- must be considered in the light of
what effect they have on the solvation of the main chromatographically
functional group—the hydroxyl group. Throughout the whole of the study
of these phenols, the mechanism of the distribution of the phenols between the various phases was considered in terms of the solvation of the
phenolic group by oxonium solvents (this solvation being discussed in
terms of hydrogen bonding), or when nonpolar solvents were used on
polar adsorbents, the adsorption of the molecule onto the surface via the
phenolic group. In an investigation into the behavior of some halogenated
phenols, and some halogeno-alkyl substituted phenols on cellulose-
polyamide thin-layers using polar solvents,[70] an ortho-effect due to the
bulk of the halogeno atoms was noted. It was seen that when the simple
monohalogeno-2-substituted phenols were chromatographed in cyclohexane–acetic acid (93:7 v/v) and in aqueous acetic acid (10% v/v),
the change in Rf-values (and hence R_M-values) due to the halogeno
substituents was in the order $F < Cl < Br < I$. If the chromatographic
behavior of the 2-monohalogenated phenols is dependent solely on the
strengths of the internal hydrogen bonds formed between the 2-halogeno
atom and the phenolic hydroxyl, *i.e.,* solely on the electrostatic and
charge transfer effects, one would expect the Rf-values to follow the
order of hydrogen bond strengths $Cl > F > Br > I$. However, the fact
that the alteration is in the same order as the change in atomic size
would suggest that steric effects are at least as important as electronic
effects.

With substituents such as nitro in the phenol, the electronic effect of
the group is paramount. The ability of such groups to form bonds with
other polar groupings outweighs their steric effects. However, when they
are placed so that they do not have an obvious and direct bond to the
phenolic group, the change in R_M, *i.e.,* $\Delta R_{M(g)}$ is linear to a first approximation. It is this restriction, caused by the small size of the benzene
skeleton, that seems to cause the apparent deviations to become as numerous as the cases where the additivity principle holds good. The ease
of delocalization of electronic effects in such mononuclear polysubsti-
tuted phenols and the variation of the effect of a substituent depending
both on its position relative to the phenolic group and to any other groups
renders the allocation of meaningful $\Delta R_{M(g)}$-values very difficult. The

steric and electronic effects of groups are not capable of being separated. If we regard the main mechanism of the chromatography of the phenols as the electronic bonding of the phenolic hydroxy group to a polar phase, then any alteration in the propensity of the group to enter into bond formation will have a consequent alteration in the R_M-value of the substance. The introduction of another methylene group into the nucleus will obviously not have the same effect as the introduction of another methylene group into a side chain. The inductive and hyperconjugative release by nuclear methyl groups will decrease the tendency of the oxygen of the hydroxyl group to cause polarization of the -O-H bond. This will be reflected in an alteration of the Rf- and hence the R_M-values. The steric effect of such a group will be to increase the hydrophobic part of the molecule; this will tend to cause the molecule to stay more with the nonpolar or less polar phase, with an attendant alteration in the Rf- and R_M-values. With an increase in chain length, there will always be a decrease in the electron release into the aromatic ring system. The hyperconjugative release will be zero; indeed, the change of the side chain from methyl to ethyl will have a profound effect on the electronic release. In general, no matter what the size of the side chain, increase in its length will cause a decrease in the inductive effect. The steric effect may not be strictly additive, depending on the size and nature of the chain.

While group parameters—average, and hence approximate values— can be allocated from these workers' results, they have not attempted to allocate strict values or to calculate expected R_M- or Rf-values. This seems to accord with the work of others who have studied this type of compound. Calculations from various results on phenols[75, 80] by the present author[81] indicate that while to a first approximation, one can allocate $\Delta R_{M(g)}$-values for such groups as *o*-methylene groups, side chain methylene groups, hydroxy groups, etc., the positional effects and the variation in the arrangement of the different group around the nucleus necessitate that some approximations be made for many compounds. The approximations are necessary to ensure that the difference between the R_M calculated and R_M experimental, when converted into Rf-values at the appropriate part of the chromatographic run, is within that expected for experimental error. Table IX indicates the spread of the differences between experimental and calculated R_M-values for a series of chloro-alkylated phenols chromatographed on cellulose impregnated with ethyl oleate and chromatographed with 37.5% v/v aqueous ethanol.[67] The ΔR_M-values for chloro groups were obtained by considering chloro phenols with chlorines at the appropriate position, and the $\Delta R_{M(CH_2)}$ were calculated from alkyl phenols. Both types of phenols had been chromatographed under identical conditions. Attempts to obtain $\Delta R_{M(s)}$-values of two types also indicated that to a first approximation linearity was achieved. The solvent was varied in two distinct methods: (1) the stationary phase was kept constant and the nature of the solvent was altered, and (2) the solvent was kept constant and the thickness of the carrier was varied. For the first method, a study of various polarities of solvents was conducted using alkyl phenols,[64] nitro phenols,[63] and halogeno phenols;[66] in all cases there was no direct correlation possible. With some simple alkyl phenols, using different concentrations of aqueous ethanol

Table IX

Comparison of experimental and calculated parameters
of phenol derivatives (ethyl oleate–37.5% v/v aq. ethanol)

	Experimental		Calculated	
	hRf	R_M	*hRf*	R_M
4-Chloro-3-methyl	56	−0.105	53.5	−0.061
4-Chloro-2,3-dimethyl	43	+0.123	32	+0.332
4-Chloro-2,5-dimethyl	45	+0.096	32	+0.332
4-Chloro-2,6-dimethyl	41	+0.158	26	+0.459
4-Chloro-3,5-dimethyl	50	0.00	38.5	+0.205
4-Chloro-2,3,5-trimethyl	29	+0.389	16.5	+0.698
4-Chloro-3-methyl-5-ethyl	34	+0.288	19	+0.639
2-Chloro-4,5-dimethyl	57	−0.123	52.5	−0.043
2,4-Dichloro-6-methyl	23.5	+0.513	26.5	+0.446
2,4-Dichloro-3,5-dimethyl	24	+0.501	21	+0.585
2,4-Dichloro-3,6-dimethyl	15	+0.760	16	+0.720
2,6-Dichloro-3,4-dimethyl	37	+0.231	46	+0.072
2,4,6-Trichloro-3,5-dimethyl	27	+0.432	31.5	+0.337

Experimental Rf-values are the means of at least four runs on plates carrying an internal standard and reproducible to ±0.01 Rf units.

as solvents, it was possible to obtain plots of R_M-values of the series of compounds: phenol; 2-,3-,4-methyl-phenol; 2-,3-,4-ethyl-phenol against the ethyl alcohol concentration in the solvent. The plots were linear over part of the range of alcohol concentrations used (between 25% and 50% v/v), but below 25% v/v ethanol there was a sharp decrease from linearity for each compound. The curves were approximately parallel, but the divergence from linearity is too great to allow accurate calculations to be made (see Table X).

When the composition of the solvent was kept constant (at 25% v/v aqueous ethanol) and the loading of the stationary phase was varied, a similar effect was noted. A like investigation of methylated phenols on thin-layers of cellulose impregnated with formamide and N-methylated formamide[74] showed the R_M-values of phenol and 19 methylated phenols

Table X

$\Delta R_{M(CH_2)}$ For solvent changes for the pairs of phenols

| $\Delta R_{M(CH_2)}$ | Ethanol concentrations (v/100 ml) | | | |
	25	30	37.5	40
2-alkyl phenols	0.397	0.344	0.367	0.368
3-alkyl phenols	0.345	0.270	0.320	0.365
4-alkyl phenols	0.367	0.284	0.330	0.336

1. 2-methyl phenol–2-ethyl phenol
2. 3-methyl phenol–3-ethyl phenol
3. 4-methyl phenol–4-ethyl phenol.
(Chromatographed with a reversed phase of ethyl oleate on cellulose powder. Various concentrations of aqueous ethanol were used as solvents.)

to be linearly related to the log of the concentration of the amide in the slurrying medium used in the preparation of the layers. Deviations from linearity were observed at high and low concentrations of amides. However, as with the ethyl oleate studies, it was not possible to obtain a general value for $\Delta R_{M(S)}$ applicable to all methylene group additions.

Amines

Another, and large, class of compounds which have been investigated are the amines. Various workers have made systematic studies of these compounds, and among the most noteworthy work is that of Gasparic and co-workers,[82, 83] who studied a systematic series of water soluble[82] and water insoluble amines[83] in a series of chromatographic systems. They used various impregnants,[83] *e.g.,* Whatman No. 3 paper impregnated with either formamide, cthylcnc glycol or dimethyl sulfoxide as 20% v/v solutions in ethanol, and various solvents—heptane, benzene, chloroform, and mixtures of these solvents. The studies were part of a larger investigation into the use of chromatography in the structural elucidation of organic compounds. Well over 200 amines were investigated and a range of Rf-values, obtained under carefully controlled conditions, were reported. It is perhaps significant that R_M-values are not reported. The results of calculations of R_M-values and subsequent calculation of $\Delta R_{M(g)}$-values and $\Delta R_{M(S)}$-values for particular groups in some simple amines from their results are given below in Table XI.

From this table it can clearly be seen that positional effects are very significant and that the substitution of a chloro atom into a nucleus at a particular position will have an effect on the R_M of the amine, depending on what substituents are already present. From a consideration of the

$\Delta R_{M(S)}$ values for -CH_2 groupings in the three systems it can be seen that there is no apparent parallel among the effects in those systems.

Similar calculation based on results reported by Bassl and co-workers[84, 85, 86] for a series of primary aromatic amines, chlorinated aromatic amines, and chlorinated and nitrated aromatic amines lead to substantially the same conclusions. The positional effects of these highly

Table XI

ΔR_M-Values calculated for aniline derivatives

$\Delta R_{M(CH_2)}$-values	System		
	1.	*2.*	*3.*
(A)–methyl-(A)*	−0.454	−0.355	−0.365
(A)-3-methyl-(A)	−0.334	−0.250	−0.355
(A)-4-methyl-(A)	−0.354	−0.250	−0.355
2-methyl-(A)–2,3 dimethyl-(A)	−0.230	−0.150	−0.145
2-methyl-(A)–2,4 dimethyl-(A)	−0.430	−0.270	—
2-methyl-(A)–2,5 dimethyl-(A)	−0.310	−0.270	−0.245
2-methyl-(A)–2,6 dimethyl-(A)	−0.500	−0.350	−0.420
$\Delta R_{M(Cl)}$-values			
(A)–2-chloro-(A)	−0.68		
(A)–3-chloro-(A)	−0.21		
(A)–4-chloro-(A)	−0.14		
2-chloro-(A)–2,4-dichloro-(A)	−0.19		
2-chloro-(A)–2,5-dichloro-(A)	+0.02		
3-chloro-(A)–3,4-dichloro-(A)	+0.05		
4-methyl-(A)–3-chloro-4-methyl-(A)	−0.27		
2-methyl-(A)–2-methyl-3-chloro-(A)	−0.21		
2-methyl-(A)–2-methyl-4-chloro-(A)	−0.15		
2-methyl-(A)–2-methyl-5-chloro-(A)	−0.17		
3-chloro-(A)–3-chloro-4-methyl-(A)	−0.41		

Aniline derivatives were chromatographed in the following systems:
  1. 20% formamide; solvent: heptane
  2. 20% formamide; solvent: heptane–benzene (1:1)
  3. 20% ethylene glycol; solvent: heptane–benzene (2:1)

   (All values were calculated by this author from Rf-values given in Reference 83.)

*(A) = aniline.

polar groups are dependent not only on the position of the substituent relative to the main chromatographically functional group but also to the order and arrangement of other substituents.

However, Oscik and Chojnacka[87] investigated the R_M-values of nitro-anilines and aminopyridines in adsorption and partition chromatography;

they used cellulose, silica gel, and alumina as layer material, and on each material used as solvents carbon tetrachloride, chloroform, various hydrocarbons, and some oxygen, containing solvents such as methyl isobutyl ketone and *n*-hexanol. The investigation was carried out for the study of some simple compounds such as 2-, 3-, 4-amino pyridines and the corresponding nitro anilines. Although they claim that their results indicate a linearity of the relationship $R_M^P = f(R_M)$ where R_M^P and R_M refer to partition and adsorption chromatography, respectively, a detailed examination of their results indicates deviations; these are attributed to the different effects of the groups in the different polarity systems.

Although some work has been reported on linear polyethylene polyamines,[88] insufficient data are available to allow detailed calculations to be made of the R_M-values for their constituent groups. There is no obvious reason why they should not behave in a manner similar to long chain polycarboxylic acids.

Steric Factors

One feature which has been brought to some prominence by the study of R_M-values is that of restriction of solvation by steric effects and the associated restriction of adsorption by steric factors. This is fairly widespread and occurs to some extent in all the classes of compounds which have been previously mentioned. The limitations arise from several causes; one is the pseudo-crystalline order which exists especially in hydrogen bonded liquids, and extends for a few molecules. This "cluster" of molecules must be regarded as the unit, and for solvation to take place at any specified point on a molecule, it is thought that there must be enough space to fit one or more of these units of solvent. This accounts to some extent for the ortho effect noticed by many workers in monohydroxy benzenes with 2:6 substituents, or with dihydroxy benzenes with the two hydroxy groups ortho to one another. This effect was noted very early by Bate-Smith and Westall.[4] Bark and co-workers in their work on phenols have used this as a method of classifying the phenols and have showed that if the simple monohydroxy benzenes are divided in accordance with the number of groups ortho to the phenolic hydroxy group, then to a first approximation the additivity principle is valid for each separate group. This is assuming that there are no internal hydrogen bonds formed involving the phenolic grouping. (The question of internal hydrogen bonding will be discussed later).

Bush[9] regards this steric hindrance as accounting for the different chromatographic mobility of the epimeric 3,16,17-estriols. A study of the work of Brewer and his colleagues[89, 90] indicates that the sequence of migration rate for these estriols is:

$$\text{estriol -3-16}\alpha\text{-17}\alpha > \text{estriol -3-16}\beta\text{-17}\beta >$$
$$\text{estriol -3-16}\beta\text{-17}\alpha > \text{estriol -3-16}\alpha\text{-17}\beta$$

It is significant that the *cis* glycols ($16\alpha,17\alpha$ and $16\beta,17\beta$) have a higher migration rate than the corresponding *trans* glycols. In these 16,17-glycols the $16\alpha,17\beta$-diol has the 17-hydroxyl group in the equatorial conformation, which is less hindered than is the axial system. The 16α-hydroxyl group has a conformation intermediate between the axial and the equatorial. Bush[9] had previously indicated that the $16\beta,17\beta$-*cis*-diol also has an equatorial and intermediate conformation of the hydroxyl groups which should cause the *cis* compound to have the same $\Delta R_{M(g)}$-value as its epimer, if the groups are behaving as they do when isolated. In fact the *trans* group has the higher $\Delta R_{M(g)}$-value. Bush gives numerous examples of this effect in the steroid systems and even calculates the probable hindrance deficit in the $\Delta R_{M(g)}$-values dependent on the conformation of the α-diol group. This factor is, of course, of great use in some cases in helping to assign directly the configuration of the steroid.

In order to study the effect of geometric isomerism on chromatographic behavior several workers have dealt with various systems. Morris *et al*[91] have studied the separation of isomeric octadecenoates on thin-layers of silica gel impregnated with silver nitrate. They achieved noteworthy separation of the *cis* and *trans* isomers of a series of octadecenoates. Green and McHale[38] report work involving the study of a long chain aliphatic C_{100}-isoprenoid alcohol (dolichol). This compound was believed to contain several *cis* olefinic linkages. From a knowledge of the chromatography of the all-*trans* alcohols, solanesol and spadicol, which differ only by one *trans*-isoprenoid unit, they were able to allocate a $\Delta R_{M(g)}$ for the *trans* unit, and hence were able by using chromatographic and other evidence, to conclude that dolichol has 15- or 16-*cis* double bonds.

Although it is possible to investigate *cis-trans* isomerism with R_M-values, as Green points out, it is necessary to be very cautious in considering low molecular weight compounds, since the steric effect is often overshadowed by the other intermolecular interactions that may arise. These often come about because of the different interfunctional group distances in the isomers. To illustrate this point they quote the work of Sanda, Prochazka, and Le Moal[92] who chromatographed a series of dicarboxylic acids on cellulose paper in a butyl acetate–water solvent. They quote ΔR_M-values for both $\Delta R_{M(CH_2)}$ and $\Delta R_{M(COOH)}$, and note that on comparing *cis* and *trans* pairs of acids the factor which determined the migration rate is probably the ease with which intramolecular hydrogen bonding can be established. The formation of internal hydrogen bonding is much more probable and energetically much more favored in the *trans* compound.

This internal hydrogen bonding also occurs in some syn- and antioximes and it has been suggested[38] that this is one of the major factors in determining the migration rate of the various oximes.

Hydrogen bonding, both intermolecular and intramolecular, plays a leading role in determining the chromatographic behavior of hydroxy compounds. It is possible to predict the qualitative effect on R_M-values of hydrogen bonding by comparing the various kinds of phenols, etc. studied. The ease of electron delocalization in the benzene nucleus facilitates variations in the polarity of the hydroxy bond with consequent variations in the type and strength of the bonds formed. This has been discussed in detail in several publications.[38, 40–45, 62–74] It is generally not possible to allocate a precise value for the $\Delta R_{M(\text{hydrogen bonding})}$, although this has been attempted on various occasions.

THE USE OF ΔR_M-VALUES FOR STRUCTURAL ELUCIDATION

From the foregoing discussion it can be seen that a large amount of work has been done on many series of compounds, and from the accumulation of the Rf-values of compounds in many chromatographic systems it should be possible to elucidate the structure of a compound provided that (a) there is a reasonable amount of knowledge available concerning its chemical properties, or if it be an unknown compound, some indication of the likelihood of which functional groups are likely to be present (postulated by analogy with the known compounds with which it is found), and (b) it is possible to obtain ΔR_M-values for groups, for modification reactions, and for solvent changes for the unknown compound.

The methods used in (a) are outside the scope of this work, and it is assumed that as much information as possible has been obtained from spectral evidence of all kinds and from chemical reactivity evidence, so that there is a reasonable probability that at least the presence of some functional groups has been established, and some approximate value of the molecular weight of the compound is available.

Thus we must consider what methods are available for and what principles are involved in obtaining ΔR_M-values likely to give structural information pertinent to the compound under investigation. Considering first the changes in R_M brought about by change of solvent in the system, it is necessary to decide which is the distribution mechanism operating— or if the distribution between the two phases is by both adsorption and partition, which is the predominant mechanism. This is particularly the case when the solute molecule has a strong polar group, such as the carboxylic acid or the phenolic group. In partition systems, the group will not be held rigidly to any particular site and the solvent molecules of either phase can approach the functional group. If, however, we consider some partition systems, where the group is fixed relatively firmly to a site, then solvent molecules have less chance of approaching the group, since they cannot pass through the solid substrate. Thus, we can envisage the case where we have two systems with the same mobile phase and with the same solutes. In one case we have "true" partition; in the other we have a mixture of partition and adsorption. (This situation can arise when the degree of loading of the reversed phase impregnant is low and the supposedly inert layer material, say, cellulose plays some part in the distribution.) If we alter the mobile phase in each by the same amount, we will not obtain the same $\Delta R_{M(S)}$ for a particular solute in the two systems. The solutes which have the more polar groups, and hence will be more strongly bound to the cellulose, will show the least effect. To obtain the maximum amount of benefit, we must know what mechanisms are determining the distribution of the solutes throughout the whole chromatographic system. With solutes having only one type of chromatographically active functional group, such as the carboxylic acid, the method is to choose two solvents which differ only in a component which reacts selectively with the functional group. If there is more than one functional group, then it is necessary to choose a component which will react strongly towards one selected functional group and not towards the others. An example of the first situation is Howe's[36] classification of the carboxylic acids by using the following two systems: (a) isopropanol–dilute aqueous ammonia, and (b) isopropanol–dilute aqueous sulfurous acid. All functional groups except acidic or basic groups are unaffected on changing the solvent, and hence identical $\Delta R_{M(g)}$-values will be found for aliphatic -OH groups, $-CH_2$, $>C = O$, etc. The change in R_M, brought about by the addition of one -COOH group, is determined by comparing the R_M-values of two acids differing only by one such group, and from this value of $\Delta R_{M(S)}$ for one -COOH group it is possible to obtain the corresponding value for a di- or tricarboxylic acid. Thus the number of acids groups can be determined. Reichl's work[58] on the phenols and homologs is a further example. Thus, if we have two systems where all group constants but one are identical, then Equation 8 for the solute in each system can be written:

$$R_{M(S)1} = K_1 + m\Delta R_{Ma1} + n\Delta R_{Mb1} + \dots\dots\dots\dots x\Delta R_{Mx1}$$
$$R_{M(S)2} = K_2 + m\Delta R_{Ma2} + n\Delta R_{Mb2} + \dots\dots\dots\dots x\Delta R_{Mx2}$$

where 1 refers to solvent system 1
      2 refers to solvent system 2

assuming that all parameters for a, b, c, etc. (except x) are constant,

then $R_{M(S)1} - R_{M(S)2} = \Delta R_{M(S)} = X(\Delta R_{Mx1} - \Delta R_{Mx2})$
or x = number of functional groups of nature X

$$= \frac{\Delta R_{M(S)}}{\Delta R_{Mx(S)}}$$

where $\Delta R_{Mx(S)}$ = change in R_M, in the system for one group X.

This idea has been used by many workers to obtain quantitative information regarding the number of groups of a particular nature in a compound. The work of Macek,[40] who determined the number of α-glycol groups in steroids by the change in R_M-values produced on adding boric acid to one solvent, has already been described. These changes are generally very great and are unambiguous. However, with more than one functional group present, especially if they are of the same nature— hydroxyl groups, phenolic and carboxylic acid groups, double bonds and other π electrons systems—then the complexities are much greater.

It is not possible to give meaningful $\Delta R_{M(s)}$ systems for groups; they must be determined for the system at hand and on compounds of known structure. For example, hydroxylic solvents such as alcohols or polar solvents such as formamides show small or negligible differences in their interactions with hydroxyl or related groups on steroid molecules, unless the hydroxyl groups are strongly hindered or are in complex formation. Thus, it is not expected that large $\Delta R_{M(s)}$-values for hydroxyl groups will occur using a series of any of these compounds as the stationary phases, since the strength of the bonds will not significantly alter. However, the use of a bulky group in a solvent, which will hinder solvation of a hydroxyl group (for example, the presence of, say, a tertiary butyl group on a solvent), will enable relatively large $\Delta R_{M(s)}$-values to be obtained.

Similarly, any solvent which has a large electron density at an atom— for example, dimethyl sulfoxide, dioxane, phosphinyl oxides—will be able to solvate most of the hydroxyl groups (unless sterically prevented from doing so), and relatively large changes in R_M-values will be noted.

CHANGES BROUGHT ABOUT BY MODIFICATION OF STRUCTURE ($\Delta R_{M(r)}$ VALUES)

As indicated earlier, the changes in the R_M-value caused by reaction of a group are characteristic for each chemical change within an organic molecule. These changes in R_M-values will be constant for other compounds of nearly similar chemical structure treated by the same reaction, provided that the same chemical changes occurred and the same molecular interactions are present in all the compounds.

Some of these chemical modifications are brought about by isolating the compound, submitting it to normal chemical reactions, and then spotting the reaction products onto a plate or paper and carrying out a normal, controlled chromatographic separation of the reaction products. One of the great advantages of chromatographic studies of this type is that it is not necessary to isolate the required reaction product or to have the reaction go to completion. The chromatographic run will be devised so that separation of the various products is obtained. From the number of products and the differences in the R_M-values of these and the parent or starting compound, it is possible to obtain much information regarding the structural nature of the starting compound. Bush gives many examples of the change in R_M produced by reaction modification using the steroids as his examples. He has compiled a list of $\Delta R_{M(r)}$-values for many compounds and many groups, obtained for such reactions as oxidation of keto groups with periodic acid or sodium bismuthate. He suggests many reactions for the characterization of such groups as hydroxyl groups, double bond systems, $\Delta 5$-3β-ols and many others. From the values quoted in his book and also that of Neher,[54] it is possible to obtain a large amount of information regarding the order of the changes in R_M expected for modification by reaction.

It is perhaps inevitable that since the hydroxy group is probably one of the most widespread of reactive groups, it has been very widely studied. Acetylation of hydroxy groups, and the resulting change in the R_M-values of compounds, is constantly referred to in much work on steroids[53, 93] and has also been used for simple phenolic compounds and sugars.[94] There is, however, one great disadvantage which occurs in modifying the steroids in this manner, and this is that sometimes the properties of the modified compounds are such that meaningful Rf-values cannot be obtained using the same solvent to chromatograph the modified compound, as was used to chromatograph the parent steroid. Thus it sometimes becomes necessary to modify the solvent and to utilize $\Delta R_{M(s)}$ changes as well as $\Delta R_{M(r)}$ changes.

Gasparič and Gemzova[95] have recently used the acetylation reaction and the consequent $\Delta R_{M(r)}$-values for the detection and determination of the number of hydroxy groups in azo dyestuffs, especially those insoluble in water but soluble in organic solvents. They list $\Delta R_{M(r)}$-values for over 30 reactions and have indicated what ranges of change correspond to certain structural features.

In the case of simple phenols, no quantitative investigations have as yet been made. This is not surprising since change of the functionality of the main chromatographically active group is accompanied by changes in electronic distribution which affect every group attached to the nucleus.

Although the reactions indicated above are all relatively easy to carry out and can often be done simply by mixing a few milligrams of the reagents in a melting point tube and allowing the reaction to proceed either at room temperature or at high temperature in a sealed tube reaction, it is much easier, and aesthetically much better, to carry out the reaction on the plate or paper. Many such examples have been reported in the literature. A few examples follow, which will show some of the scope of this type of reaction.

Edwards[96] showed that formylation can be done quite successfully by exposing the solute on the chromatographic substrate to formic acid vapors. Kaufmann[97] hydrogenated unsaturated fatty acids in the presence of colloidal palladium dropped onto the spot on the paper and exposed the still wet paper to hydrogen in a hermetically sealed vessel. Methylation can be accomplished by spraying the area of the spot with diazomethane; oxidation of easily oxidizable materials can be brought about by spotting with chromic acid–potassium iodate solution; brominations can be done by exposing the plate to bromine vapors. When reversed phase systems are used, great care must be taken not to cause a reaction with the substance of the reversed phase, and for this reason it is sometimes better to do the reactions outside the system.

Although the above methods have been quoted as methods of obtaining some quantitative evidence of the number of functional groups, it is obvious that all these can be used to obtain qualitative evidence of the existence of groups. Indeed, if only qualitative evidence is required, one may extend the range. For example, although the use of layers impregnated with silver nitrate[91, 98, 99] or other metal compounds has been advocated for the determination of the number of double bonds, it is probably best used for the detection of this group. Morris,[91] however, has classified structurally some compounds by this method. The use of ΔR_M-values for structural elucidation presupposes one important and vital fact, which is that the Rf-values produced and the ΔR_M-values calculated therefrom can be considered to be experimentally viable. The question of the experimental conditions necessary for the reproducibility of Rf-values has been discussed in detail by various workers[100] and needs no further discussion here; however, the problem still remains of how reliable values obtained over a considerable length of time are. This in turn determines whether or not they can be used routinely in laboratories.

Many workers have discussed the problems associated with the production of meaningful Rf-values when obtained during a day-to-day or routine manner. It is obvious that, although extremely highly reproducible Rf- and hence R_M-values can be obtained, these usually require more elaborate precautions and procedures than are often obtained or desired in a routine laboratory. As has been previously noted, Green and coworkers[31] advocated—for their work on phenolic compounds—that the R_M-values of selected standard substances be obtained under conditions of "tankless" chromatography. Bark and co-workers[62–74] in their work on phenols have repeatedly used a standard phenol to evaluate the results obtained on any particular chromatographic run. They chromatographed the selected standard compounds under the conditions ideally designed for reproducibility and found the mean Rf-values (usually from over 100 values). On subsequent runs, the routine conditions, although fairly rigorously controlled, were judged by comparing the Rf-values of the standard phenols with those values previously obtained under the 'standard' conditions. Any plate or paper which gave Rf-values for the standard differing by more than ±0.02Rf units from the accepted mean was rejected, and the Rf-values of all substances on this run were discounted. Although the wastage rate was not high, it is obvious that such methods have their disadvantages in normal routine procedure.

Gasparič[101] has advocated the selection of a series of standards for each chromatographic run. These standards are chosen so that their Rf-values in the system under consideration will give a solute in a particular area of the plate; any variations in the plate will be noticed, then, as variations in the Rf- of the standards. The Rf-values of the unknown can be compensated for variations in the plate or related directly to that of the standard in the same region of the plate. Bush and Crawshaw[102] reported their findings, using a technique for rapid paper chromatography of some steroids. Many of their experiments were done at ambient room temperature under poor conditions of temperature control. They attributed day-to-day variations in the Rf-values obtained with normally equilibrated papers to temperature variations. With regard to pretreated papers and the papers used for reversed phase chromatography, they considered that the variability which, in their experience, was usually greater than that found in 'untreated papers', was probably due to variation in the phase ratio, brought about by the variation in the cross-sectional area of the stationary phase. They considered that the variations in the Rf-values did not make any difference to the $\Delta R_{M(g)}$ terms, and that they could still be used for the calculation of these terms. They quote as proof of this the R_M-values for three substances obtained from chromatograms run under normal conditions and obtained from pre-equilibrated papers, under very carefully controlled conditions. These values are given in Tables XII and XIII.

Table XII

R_M-Values under different equilibration conditions*

Substance or group	$R_{M(1)}$	$R_{M(2)}$
Androst-4-ene-3,17,-dione	+0.07	+0.085
Androst-4-ene-3,11,17,-trione	+0.32	+0.495
11β Hydroxyandrost-4-ene-3,17-dione	+0.60	+0.775
	$\Delta R_{M(g)1}$	$\Delta R_{M(g)2}$
11β-Hydroxy group	+0.67	+0.69
11 Ketone group	+0.39	+0.41

Conditions (1) Normal
Conditions (2) Pre-equilibrated.

*Values are quoted from Reference 102. Courtesy of *Journal of Chromatography*.

Table XIII

$\Delta R_{M(g)}$ For 11β-hydroxy and 11-keto groups obtained for a series
of compounds chromatographed in tetralin–methanol–water (10:9:1)
on paper pre-equilibrated with the vapor phase*

Root substance	$\Delta R_{M(g)\,11\beta\text{-}hydroxy}$	$\Delta R_{M(g)\,11\text{-}keto}$
Progesterone	0.77	0.38
Androst-4-ene-3,17-dione	0.69	0.38
Aetiocholanolone	0.80	0.40

It can be seen by comparing Tables XII and XIII that the $\Delta R_{M(g)}$-values are within the range of experimental error normally expected and are better than those sometimes found under test conditions.

*Values are quoted from Reference 102. Courtesy of *Journal of Chromatography*.

They consider this a strong indication that the changes in the Rf- and R_M-values of the substances are not due to a change in the composition of the effective phase of the solvent, but are due to a change in the A_S/A_L ratio brought about by nonequilibrium conditions.

Conclusion

It may be seen from the previous discussions that the supposition expressed by Martin, that there is simply algebraic additivity of ΔR_M-values, is adequately fulfilled both in partition and adsorption chromatography *provided we can isolate and define the effect of each of the substituent groups*. For similar groups, that is, those which have similar molecular interactions within the molecule, then we have similar ΔR_M-values. From a consideration of the reasons for the apparent deviations we can see that, provided there is no effect—electronically or sterically—on the main functional group, we can obtain definite $\Delta R_{M(g)}$-values for the substituent. This can come about whether we regard the substituent as an atomic grouping or a 'molecular' grouping, such as the methylene group, the keto group, the 11α-equatorial keto group, or a structural group, *e.g.*, a double bond, *cis-trans* isomerism, or chain branching.

However, when we are dealing with chromatography of nuclear-substituted aromatic compounds such as phenols or anilines, or with adsorption systems, whether the distribution mechanism be mainly adsorption or partition, then it becomes difficult to assign all the various parameters. The ease of delocalization of electron density in simple aromatics makes the definition of a group very difficult. This in no way denies the validity of the Martin relationship or the correctness of the fundamental equation relating R_M with the number and nature of the groups present. It is simply that the number of parameters and groups has to be made so large that the determination of accurate and meaningful group values, while simple in theory, becomes difficult in practice, and for such structural analysis the use of approximate values renders the exercise meaningless. Attempts are being made to data process much of the information, and with new methods of information retrieval it should be possible to allow this type of structural elucidation to take its rightful role in the science of conformational analysis.

REFERENCES

1. Martin, A. J. P., and R. L. M. Synge, Biochem. J. **35**, 1358 (1941).
2. Consden, R., A. H. Gordon, and A. J. P. Martin, Biochem. J. **38**, 224 (1944).
3. Martin, A. J. P., Biochem. Soc. Symp. (Cambridge, Engl.) **3**, 4 (1950).
4. Bate-Smith, E. C., and R. G. Westall, Biochim. Biophys. Acta **4**, 427 (1950).
5. Mulvany, P. K., J. Am. Chem. Soc. **73**, 1255 (1951).
6. Benson, A. A., J. Am. Chem. Soc. **72**, 1710 (1950).
7. Giddings, J. C., G. H. Stewart, and A. L. Ruoff, J. Chromatog. **3**, 239 (1960).
8. Ackermann, B. J., and H. G. Cassidy, Anal. Chem. **26**, 1874 (1954).
9. Bush, I. E., *The Chromatography of Steroids* (London: Pergamon Press, 1961), p 31.
10. Reineke, L. M., Anal. Chem. **28**, 1853 (1956).
11. Neher, R., J. Chromatog. **1**, 122 (1958).
12. Green, J., and S. Marcinkiewicz, J. Chromatog. **10**, 42 (1963). See also Chromatog. Rev. **5**, 58 (1963).
13. Copius-Peereboom, J. W., Rec. Trav. Chim. **84**, 659 (1965).
14. De Zotti, G., P. Capella, and G. Jacini, Fette, Seifen, Anstrichmettel **61**, 1114 (1959).
15. Kaufmann, H. P., and E. Mohr, Fette, Seifen, Anstrichmittel **60**, 165 (1958).
16. Bark, L. S., and G. Duncan, G. Duncan, Master's Thesis, 1966 (University of Salford. In press, 1969).
17. Bark, L. S., and N. Halstead, N. Halstead, Master's Thesis, 1968 (University of Salford. In press, 1969).
18. Daly, J., Ph.D. Thesis, University of Salford, 1968.
19. Bark, L. S., and R. J. T. Graham, Unpublished results.
20. Rubin, B. L., R. I. Dorfman, and G. Pincus, J. Biol. Chem. **203**, 629 (1953).
21. Bush, I. E., *The Chromatography of Steroids* (London: Pergamon Press, 1961), p 9.
22. Kemula, W., A. Buchowski, and J. Teperek, Rev. Chim. Acad. Rep. Populaire Roumaine **7**, 295 (1962).

23. Goble, A. G., and A. G. Maddock, Trans. Faraday Soc. **55**, 591 (1959).
24. Schultz, G. V., Z. Physik. Chem. (Frankfurt) **A179**, 321 (1937).
25. Kemula, W., and H. Buchowski, Roczniki Chem. **29**, 718 (1955).
26. Soczewinski, E., and C. A. Wachmeister, J. Chromatog. **7**, 311 (1962).
27. Soczewinski, E., T. Wolski, and K. Jurkiewicz, Ann. Univ. Mariae Curie-Sklodowska, Lublin-Polonia **AA19**, 25 (1964).
28. Soczewinski, E., and J. Kuczynskie, Separ. Sci. **3**, 133 (1968).
29. Prochazka, Z., Bull. Soc. Chim. Belgrade **30**, 217 (1965).
30. Schauer, H. K., and Burlirsch, Z. Naturforsch. **106**, 683 (1955).
31. Marcinkiewicz, S., J. Green, and D. McHale, Chromatog. Rev. **5**, 65 (1963).
32. Green, J., S. Marcinkiewicz, and D. McHale, J. Chromatog. **10**, 158 (1963).
33. Long, A. G., J. R. Quayle, and R. J. Steadman, J. Chem. Soc. **1951**, 2197.
34. Inouye, Y., and M. Noda, Bull. Agr. Chem. Soc. Japan **19**, 214 (1955).
35. Inouye, Y., M. Noda, and O. Hirayama, J. Am. Oil Chemists' Soc. **32**, 132 (1955).
36. Howe, J. R., J. Chromatog. **3**, 389 (1960).
37. Isherwood, F. A., and C. S. Hanes, Biochem. J. **55**, 824 (1953).
38. Green, J., and D. McHale, Advan. Chromatogr. **2**, 99 (1966).
39. Franc, J., and J. Jokl, Collection Czech. Chem. Commun. **21**, 1161 (1956).
40. Bark, L. S., and R. J. T. Graham, Talanta **11**, 839 (1964).
41. Bark, L. S., and R. J. T. Graham, Analyst **84**, 454 (1959).
42. Bark, L. S., and R. J. T. Graham, Analyst **85**, 663 (1960).
43. Bark, L. S., and R. J. T. Graham, Analyst **85**, 905 (1960).
44. Bark, L. S., and R. J. T. Graham, Analyst **85**, 907 (1960).
45. Brenner, M., A. Niederwieser, G. Pataki, and R. Weber, *Dünnschicht-Chromatographie*, Ed. by E. Stahl (Berlin: Springer-Verlag, 1962), p 79.
46. Macek, K., and Z. Vejdelek, Nature **176**, 1173 (1955).
47. Brooks, S. G., J. S. Hunt, A. G. Long, and B. Mooney, J. Chem. Soc. **1957**, 1175.
48. Monder, C., Biochem. J. **90**, 522 (1964).
49. Lisboa, B. P., Steroids **6**, 605 (1965).
50. Pasqualini, J. R., *Contribution a l'étude Biochemique des corticosteroides* (Paris: R. Foulon et Cie, 1962).
51. Klopper, A., J. A. Strong, and L. R. Cook, J. Endocrinol. **15**, 810 (1957).
52. Knight, B. A., A. W. Roger, and G. H. Thomas, Biophys. Res. Commun. **8**, 253 (1962).
53. Lisboa, B. P., J. Chromatog. **19**, 81 (1965).
54. Neher, R., *Steroid Chromatography* (Amsterdam: Elsevier, 1964).

55. Lisboa, B. P., J. Pharm. Belg. **20**, 435 (1965).
56. Lisboa, B. P., J. Chromatog. **13**, 391 (1964).
57. Doorenbos, N. J., and R. K. Rameshwar, J. Chromatog. **29**, 393 (1967).
58. Reichl, E. R., Monatsh. Chem. **86**, 69 (1955).
59. Reichl, E. R., Mikrochim. Acta **1956**, 683.
60. Bark, L. S., J. Chromatog. In press, 1969.
61. Green, J., and D. McHale, Advan. Chromatogr. **2**, 117 (1966).
62. Bark, L. S., and R. J. T. Graham, Talanta **13**, 1281 (1966).
63. Bark, L. S., and R. J. T. Graham, Proc. Soc. Anal. Chem. Conf. Nottingham, England **1965**, 112.
64. Bark, L. S., and R. J. T. Graham, J. Chromatog. **23**, 120 (1966).
65. Bark, L. S., and R. J. T. Graham, J. Chromatog. **23**, 417 (1966).
66. Bark, L. S., and R. J. T. Graham, J. Chromatog. **25**, 347 (1966).
67. Bark, L. S., and R. J. T. Graham, J. Chromatog. **25**, 357 (1966).
68. Bark, L. S., and R. J. T. Graham, J. Chromatog. **27**, 109 (1967).
69. Bark, L. S., and R. J. T. Graham, J. Chromatog. **27**, 116 (1967).
70. Bark, L. S., and R. J. T. Graham, J. Chromatog. **27**, 131 (1967).
71. Bark, L. S., and R. J. T. Graham, Proc. 4th Intern. Symp. Chromatog. Électrophorèse Belg. Pharm. Soc. Bruxelles **1967**, 107.
72. Bark, L. S., and R. J. T. Graham, Proc. 4th Intern. Symp. Chromatog. Électrophorèse Belg. Pharm. Soc. Bruxelles **1967**, 119.
73. Bark, L. S., R. J. T. Graham, and J. Daly, Proc. 4th Intern. Symp. Chromatog. Électrophorèse Belg. Pharm. Soc. Bruxelles **1967**, 128.
74. Bark, L. S., R. J. T. Graham, and J. Daly, J. Chromatog. **33**, 107 (1968).
75. Renault, J., and M. F. Cartron, Ann. Pharm. Franc. **25**, 291 (1967).
76. Gumprecht, D. L., J. Chromatog. **30**, 528 (1967).
77. Gumprecht, D. L., J. Chromatog. **37**, 268 (1968).
78. Joschek, H. I., and S. I. Miller, J. Ann. Chem. Soc. **88**, 3276, 3279 (1966).
79. Enkvist, T., Finska Kemistsamfundets Medd. **74**, 67 (1965).
80. Scheline, R. R., J. Pharm. Pharmacol. **18**, 665 (1966).
81. Bark, L. S., Unpublished results.
82. Cee, A., and J. Gasparič, Mikrochim. Acta **1966**, 295.
83. Gasparič, J., and I. Gamzova, Mikrochim. Acta **1966**, 314.
84. Bassl, A., H-J. Heckemann, and J. Baumann, J. Prakt. Chem. **36**, 271 (1967).
85. Bassl, A., H-J. Heckemann, and J. Baumann, J. Prakt. Chem. **36**, 278 (1967).
86. Bassl, A., H-J. Heckemann, and J. Baumann, J. Prakt. Chem. **36**, 276 (1967).
87. Oscik, J., and G. Chojnacka, Chem. Anal. (Warsaw) **12**, 1213 (1967).
88. Parrish, J. R., J. Chromatog. **18**, 535 (1965).

89. Breuer, H., R. Knuppen, and G. Pangels, Z. Physiol. Chem. **317**, 248 (1959).
90. Nocke, W., H. Breuer, and R. Knuppen, Acta Endocrinol. **36**, 393 (1961).
91. Morris, L. J., D. M. Wharry, and E. W. Hammond, J. Chromatog. **31**, 69 (1967).
92. Sanda, V., Z. Prochazka, and H. Le Moal, Collection Czech. Chem. Commun. **24**, 420 (1959).
93. Neher, R., J. Chromatog. **1**, 205 (1958).
94. Dittrich, S., Mikrochim. Acta **1966**, 477.
95. Gasparič, J., and I. Gemzova, J. Chromatog. **35**, 362 (1968).
96. Edwards, R. W. H., Biochem. J. **82**, 48 (1962).
97. Kaufmann, H. P., and K. K. Chowdhury, Chem. Ber. **91**, 2117 (1958).
98. Moore, L. J., J. Lipid Res. **7**, 117 (1966).
99. De Vries, B., and G. Jurriens, Fette, Seifen, Anstrichmittel **65**, 725 (1963).
100. Proc. 3rd Intern. Symp. PC and TLC, Prague, 1967, J. Chromatog. **35** (1968).
101. Gasparič, J., J. Chromatog. **35**, 291 (1968).
102. Bush, I., and K. Crowshaw, J. Chromatog. **19**, 114 (1965).

Chapter 2

Thin-Layer
Radiochromatography
and Related Procedures

by F. Snyder

A number of reviews[1-6] on the measurement of labeled substances by thin-layer chromatography (TLC) have been published since the introduction of radioassay techniques for chromatoplates.[7-9] The types of radiometric procedures used with TLC include elution analysis, strip scanning, autoradiography and related techniques, zone analysis (*i.e.*, area scraping and zonal profile scans), beta camera detection, and combustion analysis. Illustrations of typical instruments used in these procedures are in Figures 1–6.

Labeled molecules, including those with stable isotopes,[10] have been resolved on TLC plates by adsorption, partition, molecular filtration, and ion exchange processes. The potential of these chromatographic processes can be extended by carrying out chemical reactions directly on the layers, by varying the kinds of thin-layers, and by using gradient mixtures of adsorbents on the same plate.

The techniques discussed in this review are examined in terms of the principles involved, equipment required, results obtained, and their advantages and disadvantages. The review is slanted toward users of low-energy beta isotopes, but for the most part the same procedures could be used for gamma-emitting isotopes with NaI crystals as detectors. The special section on applications of radiochromatography emphasizes methods and general sources of information on topics related to organic chemistry and biochemistry, radiation safety, radiopurity, radiolysis, mass measurements, and gas-liquid radiochromatography.

DESCRIPTION OF TECHNIQUES

Elution Analysis

Elution techniques involve the transfer of an area of adsorbent, loosened by scraping with a razor blade or spatula, to a filter disc, test tube, or beaker either manually or by special tubes containing a fritted disc attached to a vacuum (Figure 1). Such aspirator tubes are commercially available from several sources. Extracting solvents are passed over the adsorbent until the sample is quantitatively eluted. Choice of the eluting

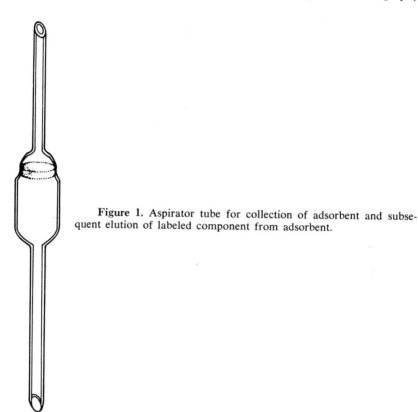

Figure 1. Aspirator tube for collection of adsorbent and subsequent elution of labeled component from adsorbent.

solvent, which is critical for quantitative recoveries, is generally made empirically. A solvent or solvent mixture that causes the sample to migrate at an Rf > 0.8 is suitable for quantitative elution: the polarity of the solvent must be greater than the polarity of the sample being eluted. The details of a typical technique are illustrated in the quantitative elution procedure that Goldrick and Hirsch[11] described for ^{14}C-labeled triglycerides.

Elution analysis is useful for isolating large quantities of labeled compounds, and it can be performed with simple and inexpensive equipment. A distinct advantage of elution procedures is that the compounds isolated can be used for additional chemical and physical measurements. On the other hand, selection of solvent(s) for quantitative elution is difficult, and the gravimetric determination of mass may not be quantitative because some adsorbents are also taken up in the eluting solvents. Moreover, most elution procedures are relatively time-consuming and do not give good resolution when radioassay by increment of an entire chromatographic lane is desired.

Strip Scanning

Strip scanning[9, 12-38] refers to procedures in which thin-layer chromatoplates containing radioactive substances pass under, over, or between radiation detector(s) (Figure 2). The detector(s) can be fixed while the chromatoplate moves, or vice versa. The detectors used are thin-window Geiger-Müller tubes, gas-flow Geiger-Müller tubes, and phototubes. The phototube detector (Figure 3) measures light produced by interaction of radioactivity with scintillator gels or solutions impregnated in the adsorbent layers.[29] Two recent reviews[2, 3] of publications related to strip scanning illustrate strip scanners that are available from several companies. Strip scans provide a linear display of the disintegrations per minute on chart paper, representing the distribution of radioactivity on

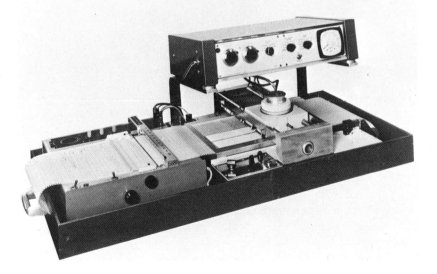

Figure 2. A thin-layer radiochromatogram strip scanner that includes versatile presentation of data, *e.g.*, tracings, integrated-count printout or interval-count printout. Reproduced by permission of Panax Equip. Ltd., Redhill, Surrey, England.

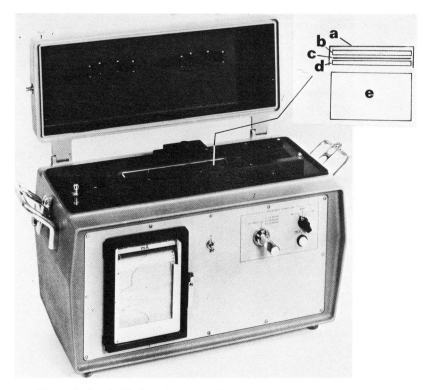

Figure 3. A scintillation photo-strip scanner (DMSL-3) for thin-layer radio-chromatograms impregnated with organic scintillator; (a) aluminum foil, (b) scintillator gel, (c) adsorbent, (d) glass chromatoplate, (e) photomultiplier. Reproduced by permission of Société d'Applications Industrielles de la Physique, Paris, France.

the chromatoplate. The speed of the recorder can be adjusted to the same speed as the TLC plate holder that passes under the radiation detector, making it possible to determine the precise location of the radioactive areas when the chromatogram is superimposed on the chart paper. When the level of radioactivity on the chromatogram is low, slow speeds or zonal assays must be used.

Strip scanning is a rapid technique when the level of radioactivity is sufficiently high. The compounds assayed are not destroyed, and the technique is especially useful for locating radioactivity on two-dimensional chromatoplates. Its main disadvantage is lack of sensitivity for detecting small quantities of low-energy beta isotopes because of self-absorption problems within the adsorbent and because 4π detection is not possible on chromatoplates. The relatively high cost of strip scanners must be considered if a wide range of sensitivities is required, *i.e.*, instrumentation of this type, satisfactory in organic chemistry, will not be practical for detecting small quantities of radioactivity in biochemical intermediates.

Autoradiography

Autoradiograms of thin-layer chromatograms[39-52] require the direct contact of the chromatographic layer with a photographic emulsion. X-Ray films are generally used, although more sensitive emulsions have been used with tritium-labeled compounds. Impregnation of adsorbent layers with nuclear emulsions or fluorographic compounds can enhance the sensitivity of autoradiography.

Fluorography[44] is possible when the TLC adsorbent is impregnated with an organic scintillator such as anthracene; it is most effective at lower temperatures. The light produced by the interaction of beta particles and the scintillator enhances the radiation effect responsible for the image on the photographic emulsion. However, fluorography is only one-tenth as sensitive as impregnation with nuclear emulsions in paper chromatography; no one has published similar comparisons with thin-layer chromatograms.

Sublimation and distillation of components from the adsorbent layer can also occur during autoradiography, causing a chemical interaction (independent of radiation) with the photographic emulsion.[52] Such interactions can be used to increase the sensitivity of detection of photographic emulsions. However, in general, it is best to eliminate these poorly characterized and poorly reproducible chemical reactions by covering the adsorbent layer with plastic or preservative coatings (artist's sprays). These coatings will also decrease the sensitivity of detection of radioactivity and should not be used when tritium is assayed.

In general, devices used for autoradiography must exclude light and provide maximum pressure contact between the adsorbent layer and the photographic emulsion. Several types of holders (Figure 4) for the preparation of autoradiograms of thin-layer chromatograms have been described and the methodology for autoradiography has been discussed in other papers.[2, 3, 39-52] An autoradiogram makes an excellent permanent record of the distribution of radioactivity on chromatograms. The degree of blackening on the film can be determined by photodensitometry, but quantitative measurements are difficult, if not impossible, for wide ranges of radioactivity.[51] Guidelines for determining exposure periods of thin-layer chromatograms containing specified quantities of radioactivity have been published.[51]

With sufficient time, the use of photographic emulsions is one of the most sensitive procedures for detecting radioactivity on chromatograms. It is inexpensive and does not require elaborate apparatus. However, autoradiograms may need extremely long periods of exposure, they are difficult to quantitate, and they can show false images due to chemical interactions with the photographic film.

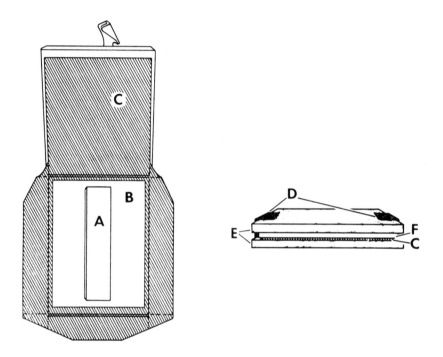

Figure 4. Example of a cassette used in the preparation of autoradiograms from thin-layer chromatograms. The components are as follows: (A) chromato-plate, (B) Kodak No-Screen X-ray film, (C) envelope for holding film and chro-matoplate, (D) spring clip, (E) ¾-in. plywood plates, and (F) ¾-in. sponge.

Zone Analysis: Area Scraping and Zonal Profile Scans by Liquid Scintillation Radioassay

The scraping of adsorbent, entire spots[7, 8, 53–57] or minute zones[34, 58–66] from chromatoplates for liquid-scintillation radioassay is the most quan-titative and sensitive procedure for detection and resolution of radioac-tivity on TLC plates. Absorption of beta energies (quenching) associ-ated with polar compounds that are adsorbed on adsorbent particles[7, 58] can be avoided by use of special scintillation solutions[2, 58, 63] or by con-trolling the particle size of the adsorbent, but when quenching occurs it must be corrected.[58] Correction factors based on internal or external standards are required if quenching problems arise.[58]

Relatively large areas of TLC adsorbent layers can be scraped by hand into scintillation vials by using a razor blade or spatula. However, the

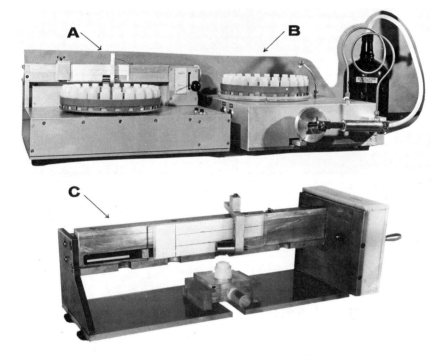

Figure 5. An automatic zonal scraper and collector (A), pipetting device (B), and manual zonal scraper (C) used to prepare ^{14}C and ^{3}H zonal profile scans of thin-layer chromatograms.

quantitative measurement of the distribution of radioactivity in small reproducible zones of adsorbent from a chromatographic lane requires precise instruments for scraping and collection. Manual[58,59] and automatic[60,61] scraping devices* have been developed for this purpose (Figure 5). The entire system of sample preparation and analysis has been completely automated[63] and the more recent change to on-line computer facilities[64,65] has permitted rapid calculations, statistical evaluations, and graphic printout of mass and radioactivity data derived from thin-layer chromatograms.

Comparisons have shown that zonal profile analysis done by liquid scintillation assay provides better data than strip scanning[34] and autoradiography.[51] The zonal system is versatile in that the scraping can be done either with simple equipment or completely automatically. However, samples cannot easily be recovered for further chemical analysis, and the procedure can be time-consuming when one is dealing with low abso-

---

*The automatic zonal scraper and collector is commercially available (Analabs Inc., P.O. Drawer 5397, Hamden, Connecticut).

lute quantities of radioactivity. The large number of samples required for analyses and the cost of the automated systems, including a liquid scintillation spectrometer, make the procedure relatively expensive.

Beta Camera

The beta camera (Figure 6) has recently been developed by Baird-Atomic (33 University Road, Cambridge, Massachusetts) for the rapid radioassay of thin-layer chromatograms. The detector in this new device consists of 1622 picture elements, equivalent to the number of individual

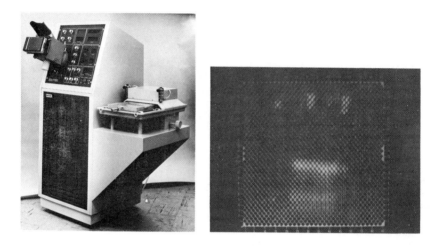

Figure 6. Beta camera depicted (Model 6000) is available from Baird-Atomic, 33 University Road, Cambridge, Massachusetts 02138. The right part of the illustration is a betagram prepared from a thin-layer chromatogram containing a standard mixture of ^{14}C-labeled compounds; light areas on the dark background designate the radioactive areas on the chromatoplate. Reproduced by permission of Baird-Atomic.

gas-flow Geiger-Müller tubes that can operate windowless or with a thin window (1.0 mg/cm^2). The radioactivity distribution on an entire plate (up to 20 × 20 cm and 0.5-cm thick) can be viewed instantaneously as a light pattern on a cathode-ray tube; a picture (Figure 6) of the display on the tube can be recorded with a Polaroid camera that is an integral part of the instrument. The background level for the beta camera is stated to be less than 0.5 cpm per detector, and the resolution claimed for this instrument ranges from 0.04 to 64 sq. in.

Inherent in the beta camera are its advantages: it provides rapid analysis (an instantaneous display of the distribution of radioactivity on the entire chromatoplate); compounds can be used for subsequent chemical analysis; and the sensitivity for detecting low-energy betas is relatively good. On the other hand, the instrumentation is extremely expensive. Furthermore, the quantitation, resolution, and sensitivity of the beta camera do not compare favorably with those attainable using liquid-scintillation scraping techniques in conjunction with liquid scintillation radioassay.

Combustion Analysis

Conventional combustion techniques[67-69] used to quantitatively convert organic matter to carbon dioxide and water can be applied to the radioassay of thin-layer chromatograms. Pullan[70] has described a spark chamber technique for evaluation of radiochromatograms. A hydrogen flame detector for mass detection on thin-layer chromatograms which has recently been described[71] could also be adapted for radioassay. Combustion of a sample eliminates quenching and self-absorption problems that are sometimes encountered with the other procedures described; however, the compounds are destroyed during the analysis.

RADIATION SAFETY APPLIED TO RADIOCHROMATOGRAPHIC PROCEDURES

All radioassay procedures used for thin-layer chromatograms present some special radiation safety problems in addition to the routine precautions[72-74] that must be used. The minute size of adsorbent particles (usually not greater than 25 microns) used for TLC makes it relatively easy for adsorbents to be dispersed throughout laboratory facilities; in certain instances, such particles can become airborne. Obviously, radioactive substances adsorbed on these particles create undesirable backgrounds that will eventually interfere with the validity of experimental data and with the safety of personnel. Adsorbent particles can also be hazardous from the point of view of respiratory disease, *e.g.*, silicosis.

Purification of radioactive compounds by thin-layer chromatography can also create contamination problems in the laboratory. Contamination may occur during preparative procedures when volatile components (for example, labeled hydrocarbons that can be present because of radiolysis[75]) are liberated from the chromatographic layers during the evaporation of solvents before visualization of the separated components. Tritiated compounds should be checked to make sure that readily exchangeable ^{3}H has been removed by standard procedures[76] before any purification steps are initiated with thin-layer chromatography. The use of fume hoods, test runs with trace quantities of the radioactive compounds, and satisfactory monitoring of all procedures will circumvent grave situations of contamination. The reader is referred to books[72-74] that cover the complete scope of recommended radiation safety practices.

RADIATION DECOMPOSITION

Self-radiation decomposition (radiolysis) is a problem encountered with the storage of radioactive compounds of high-specific activity. The degree of self-radiation decomposition inherent in a particular compound is expressed in terms of the G(-M) value, which is defined as the number of molecules of a substance permanently altered or decomposed per 100 electron volts of ionizing radiation absorbed. The G(-M) value of the system depends on the temperature, the physical state of the compound, and the nature of the radiation. The susceptibility of organic compounds to radiation decomposition varies considerably, as demonstrated by the G(-M) values for a variety of organic classes summarized by Tolbert.[77] Recently, Mangold and Sand[78] reported that randomly labeled fatty acids (100 μc/mmole) did not show any signs of radiation decomposition over a period of ten years. The fatty acids, free of solvents, were placed in vials, flushed with purified nitrogen, evacuated, sealed, and then stored in the dark at $-30°C$. The results of this study emphasize the importance of proper handling and storage conditions for labeled compounds and suggest that one cannot necessarily blame radiation decomposition for poor radiopurity after long periods of storage.

The amount and type of change brought about in organic molecules by radiation damage depends on the specific activity of the sample, the half-life, the G(-M) value, the fraction of energy absorbed, and on the components, *e.g.*, oxygen, which can influence chemical decomposition. Radiation decomposition can be minimized when labeled compounds are stored on a solid support or in solvent so that a portion of the radiation energy can be absorbed by the molecules of the support or solvent. In general, any storage condition that reduces chemical reactivity (low-temperature, oxygen-free environments, etc.) helps to reduce self-radiation decomposition.

RADIOPURITY DETERMINATIONS

Radiopurity measurements should be based on class and homolog homogeneity. Thin-layer chromatographic procedures (adsorption separations) are generally used to establish class purities, whereas the purity of individual homologs requires the use of partition, ion-exchange, or other chromatographic principles.[4] Maximum evaluation of the compound in question requires that both mass and radioactivity measurements be made; this permits the calculation of specific activities.

BIOCHEMICAL AND CHEMICAL ALTERATIONS MEASURED BY TLC RADIOCHROMATOGRAPHY

Thin-layer radiochromatography provides the biochemist with a very sensitive technique for detecting enzymatic alterations of molecules. It can monitor the time sequence, yields, and purities of labeled molecules prepared by the organic chemist. Furthermore, the same procedures can be expanded on a preparative scale so that intermediates and products of reactions can be isolated for subsequent chemical and physical studies. The isolated compounds can also be used as reactants in related studies. A specific example of the use of TLC-radiochromatography to monitor the reaction products and intermediates formed in an enzyme reaction is shown in Figure 7.

THE USE OF LABELED INTERNAL STANDARDS IN STUDIES OF CHROMATOGRAPHIC RESOLUTION

The shape of zonal profile scans is related to the molecular structure, the size of the zone assayed, the quantity of mass present, and the chromatographic environment.[62] The high degree of resolution attainable makes zonal profile scans useful for evaluating chromatographic capabilities and for detecting cross-contamination of minor components from tailing, trapping, or other phenomena. Cross-contamination can be determined by adding a specific compound of known radiopurity as an internal standard. Isotopic fractionation studies[79] have been useful in determining the ultimate resolving capabilities of a particular chromatographic process.

MASS MEASUREMENTS BY RADIOMETRIC PROCEDURES

Liquid Scintillation Quenching

A procedure for quantitating lipid mass (10–100 μg) by liquid scintillation quenching has been developed recently.[80] The method is based on the production of a color that quenches an isolated scintillation source, consisting of a small glass tube containing a scintillating plastic and a beta emitter. The source is inserted into a counting vial containing the colored solution for radioassay, and the photons are measured by phototubes in a liquid scintillation spectrometer. The decrease in counting rate as a function of color intensity is linear. Since silicic acid does not interfere, the method can also be used in conjunction with thin-layer chromato-

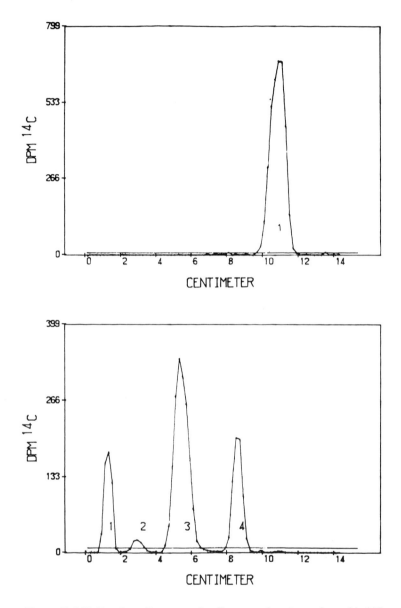

Figure 7. [14]C Zonal profile scans of a lipase-catalyzed reaction with ^{14}C-carboxyl-labeled tripalmitin as substrate. The upper scan shows the purity of the substrate before lipase attack. The lower scan shows the products obtained after a five-minute incubation at 37°C: (1) monopalmitin, (2) dipalmitin, (3) palmitic acid, and (4) tripalmitin. Separations were made on layers of Silica Gel G in hexane–diethyl ether–acetic acid (80:20:1, v/v). Reproduced from Reference 63 by permission of Marcel Dekker Inc., New York.

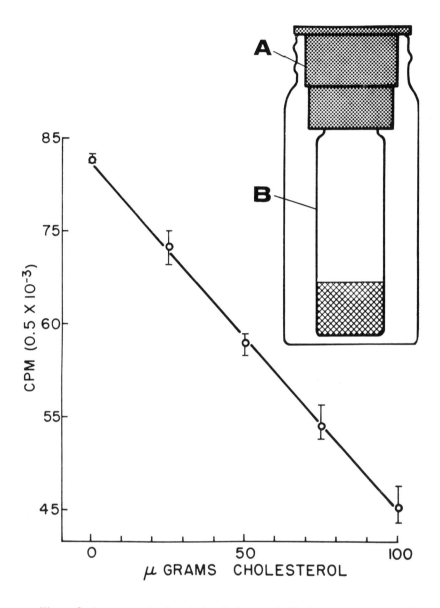

Figure 8. Arrangement of an isolated plastic scintillation source used to determine lipid mass by liquid scintillation quenching. Plastic cap (A) holds the glass tube (B) that contains plastic scintillator mixed with beta emitter. The special assembly fits commercially available liquid scintillation vials. The quenching response curve was obtained from a colored H_2SO_4 solution derived from cholesterol. Each value represents the mean of three determinations and the vertical bar bisecting each mean value represents the total range. (See Reference 80 for details.)

graphic separations. The arrangement of components in the liquid scintillation counting vial and a typical plot of the linear relation between quenching (decrease in count rate) and mass of a lipid are depicted in Figure 8.

The Use of Labeled Derivatives

Simple organic reactions with labeled reagents and functional groups of labeled compounds have been used to quantitate the mass of substances isolated by TLC. The methylation of carboxyl groups[45, 81, 82] and the acetylation of alcoholic groups[45, 81] are quantitative and offer the highest degree of sensitivity, since the sensitivity of this procedure is dependent on the detectability of radioactivity associated with the methylated or acetylated groups. Mangold[83] has reviewed a variety of reactions used in the preparation of labeled lipids; some of these reactions could be applied to quantitative measurements of mass.

ON-LINE COMPUTER MONITORING OF RADIOCHROMATOGRAPHIC MEASUREMENTS

Our group was the first to describe a computer analysis system for thin-layer chromatography. The system was developed in 1965 and described a year later.[63] In the original system, the radiometric data obtained from thin-layer chromatograms by liquid scintillation spectrometers were transmitted by means of a dedicated telephone circuit to an IBM 026 card punch.[63] The programmed analysis included the conversion of counts per minute to disintegrations per minute, the percentage distribution of radioactivity along a chromatographic lane, the recovery of total radioactivity along the entire lane, and the statistical validity of the radioactivity assay; the program also had provisions for other possibilities, such as the calculation of specific activity from radioactivity and mass data. A Benson-Lehner electroplotter provided a graphic reproduction of the radioactivity distribution so that it was on an exact-scale replica of the distances involved on the original chromatogram.

More recently, the entire radiometric system for TLC analysis has been placed on-line with a computer.[64, 65] The new system also has eliminated the need[64] for the data phone and data receiver (Western Electric Models 401A and 401J); instead, the digital data are transferred over a regular telephone line directly to the computer through the central city exchange. A more complete description of the new system appears in a recent article on thin-layer radioassay by liquid scintillation counting.[65]

SPECIFIC APPLICATIONS OF RADIOCHROMATOGRAPHY TO COMPOUNDS OF BIOLOGICAL INTEREST

Even a modest listing of literature references that describe applications of thin-layer radiochromatography to compounds of biological interest would be an impossible task. On the other hand, I feel that certain papers pertaining specifically to technical approaches should be mentioned. For example, radiochromatographic procedures developed for silicic acid adsorbents are not necessarily applicable to the ion-exchange layers that resolve nucleotides. The reader is referred to papers that illustrate some of the details associated with TLC radiochromatographic measurements of amino acids and proteins,[20, 43, 84] carbohydrates,[23, 42, 54] sterols and steroids,[13, 47, 57, 66, 85] nucleic acids,[20, 50] or lipids.[7, 8, 10, 41, 45, 51, 53, 55, 58, 60, 62, 63]

GAS-LIQUID RADIOCHROMATOGRAPHY

Although TLC provides important radiometric data, other chromatographic procedures are generally required to resolve organic compounds belonging to a homologous series. Gas-liquid chromatography (GLC) is the most successful procedure for this purpose when used in conjunction with adsorption TLC. Gas-liquid chromatography can subfractionate a homologous series according to molecular weights, functional groups, and degree of unsaturation.

Radiometric instrumentation for gas-liquid chromatography includes continuous-flow systems and collection systems, both involving combustion and noncombustion techniques or cracking of organic compounds to CH_4 in H_2 carrier gas.[86] The gas flow exiting the chromatographic column is sometimes directed through splitting devices before entering the detector, *i.e.*, a small portion passes through the mass detector and the remainder through the detection device for measurements of radioactivity. Several of the procedures are described in the following sections; three earlier reviews pertaining to methods of GLC radioactivity have been published.[3, 87, 88]

Combustion Techniques

In combustion procedures,[89–100] the mass detector or column of a gas-liquid chromatograph is connected to a furnace at 750°C containing a tube filled with a metal oxide, *e.g.*, CuO or Co_3O_4, for oxidative degradation. When organic components labeled with ^{14}C and ^{3}H are passed through these tubes, the compounds are quantitatively converted into

$^{14}CO_2$ and ^3H_2O. The water can be reduced to tritium gas by having a second tube filled with iron filings (Fe^{++}) in series with the one containing the metal oxide. Ionization chambers, proportional counting Geiger-Müller tubes, or anthracene columns inserted into liquid scintillation sample counting chambers are used for measuring the radioactivity. The special furnaces used for combustion or reduction of samples and the numerous devices housing the detectors for continuous monitoring of gas streams are commercially available. Results from continuous-flow devices are displayed on strip-chart recorders attached to rate meters on line with the radiation detector. Integrators for rapid summation of peak areas can also be included as a part of these systems.

Alternately, at preselected times based on emergence of individual components from the GLC mass detector, the $^{14}CO_2$ released by combustion can be collected in scintillation vials containing Hyamine or some other CO_2 adsorbent. An appropriate aliquot of a liquid scintillation solution is then added to the vials for ^{14}C radioassay in a liquid scintillation spectrometer. Recoveries of ^{14}C-labeled fatty acids by this procedure are quantitative.[100] Collection techniques provide greater sensitivity and higher precision than the continuous-flow systems because low-activity samples can be counted for extended periods. On the other hand, collection and subsequent radioassay are more time-consuming and the data derived are more difficult to match with the peaks obtained on the mass tracing.

Regardless of the collection or continuous-flow technique used, combustion permits gases to be transported to the collecting device or radiometric detector at room temperatures. Also, the combustion procedures eliminate problems associated with the quantitative collection of aerosols. The major disadvantages of combustion procedures are that they destroy the compounds radioassayed, preventing subsequent chemical analysis, and that although achieving complete combustion is generally not difficult, the occasional failure to do so can be a source of serious error.

Noncombustion Techniques

When one needs to measure the radioactivity of intact molecules, one passes the hot gas stream from the mass detector of a gas-liquid chromatograph directly into a radiometric detection system. Under these conditions, the temperature must be high enough to keep all compounds volatile until they leave the detector. As an alternative to the use of flow-through cells,[101–109] the compounds in the hot gas stream may be trapped continuously[110] or by fraction collection.[111–116]

The continuous collection devices (with flush-out capabilities) contain liquid scintillation solutions located in the phototube chamber of liquid scintillation spectrometers. A fresh supply of scintillation fluid is used when the buildup of residual radioactivity interferes with the measurements. Continuous monitoring of the unprocessed gas stream in a collection device (scintillation fluids) or flow-through detectors (ionization chambers of Geiger-Müller type) has not been used as often as combustion techniques, but commercial instruments for carrying out these procedures are available. The main advantages of noncombustion systems are that they are generally simple in design and that they allow the compounds to be collected for subsequent chemical and physical measurements. Data originating from the continuous monitoring of a collection device are displayed as a stepwise integral curve and results obtained with flow-through detectors are recorded as differential curves.

Long-lasting memory effects must be prevented in the flow-through systems because the buildup of residual background greatly decreases the sensitivity and accuracy of the radioassay measurement. Memory effects in flow-cell systems can be avoided by using fraction collection techniques. Organic components that emerge in the effluent gas stream from the GLC mass detector are collected in cartridges filled with anthracene or cellulose, in scintillation vials containing liquid scintillation solution, or in glass tubes. Fraction collection turntables have been used to simplify the collection of GLC samples in individual anthracene cartridges and in counting vials containing a liquid scintillation solution.

Data obtained in these collection systems are reported as amount of radioactivity associated with measured mass peaks, *i.e.*, specific activities; recoveries of radioactivity by noncombustion collection techniques are in the neighborhood of 90%. These procedures are relatively simple and inexpensive, and in general have a higher sensitivity and a higher precision than continuous-flow systems because low-activity samples can be counted with less statistical error. The samples collected can also be used for other studies. The major criticism of the noncombustion procedures is the extreme difficulty of quantitatively trapping aerosols of compounds formed at high temperatures. As with other collection techniques, the activity collected may not always be associated with GLC peaks.

REFERENCES

1. Mangold, H. K., *Thin-Layer Chromatography: A Laboratory Handbook* (New York: Academic Press, Inc., 1965), pp 58–74.
2. Snyder, F., *Advances in Tracer Methodology*, Vol. 4 (New York: Plenum Publishing Corp., 1968), pp 81–104.
3. Snyder, F., *Isotopes and Radiation Technology* 6, 381 (1969).
4. Snyder, F., and C. Piantadosi, *Advances in Lipid Research*, Vol. 4 (New York: Academic Press, Inc., 1966), pp 257–283.

5. Mangold, H. K., *Proceedings of the Second International Conference on Methods of Preparing and Storing Labelled Compounds,* Brussels, Nov. 28–Dec. 3, 1966 (Brussels: Euratom, 1968), pp 167–179.
6. Koss, F. W., and D. Jerchel, Radiochim. Acta 3, 220 (1964).
7. Snyder, F., and N. Stephens, Anal. Biochem. 4, 128 (1962).
8. Brown, J. L., and J. M. Johnston, J. Lipid Res. 3, 480 (1962).
9. Kratzl, K., and G. Puschmann, Holzforschung 14, 1 (1960).
10. Samuel, D., and I. Wasserman, Anal. Biochem. 9, 246 (1964).
11. Goldrick, B., and J. Hirsch, J. Lipid Res. 4, 482 (1963).
12. Berei, K., KFKI Koslemen. 13, 49 (1965).
13. Berthold, F., *Radioisotope Sample Measurement Techniques in Medicine and Biology,* Symposium Proceedings, Vienna, May 24–28, 1965 (Vienna: International Atomic Energy Agency, 1965), pp 303–315.
14. Bleecken, S., G. Kaufmann, and K. Kummer, J. Chromatog. 19, 105 (1965).
15. Berger, J.-A., G. Meyniel, and J. Petit, Compt. Rend. 255, 1116 (1962).
16. Boucke, G., Atompraxis 11, 263 (1965).
17. Breccia, A., and F. Spalletti, Nature 198, 756 (1963).
18. Csallany, A. S., and H. H. Draper, Anal. Biochem. 4, 418 (1962).
19. Daneels, A., D. L. Massart, and J. Hoste, J. Chromatog. 18, 144 (1965).
20. Massaglia, A., U. Rosa, and S. Sosi, J. Chromatog. 17, 316 (1965).
21. Moghissi, A., J. Chromatog. 13, 542 (1964).
22. Moye, C. J., J. Chromatog. 13, 56 (1964).
23. Moye, C. J., and R. J. Goldsack, J. Appl. Chem. 16, 209 (1966).
24. Muzzarelli, R. A. A., Talanta 13, 1689 (1966).
25. Muzzarelli, R. A. A., Talanta 13, 639 (1966).
26. Osborn, R. H., and T. H. Simpson, J. Chromatog. 35, 436 (1968).
27. Ravenhill, J. R., and A. T. James, J. Chromatog. 26, 89 (1967).
28. Rosenberg, J., and M. Bolgar, Anal. Chem. 35, 1559 (1963).
29. Roucayrol, J. C., J.-A. Berger, G. Meyniel, and J. Perrin, Intern. J. Appl. Radiation Isotopes 15, 671 (1964).
30. Roucayrol, J. C., and P. Taillandier, Compt. Rend. 256, 4653 (1963).
31. Roucayrol, J. C., J. A. Berger, G. Meyniel, and P. Taillandier, *Radioaktive Isotope in Klinik und Forschung,* Vol. 6 (München-Berlin: Urban and Schwarzenberg, 1965), pp 474–479.
32. Schulze, P.-E., and M. Wenzel, Angew. Chem. Intern. Ed. Engl. 1, 580 (1962).
33. Squibb, R. L., Nature 198, 317 (1963).
34. Snyder, F., Separ. Sci. 1, 655 (1966).
35. West, C. D., A. W. Wayne, and V. J. Chavré, Anal. Biochem. 12, 41 (1965).
36. Wilde, P. F., Lab. Pract. 13, 741 (1964).
37. Wood, B. A., *Quantitative Paper and Thin-Layer Chromatography* (New York: Academic Press, Inc., 1968), Ch. 9, pp 107–118.

38. Lowe, A. E., *Quantitative Paper and Thin-Layer Chromatography* (New York: Academic Press, Inc., 1968), Ch. 9, pp 119–122.
39. Jack, R. C. M., and W. G. Smith, Jr., Contrib. Boyce Thompson Inst. 23, 215 (1966).
40. Erismann, K. H., J. Chromatog. 20, 600 (1965).
41. Fray, G., and J. Frey, Bull. Soc. Chim. Biol. 45, 1201 (1963).
42. Jolchine, G., Physiol. Vegetale 2, 341 (1964).
43. Lambiotte, M., Atomlight 45, 10 (1965).
44. Lüthi, U., and P. G. Waser, Nature 205, 1190 (1965).
45. Mangold, H. K., R. Kammereck, and D. C. Malins, *International Symposium on Microchemical Techniques,* Vol. 2, Symposium Proceedings, University Park, Pa., Aug. 13–18, 1961 (New York: Interscience, 1962), pp 697–714.
46. Privett, O. S., M. L. Blank, D. W. Codding, and E. C. Nickell, J. Am. Oil Chemists' Soc. 42, 381 (1965).
47. Richardson, G. S., I. Weliky, W. Batchelder, M. Griffith, and L. L. Engel, J. Chromatog. 12, 115 (1963).
48. Schwane, R. A., and R. S. Nakon, Anal. Chem. 37, 315 (1965).
49. Sheppard, H., and W. H. Tsien, Anal. Chem. 35, 1992 (1963).
50. Simonis, W., and H. Gimmler, J. Chromatog. 19, 440 (1965).
51. Snyder, F., *Radioisotope Sample Measurement Techniques in Medicine and Biology,* Symposium Proceedings, Vienna, May 24–28, 1965 (Vienna: International Atomic Energy Agency, 1965), pp 521–533.
52. Wilson, A. T., and D. J. Spedding, J. Chromatog. 18, 76 (1965).
53. Abdel-Latif, A. A., and F. E. Chang, J. Chromatog. 24, 435 (1966).
54. Baker, N., R. J. Huebotter, and M. C. Schotz, Anal. Biochem. 10, 227 (1965).
55. Boberg, J., Clin. Chim. Acta 14, 325 (1966).
56. Manara, L., Eur. J. Pharmacol. 2, 136 (1967).
57. Vahouny, G. V., C. R. Borja, and S. Weersing, Anal. Biochem. 6, 555 (1963).
58. Snyder, F., Anal. Biochem. 9, 183 (1964).
59. Snyder, F., T. J. Alford, and H. Kimble, U.S. At. Energy Comm. ORINS Report 44, 1964.
60. Snyder, F., and H. Kimble, Anal. Biochem. 11, 510 (1965).
61. Snyder, F., and H. Kimble, U.S. At. Energy Comm. ORINS Report 47, 1964.
62. Snyder, F., *Advances in Tracer Methodology,* Vol. 2 (New York: Plenum Publishing Corp., 1965), pp 107–113.
63. Snyder, F., and D. Smith, Separ. Sci. 1, 709 (1966).
64. Snyder, F., and E. A. Cress, Clin. Chem. 14, 529 (1968).
65. Snyder, F., *Current Status of Liquid Scintillation Counting,* Symposium Proceedings, Cambridge, Mass., March 31–April 3, 1969 (New York: Grune and Stratton, in press, 1969).
66. Hofmann, A. F., P. A. Szczepanik, and P. D. Klein, J. Lipid Res. 9, 707 (1968).

67. Kelly, R. G., E. A. Peets, S. Gordon, and D. A. Buyske, Anal. Biochem. **2**, 267 (1961).

68. Davidson, J. D., and V. T. Oliverio, *Advances in Tracer Methodology*, Vol. 4 (New York: Plenum Publishing Corp., 1968), pp 67–79.

69. Sheppard, H., and W. Rodegker, *Advances in Tracer Methodology*, Vol. 1 (New York: Plenum Publishing Corp., 1963), pp 192–194.

70. Pullan, B. R., *Quantitative Paper and Thin-Layer Chromatography*, (New York: Academic Press, Inc., 1968), Ch. 9, pp 123–133.

71. Padley, F. D., Chem. Ind. **1967**, 874.

72. Evans, E. A., *Tritium and Its Compounds* (Princeton, New Jersey: D. Van Nostrand Co., Inc., 1966), Ch. 3, pp 70–98.

73. *Safe Handling of Radioisotopes* (Vienna: International Atomic Energy Agency, Safety Series No. 1, 1958).

74. "Safe Handling of Radioactive Materials," *Recommendations of the National Committee on Radiation Protection* (Washington, D.C.: U.S. National Bureau of Standards, Handbook 92, 1964).

75. Haigh, W. G., and D. J. Hanahan, Biochim. Biophys. Acta **98**, 640 (1965).

76. Wilzbach, K. E., *Advances in Tracer Methodology*, Vol. 1 (New York: Plenum Publishing Corp., 1963), pp 4–11.

77. Tolbert, B. M., *Advances in Tracer Methodology*, Vol. 1 (New York: Plenum Publishing Corp., 1963), pp 64–68.

78. Mangold, H. K., and D. M. Sand, Biochim. Biophys. Acta **164**, 124 (1968).

79. Klein, P. D., *Advances in Chromatography*, Vol. 3 (New York: Marcel Dekker, Inc., 1966), pp 3–65.

80. Snyder, F., and A. Moehl, Anal. Biochem. **28**, 503 (1969).

81. Mangold, H. K., Fette, Seifen, Anstrichmittel **61**, 877 (1959).

82. Schlenk, H., and J. L. Gellerman, Anal. Chem. **32**, 1412 (1960).

83. Mangold, H. K., R. Kammereck, and D. C. Malins, *International Symposium on Microchemical Techniques*, 1961 (New York: Interscience, 1962), pp 697–714.

84. Drawert, F., O. Bachmann, and K. H. Reuther, J. Chromatog. **9**, 376 (1962).

85. Benraad, J., and P. W. C. Kloppenborg, Clin. Chim. Acta **12**, 565 (1965)

86. Drawert, F., A. Rapp, and H. Ullmeyer, Chemiker Ztg. **88**, 379 (1964).

87. Drawert, F., and O. Bachmann, Angew. Chem. **75**, 717 (1963).

88. Karmen, A., J. Assoc. Offic. Agr. Chemists **47**, 15 (1964).

89. Blomstrand, R., and J. Gürtler, Acta Chem. Scand. **19**, 249 (1965).

90. Cramer, W. A., J. P. W. Houtman, R. O. Koch, and G. J. Piet, Intern. J. Appl. Radiation Isotopes **17**, 97 (1966).

91. Diehn, B., A. P. Wolf, and F. S. Rowland, Z. Anal. Chem. **204**, 112 (1964).

92. James, A. T., and E. A. Piper, J. Chromatog. **5**, 265 (1961).

93. James, A. T., and C. Hitchcock, Kerntechnik **7**, 5 (1965).

94. Karmen, A., J. Lipid Res. **8**, 61 (1967).
95. Karmen, A., J. Gas Chromatog. **5**, 502 (1967).
96. Martin, R. O., Anal. Chem. **40**, 1197 (1968).
97. Schmidt-Bleek, F., and F. S. Rowland, Anal. Chem. **36**, 1695 (1964).
98. Simon, H., G. Muellhofer, and R. Medina, *Radioisotope Sample Measurement Techniques in Medicine and Biology,* Symposium Proceedings, Vienna, May 24–28, 1965 (Vienna: International Atomic Energy Agency, 1965), pp 317–328.
99. Swell, L., Anal. Biochem. **16**, 70 (1966).
100. Pfleger, R. C., C. Piantadosi, and F. Snyder, Biochim. Biophys. Acta **144**, 633 (1967).
101. Dutton, H. J., *Advances in Tracer Methodology,* Vol. 2 (New York: Plenum Publishing Corp., 1965), pp 123–134.
102. Karmen, A., I. McCaffrey, and R. L. Bowman, J. Lipid Res. **3**, 372 (1962).
103. Mason, L. H., H. J. Dutton, and L. R. Bair, J. Chromatog. **2**, 322 (1959).
104. Schulze, H. W., and H.-K. Bothe, Atomkernenergie **9**, 363 (1964).
105. Simpson, K. L., T. O. M. Nakayama, and C. O. Chichester, J. Chromatog. **13**, 354 (1964).
106. Tolbert, B. M., *Advances in Tracer Methodology,* Vol. 1 (New York: Plenum Publishing Corp., 1963), pp 167–177.
107. White, E. R., and H. G. Davis, Anal. Chim. Acta **34**, 105 (1966).
108. Wilzbach, K. E., and P. Riesz, Science **126**, 748 (1957).
109. Wolfgang, R., and F. S. Rowland, Anal. Chem. **30**, 903 (1958).
110. Popják, G., A. E. Lowe, D. Moore, L. Brown, and F. A. Smith, J. Lipid Res. **1**, 29 (1959).
111. Bennett, M., and E. Coon, J. Lipid Res. **7**, 448 (1966).
112. Cooke, B. A., Biochem. J. **107**, 19p (1968).
113. Dutton, H. J., *Advances in Tracer Methodology,* Vol. 1 (New York: Plenum Publishing Corp., 1963), pp 147–152.
114. Iddings, F. A., and J. T. Wade, J. Gas Chromatog. **1**, 31 (1963).
115. Karmen, A., L. Guiffrida, and R. L. Bowman, J. Lipid Res. **3**, 44 (1962).
116. Thomas, P. J., and H. J. Dutton, Anal. Chem. **41**, 657 (1969).

Chapter 3

Argentation Thin-Layer Chromatography of Lipids

by L. J. Morris and B. W. Nichols

INTRODUCTION

The field of lipids, and by this we mean acyl lipids and compounds which are biogenetically very closely related to acyl lipids, has historically always been the Cinderella of chemical and biochemical research. This is because of the uniquely complicated nature of natural lipids, which generally consist of mixtures of a whole range of neutral lipid, phospholipid, and glycolipid types or classes of molecules. Many of these types or classes are very similar in structure and properties, and each comprises a whole family of distinct molecular species differing only in the chain length and the degree or type of unsaturation and/or substitution of their constituent acyl or alkyl chains. This tremendous complexity precluded adequate separation or characterization of lipid components, except in the crudest sense, by the classical techniques of organic chemistry; and, lacking the essential analytical basis, research in lipids did not progress as it had in other fields.

The resurgent state of all aspects of lipid research today is almost entirely attributable to the various forms of chromatography and, more specifically, to gas-liquid chromatography (GLC), introduced by James and Martin in the early 1950s, and to thin-layer chromatography (TLC), popularized by Stahl in the late 1950s. GLC provides rapid separation, analysis, and characterization of most of the relatively volatile alkyl constituents of lipids (fatty acids, alcohols, aldehydes, etc.), and by TLC the separation from each other of virtually all of the involatile, intact lipid classes may be fairly readily achieved. A vast amount of chemical, technological, and biochemical research on lipids was stimulated by the universal adoption of these chromatographic techniques, but it soon became clear that even more selective separations were required for many studies and that some major gaps still existed in the lipid researcher's analytical armory.

Argentation chromatography, introduced just 7 years ago, has filled one of these gaps, enabling separations of fatty acids and intact lipid classes to be made on the basis of the number and type and, to some extent, the positions of their unsaturated centers. Separations by argentation methods depend on the ability of silver ions to form weak complexes with ethylenic and acetylenic bonds. This phenomenon was first investigated quantitatively more than 30 years ago by Winstein and Lucas,[1] and since then many physico-chemical studies have been made on such interactions between unsaturated compounds and silver and other metal ions. These studies have been reviewed elsewhere,[2-4] as has the nature of the bonding in such complexes,[5] and we do not propose to review them again here.

The history of the development of chromatographic techniques based on silver ion complexes with unsaturated centers has also been reviewed.[6] Briefly, Nichols in 1952 made the first study of silver complexes of lipid materials and suggested that countercurrent distribution or paper chromatography could be adapted, by inclusion of silver nitrate in the polar liquid phase, to separate saturated and unsaturated fatty acid methyl esters and, more specifically, the *cis-trans* isomers oleate and elaidate.[7] These predictions were first directly verified in a countercurrent distribution system by Dutton, Scholfield and Jones in 1961,[8] and the use of argentation in countercurrent distribution of lipids has been reviewed.[9] Argentation adsorption chromatography was first described in 1962 simultaneously by de Vries[10] and Morris.[11] The former described separations of fatty acid methyl esters, triglycerides, and sterols on the basis of unsaturation on columns impregnated with silver nitrate, while the latter similarly separated methyl esters of fatty acids and of epoxy and hydroxy fatty acids on silver-nitrate impregnated thin-layers. At the same time, Barrett, Dallas and Padley[12] also described argentation-TLC separations of various glyceride mixtures according to their degree of unsaturation.

Argentation chromatography, particularly argentation-TLC, very rapidly gained wide acceptance and popularity, and is now a major weapon in the analytical arsenal of the lipid chemist and biochemist, third only to GLC and "normal" TLC. The applications of argentation methods to the fractionation of lipids have been summarized within a number of reviews of separations of lipids,[*e.g.*,13-18] and of particular classes of lipids,[*e.g.*,19-22] and have also been specifically reviewed several times.[6,23-27] Of these, the most recent and comprehensive is that by Morris,[6] which describes the basis and history of the development of separation methods that depend on argentation and reviews all the separations described in the literature up to about April 1966.

In this contribution we do not propose to go over again the ground covered in these earlier reviews, nor do we propose to attempt a comprehensive review of all separations by argentation methods described since April 1966. Instead, we hope to sketch in the more important types of separations of lipid materials which are possible by argentation-TLC and its related and complementary methods, and, in so doing, to stress the applications of these methods to general problems of lipid research and to point out those new areas of lipid chemistry and biochemistry which have been and are being opened up by these methods. By adopting this approach and by referring preferentially to the more recently published literature, we hope to provide a review which will complement rather than merely extend the earlier review by Morris.[6]

Although the present survey is nominally on argentation-TLC, and TLC procedures are by far the most frequently used, we also refer where appropriate to studies which have used other argentation systems, notably column chromatography and countercurrent distribution. It will of course be realized that the main advantage of column procedures is simply that of scale, and that any separations obtainable on columns will be achieved as or more readily by TLC. The converse of this, however, is not necessarily true. In the same way, separations on the large scale by argentation countercurrent distribution,[*e.g.,*9] which proceed on the basis both of chain-length and of degree and type of unsaturation, may be mimicked on the small scale by reversed phase TLC[28] or paper chromatography[29] employing silver nitrate in the solvent. Within each of these types of separation processes, variations have been proposed and utilized from time to time; for example, the use of columns of acid washed Florisil[30, 31] or of ion exchange resins[32, 33] impregnated with silver ions, the use of plates impregnated with ammoniacal silver nitrate,[34] or the incorporation of silver nitrate in the solvent rather than in the adsorbent.[35] These modifications may result in improved separations, but they were generally introduced simply to improve flow rate, stability, or some other feature of such systems.

FATTY ACIDS

Most of the fractionations carried out by argentation chromatography are of normal mixtures of fatty acid methyl esters, simply on the basis of the number of *cis* and/or *trans* double bonds of their constituents. Such separations are generally effected either to obtain simpler, defined fractions from a complex mixture, as an aid to analysis and characterization by GLC, or to isolate pure components for elucidation of structure and/or of extent or position of radioactive labeling. A number of publications describe generalized procedures for the use of argentation chromatography in conjunction with countercurrent distribution,[*e.g.,*36] or, more commonly, with GLC,[*e.g.,*37–39] for analysis and isolation of fatty acid methyl esters, followed by permanganate-periodate oxidation,[*e.g.,*38] or ozonolysis,[*e.g.,*37,39] to determine their structures. Bergelson and co-workers[40] have described one such complete scheme for structural analysis utilizing only the various forms of TLC for separations of both the fatty acids and their cleavage products. One major refinement in procedures for elucidation of structures must be mentioned here, namely the partial reduction of polyunsaturated fatty acids with hydrazine followed by isolation of the monoene products (*cis* and *trans*, if present) by argentation-TLC and characterization of each double bond type and position by oxidative or ozonolytic cleavage of these monoenes.[e.g., 36, 38, 39, 41] This is one of the most powerful and definitive methods yet devised for characterization of complex fatty acids, and some of its more specific applications will be discussed later in this review.

Argentation chromatography, in combination with these other analytical and chemical techniques, has proved most valuable in the detection, isolation, and characterization of novel or minor fatty acids, such as positionally isomeric monoenoic acids in various seed oils,[42, 43] in a phytoplankton,[44] and in the exceedingly complex fatty acid mixture from rat skin surface lipids.[45] Other more complex *cis*-unsaturated acids so separated and characterized include 4,7,10,13-eicosatetraenoic acid in rat liver phospholipids,[37] α- and γ-linolenic acids and 6,9,12,15-octadecatetraenoic acid in Boraginaceae seed oils,[e.g., 46] and leaves[47] and a whole family of C_{16}, C_{18}, and C_{20} monoenoic and polyenoic acids containing *cis*-5-unsaturation in various seed oils.[e.g., 36, 38, 39, 48]

In studies of fatty acid biochemistry, argentation-TLC has also been used mostly in the same way as in these chemical studies, namely as a highly convenient procedure in conjunction with GLC for the isolation of the individual fatty acid products of incubations with radioactively labeled substrates, to enable the extent of labeling to be determined by scintillation counting[e.g., 49–51] or to define the chemical structure and the position of specific labeling of these products.[e.g., 52–54] Chemical structure is defined by the conventional oxidative cleavage procedures described above, with or without prior partial reduction with hydrazine, while the specific position of label is effected by chemical α-oxidation after complete reduction of double bonds.[55] In each case the oxidation products are most conveniently analyzed by radiochemical GLC.[e.g., 52–55] Some additional care should be exercised in argentation chromatography of metabolic products labeled with tritium or deuterium at a position of unsaturation, as such compounds are retained somewhat less strongly by silver ion-complexing than the corresponding ^{14}C-labeled or unlabeled compounds.[56, 57]

Until quite recently natural *trans*-unsaturated fatty acids, apart from those with conjugated ethylenic systems, were considered to be confined to ruminant animals' tissues and products, but, largely by argentation methods, *trans*-ethylenic acids are now being recognized to have fairly wide distribution. Thus, for example, *trans*-3-hexadecenoic acid is now known to occur generally in the chloroplasts of green algae and all higher plants, and argentation chromatography has greatly helped in its isolation,[e.g.,58] and in studies of its biosynthesis and metabolism. [e.g.,59,60] *Cis*-9, *trans*-12-linoleic acid was detected and isolated from two seed oils by argentation-TLC;[61] a whole family of *trans*-3-enoic acids, including *trans*-3, *cis*-9-octadecadienoic and *trans*-3, *cis*-9, *cis*-12-octadecatrienoic acids, was recognized in *Aster* seed oil,[62] and in *Thalictrum verulosum* seeds there was not only a series of *cis*-5-monoenoic acids but also a family of *trans*-5-enoic acids, including *trans*-5, *cis*-9-octadecadienoic and *trans*-5, *cis*-9, *cis*-12-octadecatrienoic acids.[38]

These last three studies[38,61,62] provide excellent examples of the unequivocal elucidation of the position and the configuration of each individual double bond in *cis*, *trans*-polyunsaturated acids by partial hydrazine reduction followed by cleavage of the *cis*- and *trans*-monoene products, separately isolated by argentation-TLC. While considering the application of this excellent procedure to *cis*, *trans*-polyunsaturated acids, it seems apposite to point out that partial hydrazine reduction of allenes gives rise to the two expected monoenes but that these are produced in both their *cis* and *trans* forms. This fact was demonstrated during the characterization of 5,6-octadecadienoic (laballenic) acid[63] and *trans*-5,6,16-octadecatrienoic (lamenallenic) acid.[64] The utility of this procedure has also been convincingly demonstrated in the unequivocal characterization, after many years, of parinaric and licanic (4-keto-parinaric) acids as the *cis*-9, *trans*-11, *trans*-13, *cis*-15-octadecatetraenoic acid isomers.[65,66] Similarly, the two hydroxy-conjugated diene acids present in a number of seed oils have finally been proved to be the 9-hydroxy-*trans*-10, *cis*-12-octadecadienoic[67] and the 13-hydroxy-*cis*-9, *trans*-11-octadecadienoic[67–69] isomers, respectively.

Argentation-TLC is also very effective in separating most classes of substituted fatty acids on the basis of degree and type of unsaturation and separations of a wide range of epoxy-, halohydroxy-, hydroxy- and dihydroxy-acids have been described.[11,70] By double impregnation with silver nitrate and boric acid, dihydroxy acids can be separated on the basis not only of unsaturation but also of the *threo*- or *erythro*-configuration of the glycol groups.[11] These two impregnating agents, used separately, demonstrated the presence in *Chamaepeuce* seed oils of the new 9,10,18-trihydroxy-*cis*-12-octadecenoic acid along with its saturated analog and showed that both had the *threo*-configuration.[71] The separation of all of the known prostaglandins by combination of normal-TLC and argentation-TLC provides an excellent example of the scope and selectivity of this combination of methods.[72] Argentation-TLC is also effective for separations of the cyclopentenyl acids from chaulmoogra oil,[73] but an early claim that the cyclopropenoid acids, sterculic and malvalic, could be separated from normal saturated and unsaturated acids by this means[74] has been clearly shown to be invalid.[e.g.,27] Indeed, the deliberate treatment with silver nitrate of mixtures containing cyclopropene acids, the labile rings of which are thereby quantitatively cleaved, forms the basis of two GLC procedures for their analysis.[75,76]

A unique furanoid fatty acid has been detected and isolated from *Exocarpus cupressiformis* seed oil by argentation-TLC,[77] and the simple acetylenic acid, stearolic acid, has similarly been shown to occur in small amount in this and other Santalaceae seed oils.[e.g.,78] In such seed oils there occur major proportions of more complex acetylenic and hydroxyacetylenic acids, containing conjugated systems of acetylenic and ethylenic bonds. Silver ion chromatography has not yet achieved total resolution of such mixtures but has effected separations into fractions with and without terminal ethylenic bonds, so that the individual components of these fractions can then be characterized.[e.g.,79-82] Argentation-TLC has also been effective in chemical and biochemical studies of crepenynic (*cis*-9-octadecen-12-ynoic) acid[e.g.,83] and of the 14,15-dehydrocrepenynic acid which accompanies it in a seed oil[84] and a fungus,[85] and an extremely important role for these acids as key intermediates in the biosynthesis of large numbers of polyacetylenic secondary metabolites has been proposed.[e.g.,85] However, although the structures suggested for the dehydrocrepenynic acids from these two sources were identical, namely *cis*-9, *cis*-14-octadecadien-12-ynoic acid, there is a discrepancy in their reported migration behavior, relative to crepenynic acid, on silver nitrate-impregnated silica gel layers.[84,85]

So far, the bulk of the separations by argentation methods that have been discussed have been simply on the basis of the number of non-conjugated double bonds and whether these are *cis* or *trans;* there are a number of good, general descriptions of such separations which have not yet been cited.[e.g.,86-89] Most of the applications described have been to straightforward analytical, structural, or biochemical studies of unaltered, naturally occurring fatty acids, however unusual the structures of some of these have been. The selectivity of argentation methods, however, is such that they are also of great utility in more technological studies of chemically altered fatty acids. For example, argentation methods separate conjugated dienoic esters into *cis,cis*, *cis,trans* plus *trans,cis* and *trans,trans* fractions[e.g.,90] and conjugated trienoic acids into all-*cis*, di-*cis*,mono-*trans*, mono-*cis*,di-*trans*, and all-*trans* fractions.[90,91] The composite mixed-*cis*, *trans* fractions can then be completely resolved by capillary-GLC, thus providing the analytical basis for detailed study of alkaline isomerization of polyunsaturated fatty acids.

Another area where argentation methods are making an even greater impact is in studies of the mechanism and the intermediate products of hydrogenation of fatty acids, both under heterogeneous catalysis[e.g., 92, 93] and homogeneous catalysis,[e.g., 94, 95] and in the analysis and characterization of the constituent fatty acids of partially hydrogenated oils and fats.[e.g., 96-98] Because of the occurrence of both geometric and positional isomerization of double bonds during catalytic hydrogenation, unlike hydrazine reduction which causes no such isomerizations, the mixture of fatty acids present in a partially hydrogenated edible fat is generally extremely complex, and the full range of separatory and analytical techniques, including argentation methods, are therefore required for complete analysis and characterization. This has been an area not very amenable to detailed research until recently—but obviously of considerable importance because such fats may constitute a significant proportion of our diet and little is known of the effects of many of their constituent fatty acids. Somewhat similar complex pathways are involved in the hydrogenation of polyunsaturated fatty acids by the microbial flora of ruminant animals, giving rise to *trans* and positionally isomeric unsaturated fatty acids in their tissues and milk. These pathways of biological hydrogenation are also now being unraveled, largely with the assistance of argentation-TLC.[e.g., 99-102]

One of the major attributes of argentation chromatography which has not yet been discussed is that, superimposed upon the separations according to the number and type of unsaturated centers, separations of positional isomers can frequently be obtained. Thus, with dienoic acids, the effect of silver complexing increases with increasing separation of the two double bonds,[e.g., 86, 87] and this has been utilized, for example, in the detection of positional isomers of linoleic acids in butter fat[103] and partially hydrogenated vegetable oils.[e.g., 96] Even more remarkable is the separation of positional isomers of monoenes and of *cis,cis*-1,5-dienes. A number of instances of separations of two or three positional isomers of monoenoic esters by argentation techniques have been reported[e.g., 40, 86, 88, 104-106] and detailed studies have been made of most of the *cis*- and *trans*-octadecenoates[107] and of the entire series of positional isomers of these monoenoic acids[108] and also of the *cis, cis*-methylene-interrupted octadecadienoates.[109] The patterns of migration of these series of positional isomers were quite similar to the remarkable sinusoidal patterns obtained with similar series of positionally isomeric hydroxy-, acetoxy-, or keto-substituted aliphatic compounds.[70, 110] The anomalously high mobility of esters with *cis*-2-unsaturation,[108, 109] relative to the other *cis*-isomers and also to *trans*-2-enoic esters, has been demonstrated with other acids[106,111] but the reason for this is not known. Positional as well as geometric isomers of monoenoic aldehydes have similarly been separated by argentation-TLC.[e.g., 112]

Relatively little direct practical advantage has been gained so far from this remarkable ability of argentation-TLC to separate positional isomers. It has been used analytically to prove that only the 9-hexadecenoic and 11-octadecenoic acid isomers occurred in *Escherichia coli*[105] and that both 9- and 11-octadecenoic acid isomers were present in yeasts.[104] It has also been effective in the isolation of labeled substrates and products in studies of the metabolism and interconversions of *cis*- and *trans*-2- and -3-enoic acids in animal and plant systems.[106, 113] In two studies, however, this selectivity has played a crucial role, namely in the preparation of pure *erythro*-12,13-$^3H_2$-oleic acid and of pure *erythro*- and *threo*-12,13-$^2H_2$-oleic acids and -15,16-$^2H_2$-oleic acids.[cf. 107] Using these specifically labeled acids as substrates, the mechanism of ricinoleic (D-12-hydroxyoleic) acid biosynthesis in the castor bean was unequivocally established,[51] and it was shown that the complete stereospecificity of hydrogen removal, established for the desaturation of stearic to oleic acid,[49, 50] also applied to the desaturations introducing the 12,13- and the 15,16-double bonds of linoleic acid and linolenic acid, respectively.[50]

DIGLYCERIDES AND TRIGLYCERIDES

Although most publications describing applications of silver ion chromatography to lipids have been concerned with the separations of fatty acids, it has been realized from the beginning that this procedure is potentially of even greater importance in studies of intact lipids, notably neutral glycerides, phospholipids, and glycolipids, which are not readily analyzed by GLC. Most of the studies of neutral lipids utilizing argentation methods have been concerned with di- and triglyceride separations, but before discussing these, we can point out that all neutral lipid classes are amenable to fractionation by this means and that examples include separations of sterol esters,[114, 115] wax esters,[e.g., 25, 115] and glyceryl ethers.[e.g., 116]

Two of the original papers on argentation chromatography of lipids described separations of diglycerides and triglycerides, on columns[10] and on thin-layers,[12] based on the total number of *cis*-double bonds in each glyceride molecule and also on some *cis*, *trans*-isomeric glycerides. There was found to be little or no practical difficulty in effecting such separations, and many papers soon appeared describing fractionations of natural triglycerides by column and thin-layer argentation chromatography. These earlier papers and such practical details as quantification of separated components of triglyceride mixtures are well described in previous reviews[e.g., 6, 18, 20, 21, 26, 27] and will not again be discussed in detail here.

It became clear fairly soon that separations of triglyceride species were not simply in the order of total numbers of *cis*-double bonds in each molecule, but that one linoleic acid residue, for example, had a greater effect on retention than two oleic acid residues. Gunstone and Padley[117] determined the order of complexing affinities of triglycerides, neglecting effects of positional isomers, to be as follows (3 = linolenic, 2 = linoleic, 1 = oleic, and 0 = saturated acids): 333, 332, 331, 330, 322, 321, 320, 311, 222, 310, 221, 300, 220, 211, 210, 111, 200, 110, 100, 000. These authors assigned arbitrary values for the complexing effect of each acyl chain, namely, saturated = 0, oleic = 1, linoleic = $(2 + a)$, and linolenic = $(4 + 4a)$, where a is some fraction less than unity, to enable the order of migration of polyacyl compounds, such as triglycerides, to be predicted. Positional isomerism may result in further fractionation of some of the classes listed above.[e.g., 12]

Argentation column chromatography, which is convenient for relatively large scale separations, does not give very efficient fractionation of glycerides containing more than four double bonds per molecule,[118] but Gunstone and co-workers partly circumvented this difficulty through preliminary fractionation by low temperature crystallization from solvents containing silver nitrate.[e.g., 119] Argentation-TLC is very effective with the normal range of animal and vegetable triglycerides, but it is said to be unsuitable for highly unsaturated triglyceride mixtures; and Litchfield has developed an alternative combination of reversed phase partition-TLC with GLC for such mixtures.[120] However, since Renkonen has shown that herring lecithins with 10–12 double bonds can be resolved by argentation-TLC of the aceto-diglycerides or dimethylphosphatidates derived from them[121] (see also Volume II, this series), it seems probable that, by careful experimentation, triglycerides with these levels of unsaturation should also be separable in this way.

Natural diglyceride or triglyceride mixtures, of course, cannot be fully resolved into individual molecular species by one technique alone, and argentation chromatography of glycerides reaches its full potential utility only when used in conjunction with other chromatographic methods. Argentation-TLC has been effectively complemented by normal-TLC in studies of the composition of milk fat triglycerides[122, 123] and of seed oil triglycerides containing hydroxy fatty acids,[124] which having short chain and hydroxy acid constituents, respectively, are amenable to separation by normal adsorption. More generally, however, argentation-TLC is combined with reversed phase partition-TLC,[e.g., 125] or with GLC of the intact glyceride fractions so obtained[e.g., 126, 127] or of the azelao-glycerides produced from them by oxidative cleavage.[e.g.,118] When these sophisticated series of separatory methods are further combined with specific enzymic hydrolysis procedures to establish the positional distribution of the constituent acyl chains of the individual molecular species or of the simple mixed fractions so obtained, the lipid chemist or biochemist has available the means for detailed and discriminating analysis and characterization of all the components of these complex and hitherto intractable natural mixtures.

Up until now this tremendously powerful range of techniques has been applied largely to straightforward analysis of the triglyceride constituents of natural oils and fats.[e.g.,21,117–119,122–132] The results of some of these analytical studies[e.g.,21,117,118,127–130] have been taken to support the so-called 1,3-random, 2-random hypothesis of fatty acid distribution in natural triglycerides. However, such apparent agreement with the theory is probably fortuitous, because other similar studies based on argentation chromatography[e.g.,131,132] have called into question one of the two basic assumptions of that hypothesis, namely that the fatty acids specific for the 2-position are randomly distributed relative to the 1,3-acyl constituents. The other basic assumption of the hypothesis—that the 1- and 3-positions are equivalent and therefore identical in fatty acid composition—was disproved by the first demonstration of optical asymmetry in natural triglycerides, by a procedure based on argentation-TLC,[133,134] and by the elegant stereospecific analysis procedures of Brockerhoff[135,136] and Lands et al.[137]

Applications of argentation-TLC separations of glyceride species which are of much greater potential importance than these straightforward analytical studies take place in investigations of the biosynthesis and metabolism of diglycerides, triglycerides, phospholipids and glycolipids. Many such studies of these last two classes have been described and are discussed below. The results of the few such investigations of di- and triglyceride biosynthesis described so far suggest strongly that nonrandom synthesis of diglyceride species occurs via phosphatidic acids, with strong positional specificities for different fatty acids, followed by almost random utilization of these diglycerides for the biosynthesis of triglycerides.[138,139] It has also been shown that some triglyceride species turn over more rapidly than others, perhaps reflecting different metabolic roles.[140]

PHOSPHOLIPIDS AND GLYCOLIPIDS

Phospholipids and/or glycolipids are a major constituent of most biological membranes and are known to be essential for their integrity. The various biochemical as well as biophysical functions proposed for phospholipids and glycolipids imply that these different functions may involve individual lipids of specific fatty acid composition and that the "pure" lipid classes isolated from whole cells may represent a conglomeration of molecular species having different functions. To determine the detailed fatty acid structure of individual molecular species and to test such hypotheses as to their differing functions, it is clearly necessary to obtain specific fractionations of the kind already described for neutral glycerides. Unfortunately, the techniques of argentation chromatography which were successful for fractionations of triglycerides gave comparatively poor results at first when applied to phospholipids. Such difficulties were clearly due to the hydrophilic groups of the complex lipids, and several workers circumvented this problem by removing the phosphate moiety prior to argentation chromatography.

Van Golde and co-workers[141] hydrolyzed their phospholipid preparations with phospholipase C and subsequently achieved good separations of the resultant free diglycerides by argentation-TLC, while Renkonen[142, 143] and Dyatlovitskaya *et al.*[144, 145] preferred to chromatograph the diglycerides as their acetate or trityl derivatives. Renkonen employed two procedures for the conversion of phospholipids to the corresponding diglyceride acetates.[142] (See Volume II, Chapter 5 of this series.) The first of these involved direct acetolysis of phospholipid with a mixture of acetic anhydride and acetic acid, and was successfully applied to phosphatidyl choline, phosphatidyl ethanolamine, and dialkenyl phosphatidyl ethanolamine. The second procedure, employing phospholipase C hydrolysis followed by acetylation of the dephosphorylated residue, was applied to choline and ethanolamine plasmalogens and to sphingomyelins. This last class of phospholipid yielded ceramide acetates which were partially fractionated by argentation-TLC according to the structures of their amine and fatty acid moieties. The preferable source of phospholipase C is the growth medium from cultures of *Bacillus cereus*,[146] because such preparations dephosphorylate even the acidic phosphatides. Kuksis and co-workers[147, 148] have extended the analysis of diglyceride acetate fractions obtained from argentation-TLC to include GLC analysis of the intact acetates. In many cases, this results in the complete resolution and structural characterization of natural glycerophosphatides. These authors[147, 148] and Privett and Nutter[149] have emphasized that the diglyceride acetates must be prepared by hydrolysis with phospholipase C followed by acetylation, because direct conversion of phospholipids into their diglyceride acetates by direct acetolysis results in a partial migration of the acyl groups.

Another technique cleverly exploited by Renkonen involves diazomethanolysis of lecithins to give the corresponding dimethylphosphatidates (see Volume II, Chapter 5 of this series). Normal adsorption TLC on silica gel resolved the reaction products into two main fractions, one of which contained plasmalogenic species while diacyl lipids comprised the other. Argentation-TLC of this second fraction gave excellent resolution, including the separation of several molecular species of the same overall degree of unsaturation.[150] This procedure has also been adapted for the analysis of phosphatidyl ethanolamines; and an alternative method for the preparation of dimethyl phosphatidates from phospholipids, employing hydrolysis with phospholipase D followed by methylation of the phosphatidic acids so produced, has also been described.[151] By these procedures, phospholipids containing as many as 12 double bonds per molecule can be fractionated and characterized.[121]

Despite the undoubted superiority of the above methods for analysis and structural characterization of phospholipid species, compared to direct argentation-TLC of unmodified phospholipids, they have certain inherent disadvantages. First, removal of the phosphate or amine groups means that the method cannot be applied to studies in which the incorporation of radioactive label into these groups is under investigation. Second, they are of no value in the preparation of individual phospholipid species. Nevertheless, they can give much valuable information concerning complex lipid metabolism, especially in dietary and structural studies which do not involve the use of radioisotopes. For example, van Golde *et al.* were able to show that the changes in fatty acid composition which occur within the liver lecithin fraction when essential fatty acid-deficient rats are placed on a corn oil diet are related particularly to certain species—notably 1-palmitoyl, 2-eicosatrienoyl-, and 1-stearoyl—2-eicosatrienoyl-lecithins being replaced by 1-palmitoyl, 2-arachidonoyl-and 1-stearoyl, 2-arachidonoyl-lecithins, respectively.[152] Similarly, removal of the phosphoryl-base moieties of phospholipids is acceptable if the incorporation of labeled glycerol into lipid classes is under investigation, as in studies of *de novo* synthesis of glycerolipids. Thus, Hill and co-workers[153] made the important observation that, whereas the incorporation of fatty acids into diacyl glycerophosphate in a cell-free system from pigeon liver gave rise to an almost random synthesis of species, an entirely different pattern was obtained in the intact liver, with almost exclusive specificity of saturated fatty acids for the 1-position and unsaturated acids for the 2-position in the species synthesized.

Renkonen avoided the disadvantages of removing functional groups by converting the phosphatidyl ethanolamine fraction of hen's egg to its dinitrophenylated and methylated derivative, which was then readily separated into species by argentation-TLC[154, 155] (see Volume II, Chapter 5 of this series). More important, several research groups have shown that a rigorous control of experimental conditions can result in acceptable resolutions of unmodified, naturally occurring lecithins and phospha-

tidyl ethanolamines into species of different overall degree of unsaturation.[e.g.,156–160] Arvidson subsequently devised a reversed-phase argentation-TLC procedure which gave good separations according both to
the degree of unsaturation of the constituent fatty acids and to their
chain length.[161] The degree of resolution was equivalent to that which
might be expected if the corresponding diglycerides or diglyceride derivatives were examined by the more normal adsorption argentation-TLC.

Such techniques have been employed in several studies of the biosynthesis and metabolism of lecithin in rat liver. This tissue can synthesize lecithin by two pathways, one involving direct synthesis from
choline and diglyceride and the other forming lecithin by methylation
of endogenous phosphatidyl ethanolamine, the requisite methyl groups
being donated by L-methionine. To determine whether specific species
of diglyceride or phosphatidyl ethanolamine are preferentially utilized
in these systems, Arvidson[162] incubated rat liver with [1,2-^{14}C$_2$] choline
and L-[Me-^{14}C] methionine. By a combination of argentation-TLC and
reversed phase partition-TLC, he obtained eight different molecular
types of lecithins in which most of the label from the added choline
appeared in the palmitoyl, oleoyl- and palmitoyl, linoleoyl-lecithins,
whereas most of the L-methionine label accumulated in the tetra- and
hexaenoic lecithins, particularly the latter. This showed that the two
pathways initially synthesize lecithins of very different fatty acid composition; other groups[e.g.,163–165] have made similar observations, although
Lyman and co-workers have concluded that the methylation of phosphatidyl ethanolamine is a random process.[165]

Argentation-TLC has also been used for the enrichment of alkenyl,
acyl- and diacyl-phospholipid species from their mixtures.[e.g.,22,166,167]

The presence of trace amounts of silver nitrate in phospholipid species
eluted from silver ion chromatograms can interfere with the colorimetric
methods employed for their quantification. These impurities, however,
may be removed by a cation-exchange resin[168] or by elution from the
chromatogram with methanolic choline chloride solution.[169]

Little work has been reported so far on the fractionation of acyl
glycolipids by these techniques, although Nichols and Moorhouse have
shown that unmodified galactosyl diglyceride fractions from *Chlorella
vulgaris* may be resolved into groups of species according to overall
degree of unsaturation by argentation-TLC.[170] These authors incubated
the algal cells with [2-^{14}C] acetate and, by radiochemical-GLC of the
component fatty acids from the individual glycolipid species, found that
at any time the specific activity of a given fatty acid varied considerably
among the different species in which it occurred. These results could be
interpreted to indicate selective synthesis of specific species, but the
authors consider them more consistent with the occurrence of progressive

changes in the fatty acids esterified to the glycolipids following *de novo* synthesis.

REFERENCES

1. Winstein, S., and H. J. Lucas, J. Am. Chem. Soc. **60**, 836 (1938).
2. Chatt, J. (Ch. 8) and G. Salomon (Ch. 9), *Cationic Polymerization and Related Complexes,* Ed. by P. H. Plesch (New York: Academic Press, 1953).
3. Coates, G. E., *Organometallic Compounds*, 2nd ed. (London: Methuen, 1960), Ch. 6, p 233.
4. Bennet, M. A., Chem. Rev. **62**, 611 (1962).
5. Dewar, M. J. S., Bull. Soc. Chim. France **18**, C79 (1951).
6. Morris, L. J., J. Lipid Res. **7**, 717 (1966).
7. Nichols, P. L., Jr., J. Am. Chem. Soc. **74**, 1091 (1952).
8. Dutton, H. J., C. R. Scholfield, and E. P. Jones, Chem. Ind. (London), **1961**, 1874.
9. Scholfield, C. R., *Fatty Acids*, 2nd ed., Ed. by K. Markley (New York: Interscience Publ., 1964), p 2283.
10. de Vries, B., Presented at VIth Congress, International Society for Fat Research, London, April 1962; Chem. Ind. (London) **1962**, 1049.
11. Morris, L. J., Presented at VIth Congress, International Society for Fat Research, London, April 1962; Chem. Ind. (London) **1962**, 1238.
12. Barrett, C. B., M. S. J. Dallas, and F. B. Padley, Chem. Ind. (London) **1962**, 1050.
13. Mangold, H. K., J. Am. Oil Chemists' Soc. **41**, 762 (1964).
14. Mangold, H. K., H. H. O. Schmid, and E. Stahl, *Methods of Biochemical Analysis,* Vol. 12, Ed. by D. Glick (New York: Interscience Publ., 1964), p 394.
15. Privett, O. S., M. L. Blank, D. W. Codding, and E. C. Nickell, J. Am. Oil Chemists' Soc. **42**, 381 (1965).
16. Pelick, N., T. L. Wilson, M. E. Miller, F. M. Angeloni, and J. M. Steim, J. Am. Oil Chemists' Soc. **42**, 393 (1965).
17. Nichols, B. W., L. J. Morris, and A. T. James, Brit. Med. Bull., **22**, 137 (1966).
18. Morris, L. J., and B. W. Nichols, *Chromatography*, 2nd ed., Ed. by E. Heftmann (New York: Reinhold Publ. Corp., 1967), p 466.
19. Radin, N. S., J. Am. Oil Chemists' Soc. **42**, 569 (1965).
20. Padley, F. B., Chromatog. Rev. **8**, 208 (1966).
21. Jurriens, G., *Analysis and Characterization of Oils, Fats and Fat Products*, Vol. 2, Ed. by H. A. Boekenoogen (London: Interscience Publ., 1968), p 217.
22. Viswanathan, C. V., Chromatog. Rev. **10**, 18 (1968).
23. Morris, L. J., Lab. Pract. **13**, 284 (1964).
24. Morris, L. J., *Metabolism and Physiological Significance of Lipids*, Ed. by R. M. C. Dawson and D. N. Rhodes (London: J. Wiley and Sons Ltd., 1964), p 641.

25. Morris, L. J., *New Biochemical Separations*, Ed. by A. T. James and L. J. Morris (London: D. Van Nostrand Co. Ltd., 1964), p 295.
26. Den Boer, F. C., Z. Anal. Chem. 205, 308 (1964).
27. Jurriens, G., Riv. Ital. Sostanze Grasse 1965, 116.
28. Paulose, M. M., J. Chromatog. 21, 141 (1966).
29. Vereschagin, A. G., J. Chromatog. 17, 382 (1965).
30. Anderson, R. L., and E. J. Hollenbach, J. Lipid Res. 6, 577 (1965).
31. Willner, D., Chem. Ind. (London) 1965, 1839.
32. Wurster, C. F., Jr., J. H. Copenhaver, Jr., and P. R. Shafer, J. Am. Oil Chemists' Soc. 40, 513 (1963).
33. Emken, E. A., C. R. Scholfield, and H. J. Dutton, J. Am. Oil Chemists' Soc. 41, 388 (1964).
34. Wood, R., and F. Snyder, J. Am. Oil Chemists' Soc. 43, 53 (1966).
35. Singh, E. J., and L. L. Gershbein, J. Chromatog. 29, 229 (1967).
36. Smith, C. R., Jr., R. Kleiman, and I. A. Wolff, Lipids 3, 37 (1968).
37. Privett, O. S., M. L. Blank, and O. Romanus, J. Lipid Res. 4, 260 (1963).
38. Bhatty, M. K., and B. M. Craig, Can. J. Biochem. 44, 311 (1966).
39. Kleiman, R., G. F. Spencer, F. R. Earle, and I. A. Wolff, Chem. Ind. (London) 1967, 1326.
40. Bergelson, L. D., E. V. Dyatlovitskaya, and V. V. Voronkova, J. Chromatog. 15, 191 (1964).
41. Privett, O. S., and E. C. Nickell, Lipids 1, 98 (1966).
42. Bhatty, M. K., and B. M. Craig, J. Am. Oil Chemists' Soc. 41, 508 (1964).
43. Kuemmel, D. F., and L. R. Chapman, Lipids 3, 313 (1968).
44. Harrington, G. W., and G. G. Holz, Biochim. Biophys. Acta 164, 137 (1968).
45. Nicolaides, N., and M. N. A. Ansari, Lipids 3, 403 (1968).
46. Craig, B. M., and M. K. Bhatty, J. Am. Oil Chemists' Soc. 41, 209 (1964).
47. Jamieson, G. R., and E. H. Reid, J. Sci. Food Agr. 19, 628 (1968).
48. Powell, R. G., C. R. Smith, Jr., and I. A. Wolff, Lipids 2, 172 (1967).
49. Schroepfer, G. J., Jr., and K. Bloch, J. Biol. Chem. 240, 54 (1965).
50. Morris, L. J., R. V. Harris, W. Kelly, and A. T. James, Biochem. J. 109, 673 (1968).
51. Morris, L. J., Biochem. Biophys. Res. Commun. 29, 311 (1967).
52. Harris, R. V., P. Harris, and A. T. James, Biochim. Biophys. Acta 106, 465 (1965).
53. Howling, D., L. J. Morris, and A. T. James, Biochim. Biophys. Acta 152, 224 (1968).
54. Nichols, B. W., and B. J. B. Wood, Lipids 3, 46 (1968).
55. Hitchcock, C. H. S., and A. T. James, Kerntechnik 7, 5 (1965).
56. Sgoutas, D. S., and F. A. Kummerow, J. Chromatog. 16, 448 (1964).
57. Cvetanovic, R. J., E. J. Duncan, and W. E. Falconer, Can. J. Chem. 41, 2095 (1963).

58. Weenink, R. O., and F. B. Shorland, Biochim. Biophys. Acta **84**, 613 (1964).
59. Nichols, B. W., P. Harris, and A. T. James, Biochem. Biophys. Res. Commun. **21**, 473 (1965).
60. Bartels, C. T., A. T. James, and B. W. Nichols, Eur. J. Biochem. **3**, 7 (1967).
61. Morris, L. J., and M. O. Marshall, Chem. Ind. (London) **1966**, 1493.
62. Morris, L. J., M. O. Marshall, and E. W. Hammond, Lipids **3**, 91 (1968).
63. Bagby, M. O., C. R. Smith, Jr., and I. A. Wolff, J. Org. Chem. **30**, 4227 (1965).
64. Mikolajczak, K. L., M. F. Rogers, C. R. Smith, Jr., and I. A. Wolff, Biochem. J. **105**, 1245 (1967).
65. Bagby, M. O., C. R. Smith, Jr., and I. A. Wolff, Lipids **1**, 263 (1966).
66. Gunstone, F. D., and R. Subbarao, Chem. Phys. Lipids **1**, 349 (1967).
67. Powell, R. G., C. R. Smith, Jr., and I. A. Wolff, J. Org. Chem. **32**, 1442 (1967).
68. Tallent, W. H., J. Harris, G. F. Spencer, and I. A. Wolff, Lipids **3**, 425 (1968).
69. Serck-Hannsen, K., Acta Chem. Scand. **21**, 301 (1967).
70. Morris, L. J., and D. M. Wharry, J. Chromatog. **20**, 27 (1965).
71. Mikolajczak, K. L., and C. R. Smith, Jr., Lipids **2**, 261 (1967).
72. Green, K., and B. Samuelsson, J. Lipid Res. **5**, 117 (1964).
73. Mani, V. V. S., and G. Lakshminarayana, J. Chromatog. **39**, 182 (1969).
74. Cornelius, J. A., and G. Shone, Chem. Ind. (London) **1963**, 1246.
75. Johnson, A. R., K. E. Murray, A. C. Fogerty, B. H. Kennet, J. A. Pearson, and F. S. Shenstone, Lipids **2**, 316 (1967).
76. Schneider, E. L., P. L. Sook, and D. T. Hopkins, J. Am. Oil Chemists' Soc. **45**, 585 (1968).
77. Morris, L. J., M. O. Marshall, and W. Kelly, Tetrahedron Letters **1966**, 4249.
78. Morris, L. J., and M. O. Marshall, Chem. Ind. (London) **1966**, 460.
79. Gunstone, F. D., and A. J. Sealy, J. Chem. Soc. **1963**, 5772.
80. Morris, L. J., J. Chem. Soc. **1963**, 5779.
81. Powell, R. G., and C. R. Smith, Jr., Biochem. **5**, 625 (1966).
82. Hopkins, C. Y., A. W. Jevans, and M. J. Chisholm, J. Chem. Soc. **1968**, 2462.
83. Haigh, W. G., L. J. Morris, and A. T. James, Lipids **3**, 307 (1968).
84. Gunstone, F. D., D. Kilcast, R. G. Powell, and G. M. Taylor, Chem. Commun. **295** (1967).
85. Bu'Lock, J. D., and G. N. Smith, J. Chem. Soc. **1967C**, 332.
86. de Vries, B., and G. Jurriens, Fette, Seifen, Anstrichmittel **65**, 725 (1963).
87. Scholfield, C. R., E. P. Jones, R. O. Butterfield, and H. J. Dutton, Anal. Chem. **35**, 1588 (1963).

88. Lees, A. M., and E. D. Korn, Biochim. Biophys. Acta **116**, 403 (1966).
89. Strocchi, A., and M. Piretti, J. Chromatog. **36**, 181 (1968).
90. Emken, E. A., C. R. Scholfield, V. L. Davison, and E. N. Frankel, J. Am. Oil Chemists' Soc. **44**, 373 (1967).
91. Scholfield, C. R., R. O. Butterfield, H. Peters, C. A. Glass, and H. J. Dutton, J. Am. Oil Chemists' Soc. **44**, 50 (1967).
92. Subbaram, M. R., and C. G. Youngs, J. Am. Oil Chemists' Soc. **41**, 150 (1964).
93. Scholfield, C. R., E. P. Jones, R. O. Butterfield, and H. J. Dutton. Anal. Chem. **35**, 386 (1963).
94. Frankel, E. N., H. M. Peters, E. P. Jones, and H. J. Dutton, J. Am. Oil Chemists' Soc. **41**, 186 (1964).
95. Frankel, E. N., E. P. Jones, V. L. Davison, E. Emken, and H. J. Dutton, J. Am. Oil Chemists' Soc. **42**, 130 (1965).
96. Kuemmel, D. F., and L. R. Chapman, Anal. Chem. **38**, 1611 (1966).
97. E. P. Jones, C. R. Scholfield, V. L. Davison, and H. J. Dutton, J. Am. Oil Chemists' Soc. **42**, 727 (1965).
98. Scholfield, C. R., V. L. Davison, and H. J. Dutton, J. Am. Oil Chemists' Soc. **44**, 648 (1967).
99. Ward, P. F. V., T. W. Scott, and R. M. C. Dawson, Biochem. J. **92**, 60 (1964).
100. Wilde, P. F., and R. M. C. Dawson, Biochem J. **98**, 469 (1966).
101. Kemp, P., and R. M. C. Dawson, Biochem. J. **109**, 477 (1968).
102. Kepler, C. R., and S. B. Tove, J. Biol. Chem. **242**, 5686 (1967).
103. De Jong, K., and H. Van der Wel, Nature **202**, 553 (1964).
104. Suomalainen, H., and A. J. A. Keranen, Chem. Phys. Lipids **2**, 296 (1968).
105. Cronan, J. E., Jr., Biochim. Biophys. Acta **144**, 695 (1967).
106. Struijk, C. B., and R. K. Beerthuis, Biochim. Biophys. Acta **116**, 12 (1966).
107. Morris, L. J., D. M. Wharry, and E. W. Hammond, J. Chromatog. **31**, 69 (1967).
108. Gunstone, F. D., I. A. Ismail, and M. Lie Ken Jie, Chem. Phys. Lipids **1**, 376 (1967).
109. Christie, W. W., J. Chromatog. **34**, 405 (1968).
110. Morris, L. J., D. M. Wharry, and E. W. Hammond, J. Chromatog. **33**, 471 (1968).
111. Dutta, S. P., and A. K. Barua, J. Chromatog. **29**, 263 (1967).
112. Meijboom, P. W., and G. Jurriens, J. Chromatog. **18**, 424 (1965).
113. Davidoff, F., and E. D. Korn, J. Biol. Chem. **239**, 2496 (1964).
114. Morris, L. J., J. Lipid Res. **4**, 357 (1963).
115. Haahti, E., T. Nikkari, and K. Juva, Acta Chem. Scand. **17**, 538 (1963).
116. Wood, R., and F. Snyder, Lipids **1**, 62 (1966).
117. Gunstone, F. D., and F. B. Padley, J. Am. Oil Chemists' Soc. **42**, 957 (1965).

118. Subbaram, M. R., and C. G. Youngs, J. Am. Oil Chemists' Soc. **41**, 445 (1964).
119. Gunstone, F. D., R. J. Hamilton, and M. I. Qureshi, J. Chem. Soc. 319 (1965).
120. Litchfield, C., Lipids **3**, 170 (1968).
121. Renkonen, O., Lipids **3**, 191 (1968).
122. Blank, M. L., and O. S. Privett, J. Dairy Sci. **47**, 481 (1964).
123. Breckenridge, W. C., and A. Kuksis, Lipids **3**, 291 (1968).
124. Gunstone, F. D., and M. I. Qureshi, J. Sci. Food Agr. **19**, 386 (1968).
125. Kaufmann, H. P., and H. Wessels, Fette, Seifen, Anstrichmittel **66**, 81 (1964).
126. Litchfield, C., M. Farquhar, and R. Reiser, J. Am. Oil Chemists' Soc. **41**, 588 (1964).
127. Jurriens, G., and A. C. J. Kroesen, J. Am. Oil Chemists' Soc. **42**, 9 (1965).
128. Gunstone, F. D., and M. I. Qureshi, J. Am. Oil Chemists' Soc. **42**, 961 (1965).
129. Gunstone, F. D., and F. B. Padley, Chem. Phys. Lipids **1**, 110 (1967).
130. Gunstone, F. D., and F. B. Padley, Chem. Phys. Lipids **1**, 429 (1967).
131. Blank, M. L., B. Verdino, and O. S. Privett, J. Am. Oil Chemists' Soc. **42**, 87 (1965).
132. Blank, M. L., and O. S. Privett, Lipids **1**, 27 (1966).
133. Morris, L. J., Biochem. Biophys. Res. Commun. **20**, 340 (1965).
134. Morris, L. J., and W. G. Haigh, Lipids. In press, 1969.
135. Brockerhoff, H., J. Lipid Res. **6**, 10 (1965).
136. Brockerhoff, H., J. Lipid Res. **8**, 167 (1967).
137. Lands, W. E. M., R. A. Pieringer, P. M. Slakey, and A. Zschocke, Lipids **1**, 444 (1966).
138. Hill, E. E., W. E. M. Lands, and P. M. Slakey, Lipids **3**, 411 (1968).
139. Elovson, J., N. Akesson, and G. Arvidson, Biochim. Biophys. Acta **176**, 214 (1969).
140. Jezyk, P. F., Can. J. Biochem. **46**, 1167 (1968).
141. van Golde, L. M. G., V. Tomasi, and L. L. M. van Deenen, Chem. Phys. Lipids **1**, 282 (1966).
142. Renkonen, O., J. Am. Oil Chemists' Soc. **42**, 298 (1965).
143. Renkonen, O., Biochim. Biophys. Acta **125**, 288 (1966).
144. Dyatlovitskaya, E. V., V. I. Volkova, and L. D. Bergel'son, Biokhimiya **31**, 1189 (1966).
145. Dyatlovitskaya, E. V., V. I. Volkova, and L. D. Bergel'son, Biokhimiya **32**, 1227 (1967).
146. Chu, H. P., J. Gen. Microbiol. **3**, 255 (1949).
147. Kuksis, A., and L. Marai, Lipids **2**, 217 (1967).
148. Kuksis, A., W. C. Breckenridge, L. Marai, and O. Stachnyk, J. Am. Oil Chemists' Soc. **45**, 537 (1968).
149. Privett, O. S., and L. J. Nutter, Lipids **2**, 149 (1967).

150. Renkonen, O., *Advances in Lipid Research* Vol. 5, Ed. by R. Paoletti and D. Kritchevsky (New York: Academic Press, 1967), p 329.
151. Renkonen, O., Biochim. Biophys. Acta **152**, 114 (1968).
152. van Golde, L. M. G., W. A. Pieterson, and L. L. M. van Deenen, Biochim. Biophys. Acta **152**, 84 (1968).
153. Hill, E. E., D. R. Husbands, and W. E. M. Lands, J. Biol. Chem. **243**, 4440 (1968).
154. Renkonen, O., Acta Chem. Scand. **21**, 1108 (1967).
155. Renkonen, O., J. Lipid Res. **9**, 34 (1968).
156. Kaufmann, H. P., H. Wessels, and C. Bondopadhya, Fette, Seifen, Anstrichmittel **65**, 543 (1963).
157. Arvidson, G. A. E., J. Lipid Res. **6**, 574 (1965).
158. Arvidson, G. A. E., Eur. J. Biochem. **4**, 478 (1968).
159. Hopkins, S. M., G. Sheehan, and R. L. Lyman, Biochim. Biophys. Acta **164**, 272 (1968).
160. van Golde, L. M. G., R. F. A. Zwaal, and L. L. M. van Deenen, Koninkl. Ned. Akad. Wetenschap. Proc. Ser. B **68**, 255 (1965).
161. Arvidson, G. A. E., J. Lipid Res. **8**, 155 (1967).
162. Arvidson, G. A. E., Eur. J. Biochem. **5**, 415 (1968).
163. Balint, J. A., D. A. Beeker, D. H. Treble, and H. L. Spitzer, J. Lipid Res. **8**, 486 (1967).
164. Rytter, D., J. E. Miller, and W. E. Cornatzer, Biochim. Biophys. Acta **152**, 418 (1968).
165. Lyman, R. L., S. M. Hopkins, G. Sheehan, and J. Tinoco, Biochim. Biophys. Acta **176**, 86 (1969).
166. Hoevet, S. P., C. V. Viswanathan, and W. O. Lundberg, J. Chromatog. **34**, 195 (1968).
167. Viswanathan, C. V., S. P. Hoevet, and W. O. Lundberg, J. Chromatog. **35**, 113 (1968).
168. Kyriakides, E. C., and J. A. Balint, J. Lipid Res. **9**, 142 (1968).
169. Tinoco, J., S. M. Hopkins, D. J. McIntosh, G. Sheehan, and R. L. Lyman, Lipids **2**, 479 (1967).
170. Nichols, B. W., and R. Moorhouse, Lipids. In press, 1969.

Chapter 4

TLC Analysis of Amines as Their DANS-Derivatives

by N. Seiler and M. Wiechmann

Though the biochemistry of amines was first investigated more than a hundred years ago[1] the enormous interest in these substances during the last two decades was primarily induced by the discovery of biologically very active amines, such as epinephrine, norepinephrine, histamine and serotonin, and especially when it was observed that some of these amines play a basic role in the function of the central nervous system.[2-8] A further stimulation of this field of investigation still comes from the supposed connections of amine metabolism and some mental disorders,[9-11] and from the discovery that several amines (mescaline, dimethyltryptamine, bufotenine, D-lysergic acid diethylamide, psilocybine, amphetamine derivatives, etc.) produce in human beings hallucinations and psychotic states which resemble those in acute schizophrenic episodes.[12]

Parallel to the still growing interest in the biochemistry of the biogenic amines was the increasing demand for sensitive and simple analytical methods for their detection and quantitative determination. This demand resulted because the old methods of isolating amines, such as picrates, chloroplatinates, chloroaurates, tetraphenyloborates or in the form of other complex salts,[1] were only achievable in special cases, these methods being far too insensitive, complicated, and troublesome, and for quantitative purposes too inaccurate, for the quantitative analysis of small tissue samples. Generally the concentration of biogenic amines is within the range of $0.001-1$ μmole/g tissue.

For the quantitative determination of the most important biogenic amines, more or less specific colorimetric and fluorometric methods have been worked out. Since the fluorometric methods[13] are generally very sensitive, they are employed in many laboratories. They are the methods of choice now, though they are only available for a restricted number of amines. Their specificity is based on specific structural premises. For example, the basis of one of the fluorometric methods for the determination of epinephrine is the formation of an indole ring system by $K_3[Fe(CN)_6]$ oxidation. For this reaction the ethylamine side chain and the o-diphenol group are essential. Other molecules with these structural features react in a similar manner.

Normally with fluorometric methods of this type, only one compound can be determined in one sample, and in rare cases two or three. More generally applicable quantitative methods use the base properties of the amines. The amines are extracted from the tissue sample by an organic solvent; then the color change of an indicator dye is measured spectrophotometrically in a water-free medium,[14-16] or the reaction product of the amines with ninhydrin, fluoro-2,4-dinitrobenzene[17-19] or with 2,4,6-trinitrobenzenesulfonic acid,[20,21] among others is estimated. The handicap of these methods is the lack of specificity. The solution of the problem seems to be the combination of an efficient separation method with a generally applicable detection method. One would think first of GLC, and indeed this method can be very effective in the analysis of biogenic amines,[22] but GLC is restricted to volatile compounds. In addition there are special problems involved in the GLC of amines:[23] fewer volatile amines may be transformed into volatile substances. For example, catecholamines were separated as their trifluoro acetates.[24]

In qualitative identification, GLC is cumbersome. But reaction gas chromatography[25] and especially the combination of GLC with mass spectrometry,[26] a method for which commercially produced equipments are now available, may play a considerable role in amine analysis in the future, though the expensive equipment necessary may prohibit a general application. Since many amines are very soluble in water, their concentration to small solvent volumes, which are applicable to GLC, may in addition cause difficulties in practice.

Perry and co-workers have combined ion-exchange chromatography and PC with the ninhydrin reaction. Though this method is very time-consuming and limited by the sensitivity of the ninhydrin reaction, it demonstrated a considerable number of primary and secondary amines in different tissues and body fluids.[27-31] Ion exchange chromatography combined with dinitrophenylation was applied, for example, in the analysis of spermine, spermidine and of some related polyamines.[32-35]

The paper chromatographic or electrophoretic separation of amines and their detection with ninhydrin, in the case of primary or secondary amines, or with Dragendorff's reagent, in the case of secondary and tertiary amines, is well known.[36-38] More recently TLC was applied for amine separations,[39-50] for which different reagents are recommended.[51] The results are not convincing in any direction. If, however, preseparations are included in the analytical procedure and if specific reagents are used, then even quantitative results may be obtained on TLC with certain groups of amines.[52-55, 71] The combination of TLC and thin-layer electrophoresis was adopted by Honegger[56] for the separation of some amines.

Better amine separations have been obtained using different derivatives, most of which have also been applied in the chromatographic separation of amino acids. Teichert and others[39,57] separated the 3,5-dinitrobenzamides on Silica Gel G layers, Neurath and Doerk[58] and Heyns *et al.*[59] separated the 4'-nitroazobenzene-carbon-4-amides, and Jart and co-workers[60] separated the 4-phenylazobenzene sulfonamides. Parihar *et al.*[61] used the *p*-toluene sulfonates for the detection of amines. The same group separated charge transfer complexes of amines with 2,4,6-trinitrophenyl-N-methyl-nitramine, 2,4-dinitrochlorobenzene, 2,4,6-trinitrotoluene and with m-dinitrobenzene on TLC.[62,63] Fluoro-2,4-dinitrobenzene was also used as an amine reagent. Some urinary amines have been identified on PC as their DNP-derivatives.[64,65] The thin-layer chromatographic properties of DNP-amine derivatives were studied by several groups.[66-68,72,73] For the preparation of these derivatives, 2,4-dinitrobenzene sulfonic acid is preferred by Smith, Jepson[67] and others[69,70] because the ability of fluoro-2,4-dinitrobenzene to react with alcohols[19,74] is a disadvantage. About 5 nanomoles of DNP-amines are visible on TLC. In principle the quantitative determination of thin-layer chromatographically separated DNP-amines can be achieved spectrophotometrically or polarographically after extraction of the DNP-amine from the adsorbent, or by direct scanning of the plate. The latter method has been demonstrated to be suitable by Pataki and Strasky.[75]

Recently 7-chloro-4-nitrobenzo-2-oxa-1,3-diazole has been recommended for the fluorescence labeling of amino acids and amines.[76] This fluorescence label has to prove its usefulness in the future.

For further increase of sensitivity one could think of using [131]J-iodobenzene-*p*-sulfonyl chloride ([131]J-pipsyl chloride) as a reagent and to measure the radioactivity of the separated pipsyl-amine derivatives. This technique was used for the identification of amino acids on PC,[77] and recently pipsyl derivatives of amino acids have been separated on TLC,[78] but as far as the authors are aware, the pipsyl derivatives have only been used in the amine field for the determination of histamine.[79] It can be assumed that the chromatographic qualities of the pipsyl derivatives of amines are not so advantageous as to allow the separation of complex mixtures.

As was demonstrated first by Seiler *et al.*[52,80] and later by other groups,[75,81-90] fluorescent substances can be determined with good accuracy by direct fluorometry of the thin-layer plates. For a more general application of this method in amine analysis, it was necessary to search for a fluorescent reagent that would react quantitatively with amino groups and the derivatives of which could be separated on TLC, thus combining a sensitive detection method with an excellent separation technique. The reagent of our choice was 1-dimethylamino-naphthalene-5-sulfonyl chloride (dansyl chloride, DANS-Cl). Dansyl chloride was introduced by Weber,[91] who prepared fluorescent protein conjugates for the study of size and shape of the macromolecules. Later on it was used for the histochemical localization of antigens in immuno-chemistry, virology, and bacteriology,[92-99] and for the study of active centers of enzymes.[100-108] The most important application for this substance was found by Gray and Hartley,[109] who introduced it as a sensitive end-group reagent in peptide and protein chemistry. It is used in a fashion analogous to fluoro-2,4-dinitrobenzene, the reagent introduced by Sanger.[110-113,145]

REACTION OF DANSYL CHLORIDE WITH AMINES, PHENOLS, AND OTHER COMPOUNDS

Reactivity of Different Functional Groups

Primary and secondary amines, imidazoles, and phenols generally react swiftly with dansyl chloride under suitable conditions to produce the corresponding sulfonamides and phenol esters.[114] The reactions are formulated in Scheme I.

While free amino acids are partially fragmented to DANS-NH$_2$, CO and the aldehyde or ketone with one less carbon atom than the parent amino acid,[115] amines and phenols normally react stoichiometrically

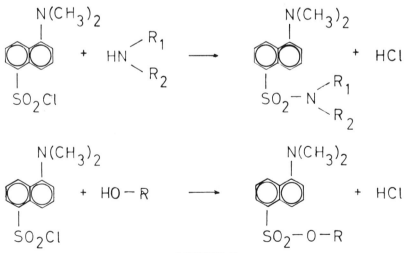

SCHEME I

with DANS-Cl on both preparative[114] and micro scale.[114,116] If one molecule has more than one functional group, all these groups are dansylated. The dansyl chloride consumption during the reaction can be easily determined by continuous titration. In Figure 1, titration curves are shown of a mono-, a di-, and a trifunctional molecule under favorable dansylation conditions.

Alcoholic hydroxyl groups normally react only to a small extent, although there are some alcohols, for example choline, which are readily dansylated quantitatively under the conditions to be discussed in detail later.[117,118] Though thiol groups react with dansyl chloride, the corresponding disulfides are obtained as the reaction products. For example the dansylation of thiophenol produced diphenyl-disulfide in a fast reaction, and during the dansylation of cysteamine (2-mercaptoethylamine), 2 moles of DANS-Cl per mole cysteamine were consumed, but the reaction product obtained was identical with that obtained from cystamine, the corresponding disulfide, namely, bisDANS-2,2'-dithio-bis(ethylamide) (bisDANS-cystamine).

Under the pH conditions favorable for the dansylation of amino acids and amines, guanidino groups and aliphatic alcohols are present almost exclusively as the unreactive conjugate acids, so that arginine, for instance, reacts under these circumstances preferentially with the α-amino group. If the pH is raised above 10, the guanidino group is also reacting. Thus we obtained from guanidine hydrochloride DANS-guanidine in 60% yield. If agmatine (γ-guanidino butyramine) was reacted with 4M DANS-Cl 27% monoDANS-agmatine, 10% bisDANS-agmatine and 25% bisDANS-putrescine was isolated from the reaction mixture in pure state. The reaction of methylguanidine with DANS-Cl produced DANS-methylamide as a fragmentation product. Arginine is also partially fragmented under these reaction conditions, but the fragments have not been identified yet.

The reactivity of basic substances towards dansyl chloride is mainly dependent upon their strength as bases,[110] but steric factors may also influence the reaction velocities, as can be seen by comparison of the reaction rates of different N-substituted amino acids with DANS-Cl.[119] From the reactivity of dansyl chloride towards different functional groups, it can be concluded that a large number of substances with a great structural variety (primary and secondary aliphatic, aromatic, and heterocyclic amines, hydrazine and hydrazine derivatives, unsubstituted and N-monosubstituted amino acids, purine bases, different alkaloids, choline, and some other aliphatic alcohols including sugars) are capable of reacting with dansyl chloride to give fluorescent derivatives. In Table I different examples of DANS-derivatives, which have been obtained in pure crystalline state, are presented.

Table I

Elemental analysis and some properties of DANS-amides and of DANS-phenol esters

Amine or phenol		Mol. wt.	Elemental analysis						M.P.	color of the crystalline DANS-derivative
			theoretical			experimental				
			C	H	N	C	H	N		
ammonia	$C_{12}H_{14}N_2O_2S$	250.3	57.56	5.64	10.98	57.45	5.66	10.98	218	colorless
hydrazine (monoDANS)	$C_{12}H_{15}N_3O_2S$	265.4	54.32	5.70	15.84	54.57	5.65	16.07	126	pale yellow
methylamine	$C_{13}H_{16}N_2O_2S$	264.4	59.07	6.10	10.60	58.90	6.20	10.66	112	greenish yellow
guanidine	$C_{13}H_{16}N_4O_2S$	292.4	53.41	5.52	19.17	52.84	5.31	18.98	270	greenish yellow
ethylamine	$C_{14}H_{18}N_2O_2S$	278.4	60.40	6.52	10.06	60.65	6.46	10.09	135	pale yellow
dimethylamine	$C_{14}H_{18}N_2O_2S$	278.4	60.40	6.52	10.06	60.58	6.49	10.31	102	greenish yellow
ethanolamine	$C_{14}H_{18}N_2O_3S$	294.4	57.12	6.16	9.52	56.97	5.95	9.66	102	greenish yellow
cysteamine**	$C_{28}H_{34}N_4O_4S_4$	618.9*	54.34	5.54	9.05	54.16	5.84	9.02	71	yellow
cystamine		618.9*				54.65	5.68	9.21	71	yellow
ethylenediamine (monoDANS)	$C_{14}H_{19}N_3O_2S$	293.4	57.31	6.53	14.32	57.25	6.54	14.79	152	pale yellow
ethylenediamine (bisDANS)	$C_{26}H_{30}N_4O_4S_2$	526.7	59.29	5.74	10.64	59.69	5.75	10.18	178	yellow
imidazol	$C_{15}H_{15}N_3O_2S$	301.4	59.78	5.02	13.94	60.02	5.00	14.22	98	yellow
homocysteine-thiolactone	$C_{16}H_{18}N_2O_3S_2$	350.5	54.83	5.18	7.99	54.74	5.36	7.90	132	yellowish
tetramethylenediamine (putrescine) (bisDANS)	$C_{28}H_{34}N_4O_4S_2$	554.7	60.60	6.17	10.09	60.60	6.25	10.10	187	colorless
adenine	$C_{17}H_{16}N_6O_2S$	368.4	55.42	4.38	22.81	55.33	4.62	23.12	216	deep yellow
histamine (bisDANS)	$C_{29}H_{31}N_5O_4S_2$	577.7	60.29	5.41	12.12	59.95	5.63	11.08	71	deep yellow

Compound	Formula	Mol. wt.	Found C	Found H	Found N	Calc. C	Calc. H	Calc. N	Yield	Color
piperidine (monoDANS)	$C_{17}H_{22}N_2O_2S$	318.5	64.11	6.96	8.80	63.95	6.88	8.96	110	colorless
agmatine (monoDANS)	$C_{17}H_{25}N_5O_2S$	363.5	56.17	6.93	19.27	55.34	6.71	18.21	214	colorless
agmatine (bisDANS)	$C_{29}H_{36}N_6O_4S_2$	596.8	58.36	6.08	14.08	58.32	5.89	13.70	112	pale yellow
hexamethylenediamine (bisDANS)	$C_{30}H_{38}N_4O_4S_2$	582.8	61.83	6.57	9.61	62.54	6.69	9.39	115	yellow
glucosamine (monoDANS)	$C_{18}H_{24}N_2O_7S$	412.5	52.42	5.87	6.79	52.31	5.83	7.33	185	yellow
N-methyl-adenine	$C_{18}H_{18}N_6O_2S$	382.5	56.53	4.74	21.98	56.99	5.14	21.27	166	deep yellow
phenol (HCl)	$C_{18}H_{18}ClNO_3S$	363.9	59.42	4.99	3.58	59.99	5.52	4.10	141	colorless
catechol (bisDANS)	$C_{30}H_{28}N_2O_6S_2$	576.7	62.48	4.89	4.86	62.06	4.87	4.97	126	deep yellow
spermidine (triDANS)	$C_{43}H_{52}N_6O_6S_3$	845.1	61.11	6.20	9.95	60.57	6.29	10.14	93	pale yellow
β-phenylethylamine	$C_{20}H_{22}N_2O_2S$	354.5	67.77	6.26	7.90	67.91	6.34	7.96	106	colorless
tyramine (bisDANS)	$C_{32}H_{33}N_3O_5S_2$	603.8	63.64	5.51	6.96	62.91	5.92	6.85	73	deep yellow
pyridoxamine (bisDANS)	$C_{32}H_{34}N_4O_6S_2$	634.9	60.55	5.40	8.83	59.39	5.18	8.90	141	deep yellow
epinephrine (triDANS)	$C_{45}H_{46}N_4O_8S_3$	883.1*	61.18	5.24	6.34	62.46	5.73	6.06	87	deep yellow
5,6-dimethyl-benzimidazol	$C_{21}H_{21}N_3O_2S$	379.5	66.47	5.78	11.07	66.86	5.65	12.19	140	deep yellow
spermine (tetraDANS)	$C_{58}H_{70}N_8O_8S_4$	1135.5	61.35	6.21	9.87	61.44	6.37	9.56	103	pale yellow
hordenine (N-dimethyltyramine) (2HCl · H₂O)	$C_{22}H_{30}Cl_2N_2O_2S$	489.5	53.98	6.18	5.72	54.51	6.21	5.72	197	colorless
tryptamine	$C_{22}H_{23}N_3O_2S$	393.5	67.15	5.89	10.68	67.04	5.94	10.52	57	yellow
mescaline	$C_{23}H_{28}N_2O_5S$	444.6	62.13	6.35	6.30	62.04	6.42	6.20	157	yellowish
bufotenin (2HCl · 2H₂O)	$C_{24}H_{33}Cl_2N_3O_5S$	546.5	52.74	6.09	7.69	52.48	5.63	7.87	117	colorless

101

* Mol. wt. determined by mass-spectrometry.
** Cysteamine and cystamine give identical reaction products.

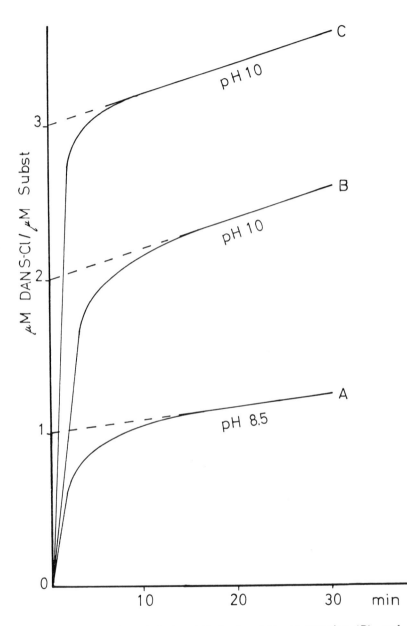

Figure 1. Reaction of β-phenylethylamine (*A*), of tyramine (*B*), and of epinephrine (*C*) with DANS-Cl. Reaction conditions: 0.01M amine; 0.03M DANS-Cl per functional group in 25 ml solvent of acetone–water (7:3) at 25°C. Reaction velocity was measured by continuous titration with 0.01N NaOH.

In addition to the substance classes mentioned above, there are other compounds which may react with dansyl chloride. For example, a rapid reaction is observed with dimethylsulfoxide at room temperature.[120] DANS-OH and chlorodimethylsulfide are formed during this reaction according to Scheme II.

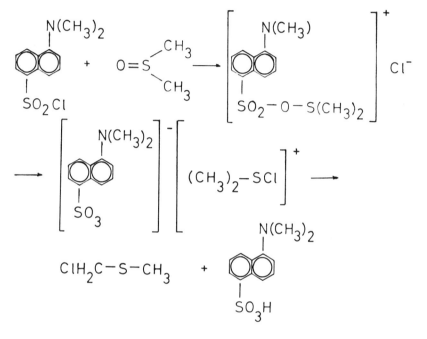

SCHEME II

Reaction Conditions

Dansyl chloride is not readily soluble in water. Dansylation is therefore performed in mixtures of water with an organic solvent. Most widely used are acetone–water mixtures, but ethanol– or dioxane–water mixtures are also suitable. A high proportion of acetone in the mixture considerably lowers the absolute reaction rate, but the rate of hydrolysis of DANS-Cl to DANS-OH is slowed down. Thus changes of the composition of the acetone–water mixture are of little influence to the extent of dansylation. In many experiments an acetone–water ratio of 7:3–1:1 proved most suitable.

The velocity of the dansylation process increases with increasing pH, but the reaction is paralleled by an increasing hydrolysis rate of dansyl chloride. Optimal conditions are those under which the reactive groups most effectively compete with hydrolysis for the limited amount of reagent. As can be seen from Figure 2, at pH values below 7, amines react too slowly—because the unreactive protonated form of the amino group predominates—to complete reaction in a reasonable time. The reaction velocity of phenols with DANS-Cl is too low even at pH 8.5. For the labeling of amines, amino acids and phenols, a.pH of 9.5–10.5 at room temperature proved to be optimal. At higher pH values the hydrolysis of DANS-Cl is very rapid. In addition fragmentation reactions increase.

Labeling of Amines and Phenols in the Nanomole Scale

To one volume of amine solution (in water or 0.2N HClO$_4$) with 10–0.01 nmoles amine 3 volumes of a solution of DANS-Cl in acetone is added. The amount of DANS-Cl should be present in a several-fold excess and its concentration should not be below 5 mM in the final reaction mixture. Which amount of DANS-Cl is achieved depends therefore on the concentration of the substances that can react with dansyl chloride and the volume of their solution. Solutions of 5–45 mg DANS-Cl per ml acetone have been used in practical labeling experiments. If amines or amino acids are to be dansylated, the reaction mixture is saturated with sodium bicarbonate; if phenols or similar compounds are to be reacted, the reaction mixture is saturated with sodium carbonate to increase the pH.[114] Solid sodium bicarbonate and sodium carbonate may be substituted by 0.5–1M solutions of KHCO$_3$ or Na$_2$CO$_3$, or even by other strong bases—triethylamine, for example. Most easily handled are solutions with 1–5 nmoles amine in 0.1–0.5 ml. In this case the reaction is carried out in 10-ml centrifuge tubes with ground glass stoppers. Though in principle the reaction volume is not limited, it is more convenient to work with amine solution volumes not exceeding 1 ml. Salts or buffer components without reacting groups do not disturb the reaction. Oxidizing or strong reducing agents have to be excluded from the reaction mixture. In most cases larger volumes of the amine solutions can easily be brought to a small volume without losses by evaporation in a desiccator or in a stream of air or nitrogen.

As can be seen from Figure 1 and 2, the reactions are complete within a few minutes under favorable conditions. To ensure quantitative dansylation even of substances with low reaction velocities, the reaction mixtures are stored at room temperature for 3 to 4 hours or overnight in a dark place. After this time the excess of dansyl chloride is hydrolyzed to DANS-OH. In special cases of quantitative analysis, the dansyl chloride excess is chosen very high, so that even after a 16-hour storing of the reaction mixture a DANS-Cl excess may be present. In this case a solution of proline (or glutamic acid) in water is added to the reaction mixture to eliminate the DANS-Cl. Dansyl chloride would cause blue-

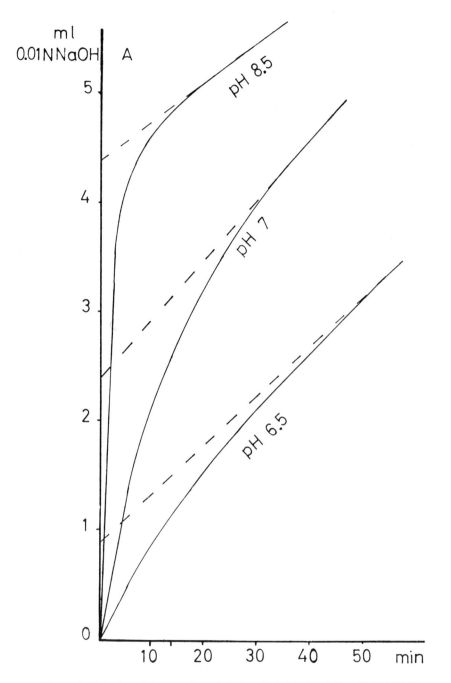

Figure 2. Velocity of the reaction of β-phenylethylamine (A) with DANS-Cl dependent on the pH value, as measured by continuous titration. Reaction medium: acetone–water (7:3) at 25°C (Seiler and Wiechmann).[114]

green fluorescing streaks on the chromatograms, since it is easily hydrolyzed on the silica gel layers.

Most of the DANS-derivatives of amines are soluble in benzene or
ethyl acetate, and can be extracted from the alkaline reaction mixtures
by shaking with these or similar solvents and separating the solvent
phases by centrifugation. The extraction of the DANS-amides with 5 ml
benzene is practically quantitative from a reaction mixture composed
of 0.5 ml amine solution, 1.5 ml dansyl chloride solution in acetone and
saturated with sodium carbonate. Normally 20-μl aliquots of the benzene or ethyl acetate extract are applied to the chromatograms for
identification of the DANS-amides, if the amounts of amines in the
reaction mixture were in the range 1–5 nmoles. If smaller amounts of
amine have to be detected, the organic phase can be evaporated to
dryness, redissolved in a small solvent volume and quantitatively spotted
to the thin-layer plates. But in this case it is preferable to dansylate as
many concentrated amine solutions as possible, since with the increased
reaction volumes more reagents are applied, so that the absolute amount
of impurities increases in the reaction mixture. As small as 50-μl amine
solution samples can very easily be processed in small tubes (4 x 50
mm). Working with small sample volumes is essential in the case when
DANS-derivatives are determined, which cannot be extracted by nonpolar organic solvents, for example, in the case of DANS-choline, amino
sugars, and similar compounds. After completion of the dansylation
reaction in these cases, a five to tenfold volume of acetone is added to the
samples. The salt-saturated water phase is separated by centrifugation
and aliquots or the total acetone phase is applied to the thin-layer plates.
Though the DANS-OH which is formed during the reaction by hydrolysis of DANS-Cl should be enriched in the water phase, a considerable
amount is extracted by acetone and has to be separated later on by
chromatography; this can cause a serious problem. With small reaction
volumes, the DANS-OH formation is reduced.

Though some DANS-amino acid derivatives are extracted together
with the amine derivatives from the alkaline reaction mixture, even with
benzene, and considerably higher amounts with ethyl acetate, the DANS-
amino acid derivatives normally do not disturb the chromatographic
separation of the DANS-amides.[121] If it is desired to extract the DANS-
amino acid derivatives together with the amine derivatives, the reaction
mixture should be brought to pH 3 with NaH_2PO_4 and extracted with
ethyl acetate. DANS-Glutamic acid, DANS-aspartic acid, DANS-cysteic
acid, DANS-taurine and the monoDANS-derivatives of the basic amino
acids are not extracted under these conditions. They can be isolated by
acetone extraction.

Synthesis of DANS-derivatives in Preparative Scale

In the last few years a series of DANS-amine derivatives have been prepared in our laboratory (see Table I). Weber has described the preparation of DANS-NH$_2$ and the synthesis of the DANS-derivatives of aniline and of benzylamine.[91] In principle the dansylation of amines in preparative scale can be achieved in analogy to the reaction of nano-mole amounts of amines with DANS-Cl; however, because of economic considerations, the excess of DANS-Cl applied is normally only twofold. To the solution of 1 mmole of an amine or an amine hydrochloride, sulfate, etc. in water (concentrations selected as high as possible) 3 volumes of acetone with 1.5–2 mmoles of DANS-Cl per functional group of the amine or phenol are added. The solution is saturated with Na$_2$CO$_3$ 10H$_2$O and the reaction mixture shaken at room temperature until the deep yellow color of the dansyl chloride disappears. Normally the reactions are complete within 1–2 hours; excess DANS-Cl is hydrolyzed by storing the reaction mixture at room temperature.

Addition of ethyl acetate (or benzene) causes the water layer to separate. An additional extraction of the water phase completes the quantitative isolation of the DANS-derivative. The organic layer is washed to neutral, dried with sodium sulfate, and evaporated to dryness under reduced pressure. One or two crystallizations from a suitable solvent give normally pure samples in 85–95% yield.

Most of the DANS-derivatives isolated hitherto in pure state (see Table I) have been prepared in this manner. In some cases, however, especially if it is doubtful how many groups will react with the dansyl reagent in a polyfunctional molecule under certain reaction conditions, it is advisable to measure the reaction velocity and the consumption of DANS-Cl. This is achieved by titration, since during the reaction of 1 mole DANS-Cl with an amino group, etc. 1 mole of HCl is liberated.

The solution of DANS-Cl in acetone–water (7:3) is brought to the desired pH by adding a few drops of 2N NaOH with the aid of a glass electrode. This pH is maintained in the stirred solution by adding concentrated NaOH (1–2N, if 1 mmole amine shall be dansylated) from a microburette. The consumption of the NaOH per minute is a measure of the velocity of the DANS-Cl hydrolysis. After 5–10 minutes the amine solution (likewise in acetone–water, 7:3, and brought exactly to the same pH value as the DANS-Cl solution) is added to the DANS-Cl solution, and the reaction mixture is maintained under stirring at constant pH by addition of NaOH until the NaOH consumed is negligibly low. (The volume of the NaOH solution added should be small in comparison to the volume of the reaction mixture, so that the reaction

velocity remains unaffected.) Titration curves are obtained analogous
to those in Figures 1 and 2, from which the DANS-Cl consumption can
be estimated. More convenient for continuous titration is the application
of automated equipment, which is suitable for the pH-stat technique.
Several types are available commercially.

In those cases when free bases or solutions of free bases in water
(which are advantageously cheap) are to be dansylated, a very convenient dansylation technique can be applied, since the base can be used
as proton acceptor: to an excess of the base (in water–acetone) a
concentrated solution of DANS-Cl in acetone is added by drops with
stirring. The reaction velocity dictates in this case the velocity of DANS-
Cl addition. The isolation of the reaction product is achieved in the
same manner as has been described above. This simple dansylation
procedure was applied for the preparation of DANS-methylamide and
-ethylamide; monoDANS-hydrazine, mono- and bisDANS-1,2-diamino
ethane, among others. MonoDANS-1,2-diamino ethane was easily
separated from the disubstituted product by adjusting the reaction mixture (after completion of the dansylation reaction) to pH 6 with
NaH_2PO_4. At this pH only the disubstituted ethylenediamine was extracted. After saturation of the water phase with sodium carbonate, the
monosubstituted diamine could be extracted with ethyl acetate practically in a pure form.

Normally the DANS-amides can be purified by crystallization. In
those cases when more than one reaction product is obtained (for
example, if a polyfunctional amine is dansylated with too low amounts
of DANS-Cl, so that partially dansylated derivatives are formed, or if
a molecule is fragmented during the dansylation reaction), the separation of the different reaction products is achieved by chromatography on
silica gel columns, using the solvents similar to those applied in thin-layer
chromatographic separations (see Table II).

Preparation of 1-Dimethylamino-naphthalene-5-sulfonyl Chloride

The following procedure is essentially that described by Weber,[91] with
certain modifications used in our laboratory. Two g of 1-dimethylamino-
naphthalene-5-sulfonic acid (DANS-OH) is ground in a mortar with
3.5 g PCl_5 for 3–5 minutes. After this time the reaction is complete (HCl
production ceased). The mixture is poured onto cracked ice. The
reaction product is extracted with ethyl acetate or diethyl ether, and
the organic layer is thoroughly washed until neutral and then evaporated
to dryness under reduced pressure. If the DANS-OH applied for the
preparation was pure, the reaction product (DANS-Cl) crystallizes
immediately. It may be further purified by recrystallization from benzene. Yield: 80% (M.P. 69°C).

For the preparation of DANS-OH three methods have been recommended: methylation of 1-amino-naphthalene-5-sulfonic acid with
methyliodide according to Fussgänger;[122] methylation of this acid with
dimethylsulfate in alkaline solution;[100] and sulfonation of 1-dimethyla-
mino-naphthalene with oleum at -5 °C.[123] Purification in each case is
achieved by repeated crystallization from water. DANS-OH decomposes
at 315 °C. DANS-Cl is now available commercially.

Some Side Reactions

If dansyl chloride is hydrolyzed in acetone–water with sodium carbonate or bicarbonate under the conditions favorable for the dansylation reaction, the chromatographic separation of the benzene extract of
this reaction mixture always shows some yellow fluorescing spots. The
most intense behaves in all solvents like DANS-dimethylamide. The
mechanism of the DANS-dimethylamide formation during the hydrolysis of DANS-Cl was not studied extensively, but it might be assumed
that the C-N bond between the naphthalene ring and the dimethylamino
group is cleaved hydrolytically by a mechanism analogous to that of
the Bucherer reaction.[124, 125]

A considerably smaller spot is found on the chromatograms which
behaves like DANS-methylamide. A third spot that moves in all chromatographic systems near the solvent front is sensitive to hydrolysis. This
suggests that it is a DANS-ester, probably the DANS-derivative of 2-
methyl-2-hydroxy-pentane-4-one, an alcohol that could be formed from
acetone by an aldol condensation.

Since ammonia cannot be completely excluded from the reagents,
DANS-NH_2 is also found somewhat. To avoid mistakes, it is advisable
in the qualitative analysis of amines to run in parallel a blank reaction
under identical reaction conditions in which only the solution of the
sample is replaced by the adequate solvent volume.

As was stated before, some compounds give rise to side reactions
with dansyl chloride. The best known example so far is the fragmentation of the amino acids.[115] From most of the amino acids, only
DANS-NH_2 is formed as a fluorescent reaction product, and therefore they do not influence the DANS-amide identification. But from the
basic amino acids, dansylated fragments are produced apart from DANS-
NH_2. For example, lysine and ornithine gave DANS-5-amino-*n*-valer-
aldehyde and DANS-4-amino-butyraldehyde respectively as decomposition products; these have been identified by mass spectrometry.[119, 126]
Histidine and arginine also produce, in minor amounts, fluorescing
decomposition products with dansyl chloride under the usual reaction
conditions. These dansylated fragments are found together with the
DANS-amine derivatives on the TLC, whereas DANS-amino acids do

not move far from the origin under the chromatographic conditions applied for the amide separations. This is also the case with the reaction product of γ-aminobutyric acid, which reacts with a large excess of dansyl chloride to form a dansylated γ-lactam[127] according to Scheme III. The structure of the lactam was proved by elemental analysis and IR spectroscopy. Under suitable conditions the lactam formation is quantitative and can be used for the microdetermination of γ-amino-butyric acid and of β-hydroxy-γ-aminobutyric acid in tissues. Ornithine

$$H_2N\text{-}CH_2CH_2CH_2COOH \xrightarrow[\text{-HCl}]{^+DANS\text{-}Cl} DANS\text{-}HN\text{-}CH_2CH_2CH_2COOH$$

$$\xrightarrow[\text{-HCl}]{^+DANS\text{-}Cl} DANS\text{-}HN\text{-}CH_2CH_2CH_2CO\text{-}O\text{-}DANS \xrightarrow[\text{-DANS-OH}]{}$$

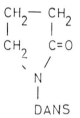

SCHEME III

does not produce analogously a δ-lactam. It must be pointed out that dansylated fragments of amino acids and certain reaction products have to be taken into account if the dansyl method is applied for tissue analysis, though normally the separation of amines and amino acids before dansylation is unnecessary.

The fragmentation of agmatine and of similar guanidine derivatives has been mentioned already. In the case of amino sugars we also always observed several reaction products, and a similar situation occurs with 5-amino-4-imidazole carboxamide. It is to be assumed that further examples of side reactions of amines and other compounds will be found during dansylation in the future. Though these side reactions are limitations of the applicability of the dansyl reaction, they do not impair the usefulness of the dansyl method in principle.

TLC SEPARATION OF DANS-AMIDES

DANS-Derivatives of amines, especially of amines of biological interest, were first separated by Seiler and Wiechmann.[121] The paper chromatographic separation of some DANS-amides, phenolic compounds, and of the DANS-derivatives of pyridoxamine and pyridoxal was also described.[128–130] A disadvantage of the latter technique is that DANS-amine and DANS-amino acid derivatives move together on the PC, so that preseparation of these two groups of compounds is necessary for their unequivocal identification.

On Silica Gel G layers, DANS-amino acids move only in rather polar systems.[113, 131] However, they remain near the origin in the systems suitable for the separation of the DANS-amine and DANS-phenol derivatives, as has been briefly mentioned. Apart from these separation methods only some preliminary thin-layer electrophoretic separations on 250μ cellulose layers have been performed.[132]

General Considerations

All the TLC separations of DANS-amides have been performed on $200–250\mu$ Silica Gel G layers. Other layers have not been investigated in this respect systematically, though there may of course be other suitable adsorbents. The thin-layers were prepared in the usual manner on 20 x 20-cm glass plates with one of the commercially available spreaders. The plates were dried at room temperature and then activated for 1–2 hours at 110°C. On principle commercially prepared plates are suitable for the separation of DANS-derivatives, but the separations obtained with freshly prepared layers are not exactly the same as those made with commercially made plates. The most effective conditions must be found by trial and error for each type of layer. The mechanical stability of commercially prepared silica gel layers is advantageous, since it makes the handling of these plates more convenient, but the usual slow mobility of the solvent is undesirable; it can cause spot enlargement by diffusion.

For all thin-layer chromatographic separations of DANS-derivatives conventional chromatographic tanks were used, suitable for 20 x 20-cm plates. The insides of these tanks were lined with filter sheets to ensure a solvent vapor-saturated atmosphere within the tanks. The solvent mixtures were prepared at least daily. Normally two plates were put simultaneously in a tank which contained 100–120 ml solvent. One-dimensional (ascending) chromatography was used for the quantitative determination of certain compounds in tissues.[118, 127, 133, 134] For a more complete resolution of all the fluorescent components of a complex mixture, two-dimensional chromatography is more effective than multiple development in one direction.

The mixture of DANS-derivatives is applied to the chromatograms as a very small spot (diameter not exceeding 3 mm), at a distance of 3 cm from two edges of the plate. Chromatography is performed in the first direction with a suitable solvent until the solvent front reaches the line, drawn into the layer at a distance of 13 cm from the starting point. Reactivation of the layer at elevated temperature before the second run—as was recommended for the two-dimensional separation of DANS-amino acids—[131] is not necessary in the case of the separation of DANS-amides, since these substances are moved on the chromatograms in rather nonpolar solvents. Three to five minutes drying at room temperature is normally adequate before chromatography in the second direction.

A good solvent can be considered to be useful if its sensitivity to environmental influences is not high, thus enabling an approximate identification of unknown substances to be made with the aid of spot maps as obtained with marker mixtures (see Figures 3–8). A more definite identification of an unknown dansyl derivative should always be made by cochromatography parallel to marker mixtures with the unknown on the same chromatogram. On two-dimensional chromatograms the marker mixtures can be applied to the plates in the manner indicated in Figure 4. This technique is useful for a first orientation. A more thorough comparison of the chromatographic behavior of substances is obtained after extraction of the spots to be identified from a two-dimensional chromatogram, application of these unknown samples between samples of the reference substances, and chromatography with one solvent or with different solvent systems, which are used successively in the same direction. It should be pointed out here, that a really definite identification can never be obtained by chromatographic or electrophoretic procedures alone. It is one of the main advantages of the dansyl derivatives that they are recoverable from chromatograms and are therefore accessible for further identification by optical methods[114] or by mass spectrometry.[126, 135, 140]

Generally Applicable Separating Systems

One pair of the solvents published in 1965 by Seiler and Wiechmann,[121] proved to be widely applicable for the separation of DANS-amides. In these solvents of medium polarity (and in other solvents described below) the chromatographic behavior of approximately 100 DANS-derivatives (see Table III) was studied. These especially include derivatives of amines of biological or pharmacological interest. In Figure 3 the chromatographic map obtained from separations of these

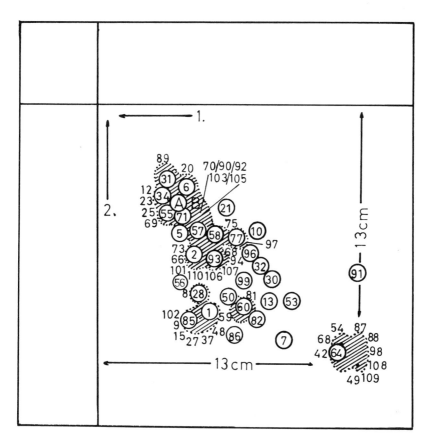

Figure 3. Two-dimensional separation of DANS-derivatives. Adsorbent: 200µ Silica Gel G. First dimension: cyclohexane–ethyl acetate (2:3); second dimension: benzene–triethylamine (5:1). The DANS-derivatives of the substances marked by an asterisk in Table III have been separated simultaneously on this chromatogram. A = DANS-5-amino-*n*-valeraldehyde (fragmentation product of lysine); B = DANS-4-amino-*n*-butyraldehyde (fragmentation product of ornithine). For the further code numbers of the different spots see Table III (Seiler).[113] Reproduced from Reference 113 by permission of Interscience Pubs., Inc., New York.

DANS-derivatives is shown. The positions of the most important dansylated fragmentation products of amino acids are also shown in this map as well as the positions of amino acid derivatives that move under the chromatographic conditions to be discussed. Normal amino acid derivatives remain near the start.

The chromatographic map (Figure 3) is well reproducible, even if tissue extracts are separated, so that it proved a useful aid in the identification of amines from different tissues, body fluids or urine.[119, 126, 127, 135–138] The chromatograms were first run with cyclohexane–ethyl acetate (2:3) (solvent III, Table II), and after drying for 3 minutes at room temperature in the second direction with benzene–triethylamine (5:1) (solvent XXIV, Table II). In a similar system—solvent III was substituted by solvent V (Table II)—the chromatographic behavior of a number of synthetic catecholamine analogs was studied.[139] Another pair of solvents suitable for a survey on the composition of an amine mixture is solvent III combined with solvent XXVI (Table II).

A further characterization, especially of the less polar DANS-derivatives, is achieved by chromatography either with solvent VIII in the

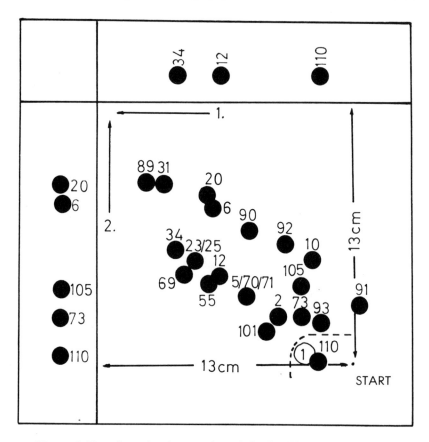

Figure 4. Two-dimensional separation of the DANS-derivatives of aliphatic amines and of other DANS-derivatives of relatively low polarity. Adsorbent: 200μ Silica Gel G. First dimension: cyclohexane–butyl acetate (8:3); second dimension: tetrachloromethane–triethylamine (5:1), twice in each direction. The DANS-derivatives of the substances in Table III marked by an asterisk have been separated simultaneously. Those dansyl derivatives of this group, which are not shown in Figure 4, stay in the zone marked by a dotted line. For the code numbers of the different spots, see Table III (Seiler and Wiechmann).[132] Reproduced from Reference 132 by permission of Elsevier Publishing Co., Amsterdam.

first dimension and with solvent XVII in the second dimension (the plates are run two times in each direction) (Figure 4), or with solvent IX in the first dimension (one time) and then successively with diisopropylether and solvent XX (see Table II) in the second dimension (two times each) (Figure 5). While the DANS-derivatives of the aliphatic amines and of some β-phenylethylamines are well separated under these conditions, the more polar DANS-derivatives of N-acetylated phenolamines or of monoacetyl diamines (*e.g.*, DANS-N-acetyl-dopamine, O-DANS-N-acetyl-tyramine, DANS-N-acetyl-histamine, DANS-

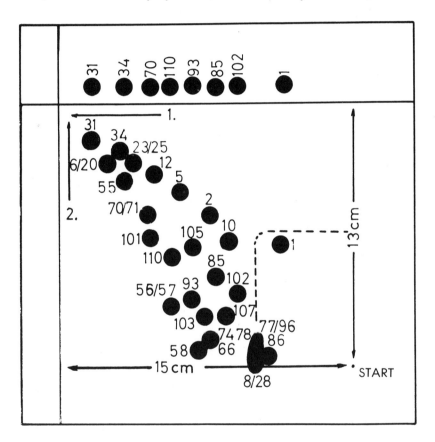

Figure 5. Two-dimensional separation of DANS-amides of medium and low polarity. Adsorbent: 200μ Silica Gel G. First direction: chloroform–butyl acetate (5:1); second direction: (a) diisopropylether, twice, and (b) diisopropylether–triethylamine (5:1) twice. The DANS-derivatives of the substances in Table III marked by an asterisk have been separated simultaneously. Those dansyl derivatives of this group, which are not shown in Figure 5, stay in the zone marked by a dotted line. For the code numbers of the different spots see Table III (Seiler and Wiechmann).[132] Reproduced from Reference 132 by permission of Elsevier Publishing Co., Amsterdam.

N-acetyl-serotonin), of aminophenols with tertiary amino groups (*e.g.*, DANS-N-methyl-epinephrine, DANS-hordenine, DANS-bufotenine) and of DANS-1-methyl-histamine possess little mobility in these chromatographic systems and remain therefore within the zones marked by

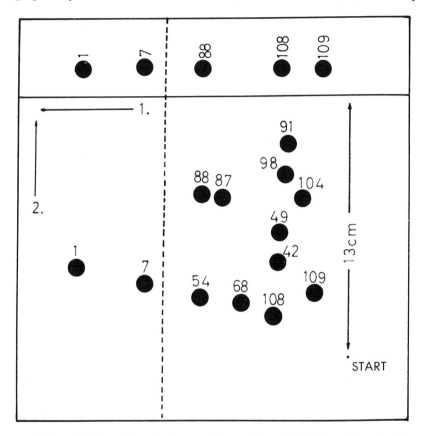

Figure 6. Two-dimensional separation of dansylated N-acetyl–polyamines or –aminophenols, of aminophenols with a tertiary amino group and of hydroxy-phenyl–glycols. Adsorbent: 200µ Silica Gel G. First dimension: (a) butyl acetate–ethyl acetate (1:5) and (b) twice with benzene–methanol (9:1); second dimension: chloroform–triethylamine (5:1). The DANS-derivatives of the substances in Table III which are marked by an asterisk have been separated simultaneously. Those dansyl derivatives of this group, which are not shown in Figure 6, move above the boundary marked by a dotted line. 1 = DANS-NH$_2$, 7 = DANS-ethanolamine, 42 = DANS-1-methyl-histamine,   49 = DANS-N-acetyl-histamine,   54 = DANS-3,4-dihydroxy-β-phenyl-glycol,   68 = DANS-3-methoxy-4-hydroxy-β-phenyl-glycol, 87 = DANS-N-acetyl-tyramine,   88 = DANS-N-acetyl-dopamine,   91 = DANS-hordenine,   98 = DANS-N-methyl-epinephrine,   104 = DANS-N-methyl-metane-phrine,   108 = DANS-N-acetyl-serotonin,   109 = N-acetyl-bufotenine (Seiler and Wiechmann).[132] Reproduced from Reference 132 by permission of Elsevier Publishing Co., Amsterdam.

dotted lines in Figure 4 and Figure 5 near the start.[132] These latter DANS-derivatives can be well-separated by performing chromatography two times: first with solvent II and with solvent XXIII in the first direction of a two-dimensional chromatogram, followed by chromatography with solvent XIV (see Table II) in the second direction.[132] The non-polar DANS-derivatives of Table III move beyond the boundary marked by a dotted line in Figure 6, which is drawn behind the spot representing DANS-ethanolamine. (The other DANS-amine derivatives have been omitted from Figure 6.) In addition to the polar amine derivatives mentioned above, the DANS-derivatives of some alcohols, biologically derived from catecholamines (for example, 3,4-dihydroxy-phenyl-ethanol and 3,4-dihydroxy-phenyl-glycol), are also separated under the same conditions, as can be seen from Figure 6.

Catechol Derivatives

Since the concentrations of the different amines vary in a wide range in tissue samples and body fluids, it may be necessary in many cases to use preseparation techniques or to enrich certain substances before their quantitative determination can be achieved. This is the case, for example, with the biologically extremely important catecholamines, if they are to be determined in urine or in brain tissue. A preseparation method which depends on the *o*-diphenol group of these substances has been proposed,[152] namely, the adsorption of the catechol derivatives on Al_2O_3 from weak alkaline solution, thus separating them from other amines and from amino acids. Other suitable separation methods may be used as well.

For the separation of the DANS-derivatives of the most important catecholamines and their metabolites as well as for some pharmacologically important catecholamines, several thin-layer chromatographic separation systems have been worked out.[132] It should be pointed out that the systems described below are suitable for the separation of the catecholamines from their corresponding α-methyl derivatives. The separations shown in Figure 7 are achieved by chromatography first with diisopropylether followed (two times) by solvent X (see Table II). Solvent XXI is used twice in the second direction. For a further chromatographic characterization of the catecholamines the following procedure may be used: chromatography with chloroform (twice) in the first direction and with solvent VII (twice) in the second direction. The separations obtained under these conditions can be seen from Figure 8.

As has been mentioned already, the chromatographic behavior of a series of catechol derivatives has been investigated[139] in the slightly modified systems of Seiler and Wiechmann.[121]

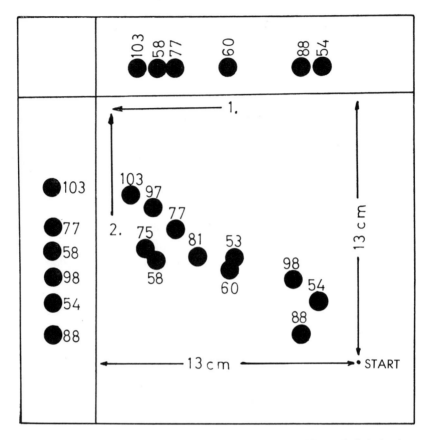

Figure 7. Two-dimensional separation of some DANS-catechol derivatives. Adsorbent: 200μ Silica Gel G. First direction: (a) diisopropylether; (b) butyl acetate–triethylamine (5:1), twice; second direction: diisopropylether–triethylamine (1:5), twice. For the code numbers of the different spots see Table III (Seiler and Wiechmann).[132] Reproduced from Reference 132 by permission of Elsevier Publishing Co., Amsterdam.

Aliphatic Diamines

Among the aliphatic diamines, putrescine (tetramethylenediamine) and cadaverine (pentamethylenediamine) play a certain role in biochemistry. In the standard system (combination of solvents III and XXIV, Figure 3) the DANS-derivatives of these and of some other diamines move similarly as DANS-NH$_2$, so that they cannot be identified on such a chromatogram. However, if the area containing ammonia, tryptamine and the diamines is scraped off the chromatogram and the extract once more applied to a thin-layer plate, the aliphatic diamines (up to hexamethylenediamine) can be separated first with solvent XV followed by solvent XXII (see Table II) in the first direction and then with solvent

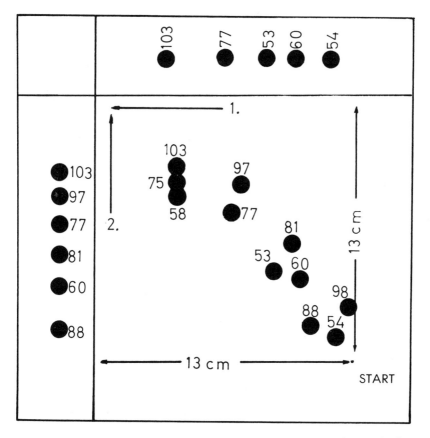

Figure 8. Two-dimensional separation of some DANS-catechol derivatives. Adsorbent: 200µ Silica Gel G. First dimension: chloroform; second dimension: cyclohexane–butyl acetate–ethyl acetate–triethylamine (10:11:4:4), twice in each direction. For the code numbers of the different spots see Table III (Seiler and Wiechmann).[132] Reproduced from Reference 132 by permission of Elsevier Publishing Co., Amsterdam.

XIII in the second direction. A still better separation is obtained by chromatographing five times with solvent XVI in the first dimension and with solvent XIII (see Table II) in the second dimension (Figure 9).[132] Solvent XVIII (Table II) proved to be useful for the separation of bisDANS-putrescine from triDANS-spermidine and tetraDANS-spermine as well as from other fluorescing substances in a culture of tumor cells.[119]

Choline

The chromatographic behavior of quaternary bases, which possess functional groups capable of dansylation, has scarcely been studied.

Table II

Composition of the solvent systems used
for the TLC separation of DANS-amides

Solvent	Solvent Composition	References
I	ethyl acetate	—
II	butyl acetate–ethyl acetate (1:5)	132
III	cyclohexane–ethyl acetate (2:3)	121
IV	cyclohexane–ethyl acetate (1:1)	133
V	cyclohexane–ethyl acetate (2:1)	139
VI	cyclohexane–ethyl acetate–triethylamine (50:50:1)	133
VII	cyclohexane–butyl acetate–ethyl acetate–triethylamine (10:11:4:4)	132
VIII	cyclohexane–butyl acetate (8:3)	132
IX	chloroform–butyl acetate (5:1)	132
X	butyl acetate–triethylamine (5:1)	132
XI	chloroform	132
XII	cyclohexane–chloroform (1:19)	133
XIII	chloroform–triethylamine (10:1)	132
XIV	chloroform–triethylamine (5:1)	132
XV	trichloroethylene–methanol (19:1)	132
XVI	tetrachloromethane–methanol (45:3)	132
XVII	tetrachloromethane–triethylamine (5:1)	132
XVIII	cyclohexane–diethyl ether (1:9)	—
XIX	diisopropyl ether	132
XX	diisopropyl ether–triethylamine (5:1)	132
XXI	diisopropyl ether–triethylamine (1:5)	132
XXII	benzene–methanol (19:1)	132
XXIII	benzene–methanol (9:1)	132
XXIV	benzene–triethylamine (5:1)	121
XXV	cyclohexane–benzene–methanol (15:85:2)	127
XXVI	cyclohexane–benzene–methanol (2:17:1)	121
XXVII	cyclohexane–benzene–tetrachloromethane–methanol (10:45:40:4)	133
XXVIII	petroleum ether–*tert*. butanol–acetic acid (15:3:3)	141
XXIX	ethyl acetate–pyridine–water (61:31:8)	141
XXX	chloroform–benzyl alcohol–acetic acid (70:30:3)	142

According to their polar character these DANS-derivatives should move chromatographically together with DANS-amino acids. Thus dansyl choline can be separated from the DANS-amino acids using the solvents recommended earlier for the separation of DANS-amino acids[131] or instead by thin-layer electrophoresis.[117] It can easily be distinguished from most other DANS-derivatives because of its deep orange fluorescence. Though choline reacts quantitatively with dansyl chloride under suitable conditions,[118] it is sensitive to hydrolysis, so that losses may occur even during chromatography.

Amino Sugars

As it is with the DANS-derivatives of quaternary bases, the DANS-derivatives of amino sugars co-chromatograph with the DANS-amino

Table III

List of the DANS-derivatives that were chromatographically investigated and their hRf-values in different solvents

Code No.	Formula	Substance	Solvent Number / hRf-Values																				
		Average Time of Chromatography (min)	I 33	II 36	III 31	IV 36	VII 55	VIII 61	IX 62	X 53	XI 37	XII 39	XIV 60	XV 33	XVII 67	XVIII 35	XIX 33	XX 39	XXIII 38	XXIV 38	XXV 38	XXVI 35	XXVII 49
1	H_3N	*ammonia	65	75	45	40	30	7	20	50	10	8	27	15	2	51	18	8	33	12	7	19	11
2	C_1H_5N	*methylamine	65	72	50	46	48	12	43	61	24	22	68	38	11	57	22	15	52	39	21	40	30
3	$C_1H_5N_3$	guanidine	27	28	5	4	1	0	1	4	0	0	1	3	0	2	0	0	13	0	0	3	1
4	$C_2H_6N_2O$	glycinamide	16	16	1	4	1	0	7	4	0	0	1	1	0	2	0	0	17	0	0	4	1
5	C_2H_7N	*ethylamine	66	76	56	53	62	18	52	72	28	26	81	45	18	64	28	23	56	49	26	50	37
6	C_2H_7N	*dimethylamine	64	74	53	53	70	26	78	76	48	48	95	65	50	70	34	39	70	66	48	65	61
7	C_2H_7NO	*ethanolamine	43	48	17	14	6	1	4	15	2	1	16	8	1	15	2	1	25	5	2	8	6
8	C_2H_7NS	*2-mercapto-ethylamine (cysteamine)	69	77	48	41	30	3	23	52	10	6	60	37	7	40	4	1	60	24	13	32	23
9	$C_2H_8N_2$	*ethylenediamine	65	74	43	36	20	3	17	39	6	4	34	32	1	34	4	1	55	13	9	26	20
10	$C_3H_4N_2$	*imidazole	47	53	28	27	50	4	30	61	21	17	89	53	25	30	13	16	59	49	21	36	39
11	C_3H_9N	N-methyl-ethylamine	68	79	64	57	74	34	83	80	61	52	92	72	57	68	41	48	69	72	54	66	60
12	C_3H_9N	*n-propylamine	71	82	64	59	69	30	64	69	40	30	80	52	23	64	34	29	60	55	34	52	39
13	C_3H_9NO	*N-methyl-ethanolamine	42	49	22	16	16	2	13	24	6	5	51	22	0	18	3	4	38	15	7	19	12
14	C_3H_9NO	3-hydroxy-propylamine-(1)	40	46	17	11	9	0	5	15	1	1	21	9	0	13	1	1	24	5	2	9	3
15	$C_4H_{10}N_2$	trimethylenediamine	66	76	45	30	24	2	17	40	6	4	45	30	0	29	3	2	51	13	9	27	14
16	$C_4H_6N_2O$	4-hydroxymethyl-imidazole	19	21	6	5	8	2	4	16	2	0	42	12	3	5	1	1	24	7	3	9	6
17	$C_4H_6N_2O$	4-amino-5-imidazole-carboxamide	20	22	6	5	7	0	4	14	3	0	30	21	1	5	0	1	28	5	3	13	8
18	C_4H_7NOS	2-amino-4-butyro-thiolactone	70	79	53	47	46	11	46	59	30	23	76	51	9	50	13	8	60	38	31	52	36
19	$C_4H_7NO_2$	2-amino-4-butyrolactone	63	72	38	30	26	3	22	41	12	8	43	28	0	28	3	1	47	15	13	31	17
20	C_4H_9N	*pyrrolidine	71	79	61	58	70	32	80	71	56	51	93	70	56	60	36	43	71	67	51	67	60
21	$C_4H_9NO_2$	4-amino-butyric acid	60	66	38	33	44	5	48	53	31	27	88	56	19	30	6	12	65	59	35	57	43
22	$C_4H_9NO_3$	3-hydroxy-4-amino-butyric acid	37	40	9	9	3	0	6	6	1	1	15	19	0	7	1	0	29	3	3	12	6
23	$C_4H_{11}N$	*n-butylamine	75	81	65	62	75	37	78	75	43	35	90	54	30	72	42	33	62	57	37	55	48
24	$C_4H_{11}N$	*diethylamine	71	82	65	62	75	40	82	74	57	52	91	72	60	66	46	50	70	71	56	69	63
25	$C_4H_{11}N$	*isobutylamine	75	81	65	63	75	37	78	76	42	35	90	54	30	72	42	33	62	58	37	55	48
26	$C_4H_{11}NO$	4-hydroxy-butylamine-(1)	42	41	13	10	10	1	3	21	2	1	27	7	1	13	2	3	22	7	1	7	5

Table III (continued)

Code No.		Substance	Solvent Number — hRf-Values																				
		Average Time of Chromatography (min)	I 33	II 36	III 31	IV 36	VII 55	VIII 61	IX 62	X 53	XI 37	XII 39	XIV 60	XV 33	XVII 67	XVIII 35	XIX 33	XX 39	XXIII 38	XXIV 38	XXV 38	XXVI 35	XXVII 49
27	$C_5H_{12}N_2$	*tetramethylenediamine	70	80	50	36	28	0	15	47	4	2	52	23	1	33	3	1	39	15	5	22	17
28	$C_4H_{12}N_2S_2$	*2,2'-dithio-bis(ethylamine) (cystamine)	69	77	48	41	30	3	23	52	10	6	60	37	7	40	4	1	60	24	13	32	23
29	$C_5H_5N_5$	adenine	31	26	9	6	12	0	3	21	0	1	24	18	2	9	1	1	28	6	2	11	16
30	$C_5H_9N_3$	*histamine	54	56	25	16	26	0	11	41	1	7	80	43	3	17	1	1	48	26	7	33	19
31	$C_5H_{11}N$	piperidine	67	80	70	65	77	41	90	81	58	55	95	75	60	76	49	56	75	77	53	73	73
32	$C_5H_{11}NO$	*3-hydroxy-piperidine	47	58	34	25	30	2	15	40	5	6	65	26	8	27	3	8	40	25	4	20	22
33	$C_5H_{11}N_3O_2$	4-guanidino-butyric acid	53	65	36	26	46	2	28	58	11	15	91	45	12	22	4	8	58	50	12	37	39
34	$C_5H_{13}N$	*isoamylamine	69	83	73	65	76	39	81	83	37	45	96	58	35	77	48	41	64	66	36	53	56
35	$C_5H_{13}NO$	5-hydroxy-pentylamine-(1)	37	46	19	13	17	1	4	27	0	1	27	8	1	13	2	3	24	8	0	7	7
36	$C_5H_{14}N_2$	3-N-dimethylamino-propyl amine-(1)	0	1	0	0	11	0	0	15	0	1	32	1	3	0	2	2	4	11	0	0	0
37	$C_5H_{14}N_2$	*pentamethylenediamine (cadaverine)	64	81	53	39	39	3	15	55	5	3	66	29	1	37	3	2	48	22	4	23	21
38a	$C_6H_{14}N_4$	agmatine (bisDANS)	5	0	8	4	0	0	0	2	0	0	0	3	0	1	0	0	19	1	0	3	2
38b	$C_6H_{14}N_4$	agmatine (monoDANS)	0	0	1	1	0	0	0	0	0	0	0	0	0	0	0	0	0	0	0	0	0
39	C_6H_6O	phenol	66	84	70	66	77	54	97	76	61	73	95	75	60	77	52	53	77	76	67	73	77
40	$C_6H_6O_2$	o-diphenol (catechol)	61	78	56	50	54	18	89	63	41	63	93	75	33	60	21	15	77	66	57	70	73
41	$C_6H_7N_5$	N-methyl-adenine	38	39	17	14	24	1	8	37	2	5	62	40	6	16	15	1	57	20	8	26	26
42	$C_6H_{11}N_3$	*1-methyl-histamine	3	4	0	0	3	0	1	5	0	0	23	6	0	0	0	0	18	2	0	3	2
43	$C_6H_{13}NO_5$	galactosamine	4	4	0	0	0	0	0	0	0	0	0	0	0	0	0	0	6	0	0	0	0
44	$C_6H_{13}NO_5$	glucosamine	5	4	0	0	0	0	0	0	0	0	0	0	0	0	0	0	6	0	0	0	0
45	$C_6H_{13}NO_5$	mannosamine	5	5	0	0	0	0	0	0	0	0	0	0	0	0	0	0	6	0	0	0	0
46	$C_6H_{14}N_2O$	mono-N-acetyl-putrescine	6	6	1	0	3	0	0	6	0	0	11	4	0	0	0	0	20	0	0	2	1
47	$C_6H_{15}N$	*n-hexylamine	82	88	74	68	77	47	83	80	33	33	94	61	35	77	50	39	68	63	42	58	56
48	$C_6H_{16}N_2$	*hexamethylenediamine	79	85	57	41	42	3	25	61	3	3	76	31	1	42	5	3	51	28	5	27	20
49	$C_7H_{11}N_3O$	*β-(imidazolyl-4)-äthyl-acetamide (N-acetyl-histamine)	4	2	0	0	3	0	0	6	0	0	27	8	0	0	0	0	23	3	0	3	3
50	$C_7H_{19}N_3$	*spermidine	75	80	45	25	23	0	13	47	2	2	76	38	0	22	0	1	60	23	3	29	25
51	C_8H_7NO	5-hydroxy-indole	75	80	56	41	20	15	70	33	28	35	48	43	3	53	24	6	61	23	34	48	39

No.	Formula	Name	Data
52	C₈H₉NO₃	pyridoxal	25 25 10 5 12 0 3 22 1 0 50 13 5 8 1 4 25 17 0 8 9
53	C₈H₁₀O₃	*3,4-dihydroxy-β-phenylethanol	31 41 16 8 9 0 15 18 4 6 55 27 2 11 2 1 45 14 7 25 21
54	C₈H₁₀O₄	*3,4-dihydroxy-β-phenylglycol	16 17 3 2 0 3 4 0 13 8 0 2 1 1 21 1 1 8 6
55	C₈H₁₁N	β-phenylethylamine	71 88 72 61 66 35 73 74 35 45 95 61 76 36 26 65 55 38 57 50
56	C₈H₁₁NO	*β-hydroxy-β-phenylethylamine	71 77 54 41 35 8 18 53 6 5 59 27 7 15 8 40 29 7 22 15
57	C₈H₁₁NO	*4-hydroxy-β-phenylethylamine	66 83 60 43 43 7 54 57 19 24 91 60 6 9 5 66 46 28 54 45
58	C₈H₁₁NO₂	*3,4-dihydroxy-β-phenylethylamine (dopamine)	62 80 50 33 30 3 41 50 16 15 91 63 3 3 1 69 42 24 54 47
59	C₈H₁₁NO₂	*4-hydroxy-β-hydroxy-β-phenylethylamine (octopamine)	62 71 37 26 12 0 13 30 1 4 46 31 0 3 3 1 51 13 5 25 18
60	C₈H₁₁NO₃	*norepinephrine	59 67 32 20 8 0 12 24 0 3 46 34 0 1 1 0 58 12 5 26 21
61	C₈H₁₁NO₃	pyridoxine	19 19 5 3 5 0 4 17 0 1 40 16 0 0 0 0 38 2 2 13 12
62	C₈H₁₁NO₃	2,4,5-trihydroxy-β-phenylethylamine	62 74 44 28 39 2 41 58 34 13 91 74 8 2 2 1 78 55 26 58 54
63	C₈H₁₁NO₃	3,4,5-trihydroxy-β-phenylethylamine	65 74 41 29 28 2 37 55 22 16 88 64 3 2 0 75 49 18 54 47
64	C₈H₁₂N₂O₂	*pyridoxamine	16 15 4 3 7 0 1 6 0 0 14 12 0 0 0 29 2 0 9 7
65	C₉H₁₀N₂	5,6-dimethyl-benzimidazole	63 68 48 44 66 11 68 62 21 38 91 67 40 17 27 70 55 31 55 50
66	C₉H₁₁NO₃	adrenalon	67 73 3 3 8 51 57 14 14 76 47 6 15 1 55 1 20 46 26
67	C₉H₁₁N₃O	kynuramine	73 79 52 48 52 0 50 57 10 0 76 47 6 15 9 60 34 20 5 27
68	C₉H₁₂O₄	*3-methoxy-4-hydroxy-β-phenylglycol	16 11 3 3 2 0 3 3 0 0 7 5 0 0 0 17 3 0 5 3
69	C₉H₁₃N	*2-amino-3-phenyl-propane (amphetamine)	74 80 72 65 77 34 80 75 31 30 92 59 26 36 27 67 56 40 60 47
70	C₉H₁₃NO	*3-methoxy-β-phenylethylamine	72 78 64 56 64 16 68 66 18 20 90 59 17 26 18 67 49 36 59 43
71	C₉H₁₃NO	*4-methoxy-β-phenylethylamine	72 78 64 56 64 16 68 65 18 20 89 59 16 27 17 67 49 36 59 43
72	C₉H₁₃NO	N-methyl-β-hydroxy-β-phenylethylamine	71 75 57 47 56 11 35 68 22 38 86 50 30 23 24 55 55 21 44 37
73	C₉H₁₃NO	*nor-pseudoephedrine (cathin)	72 78 60 49 52 9 30 57 4 3 70 25 10 20 16 49 35 9 33 15
74	C₉H₁₃NO₂	*3-methoxy-4-hydroxy-β-phenylethylamine	67 73 48 33 36 2 47 47 7 9 81 50 3 4 3 68 46 20 56 27
75	C₉H₁₃NO₂	*α-methyl-dopamine	67 73 51 37 43 2 50 52 6 10 87 57 4 3 2 71 38 22 61 31
76	C₉H₁₃NO₂	N-methyl-4-hydroxy-β-hydroxy-phenylethylamine (synephrine)	67 72 46 32 30 2 34 40 5 7 78 43 7 6 4 66 41 14 52 22
77	C₉H₁₃NO₃	*epinephrine	64 68 39 24 19 1 29 35 3 6 75 46 3 2 1 69 45 12 52 22
78	C₉H₁₃NO₃	2,4-dihydroxy-5-methoxy-β-phenylethylamine	65 70 44 26 27 1 33 46 20 11 82 61 4 2 1 72 43 19 52 45

Table III (continued)

Code No.	Substance	Average Time of Chromatography (min)	I 33	II 36	III 31	IV 36	VII 55	VIII 61	IX 62	X 53	XI 37	XII 39	XIV 60	XV 33	XVII 67	XVIII 35	XIX 33	XX 39	XXIII 38	XXIV 38	XXV 38	XXVI 35	XXVII 49
												hRf-Values											
79	C₉H₁₃NO₃ 3,5-dihydroxy-4-methoxy-β-phenylethylamine		67	79	51	39	41	3	48	64	20	18	90	66	6	51	4	3	77	54	26	58	52
80	C₉H₁₃NO₃ 3,4-dihydroxy-5-methoxy-β-phenylethylamine		61	70	34	21	14	1	27	35	16	12	79	49	1	24	2	0	71	30	13	45	34
81	C₁₀H₁₃NO₃ *α-methyl-norepinephrine		64	71	41	24	17	1	19	33	3	2	55	36	1	28	2	0	55	21	6	34	14
82	C₁₀H₁₃NO₃ *nor-metanephrine		60	66	28	15	8	1	12	19	2	1	34	22	1	20	1	0	44	10	3	22	8
83	C₁₀H₁₃N₄O₂ tyrosineamide		37	38	8	4	3	0	4	6	1	0	5	9	0	2	0	0	26	1	1	8	2
84	C₁₀H₁₁NO₂ 5-hydroxy-tryptophol		36	38	11	6	3	0	7	7	2	0	10	8	0	10	1	0	25	4	2	10	3
85	C₁₀H₁₂N₂ *tryptamine		84	84	49	42	25	11	48	40	18	10	40	34	2	53	17	3	51	17	15	37	16
86	C₁₀H₁₂N₂O *5-hydroxy-tryptamine (serotonin)		63	77	33	23	9	2	26	20	4	3	28	24	1	28	3	0	49	10	8	29	9
87	C₁₀H₁₃NO₂ *N-acetyl-tyramine		9	9	3	2	5	0	6	9	2	0	32	11	0	3	0	0	26	5	1	10	4
88	C₁₀H₁₃NO₃ *N-acetyl-dopamine		7	6	2	2	3	0	5	5	2	0	32	14	0	2	0	0	30	5	1	10	4
89	C₁₁H₁₅N *2-methylamino-3-phenyl-propane (pervitine)		74	88	64	64	80	53	94	78	62	63	93	75	59	77	47	52	77	77	55	70	64
90	C₁₀H₁₅NO *ephedrine		72	85	58	53	64	23	49	70	15	12	83	51	34	70	34	34	62	52	20	48	31
91	C₁₀H₁₅NO *hordenine (N-dimethyl-tyramine)		0	0	0	0	17	0	0	24	0	0	65	2	12	0	0	6	5	24	0	0	0
92	C₁₀H₁₅NO *pseudo-ephedrine		63	83	63	50	62	11	54	71	29	27	90	52	29	72	23	30	62	53	23	50	41
93	C₁₀H₁₅NO₂ *3,4-dimethoxy-β-phenylethylamine		62	78	50	37	47	4	54	62	31	25	89	49	9	52	6	9	58	38	15	42	32
94	C₁₀H₁₅NO₃ 3,4-dimethoxy-5-hydroxy-β-phenylethylamine		63	74	46	33	32	2	37	54	20	9	85	54	3	45	3	1	69	47	23	47	43
95	C₁₀H₁₅NO₃ 3,5-dimethoxy-4-hydroxy-β-phenylethylamine		62	70	41	28	23	2	39	48	18	10	80	42	2	39	3	1	64	31	16	43	35
96	C₁₀H₁₅NO₃ *metanephrine		58	74	35	20	21	1	23	40	15	7	78	41	4	35	3	3	60	29	9	38	27
97	C₁₀H₁₅NO₃ *α-methyl-epinephrine		62	80	46	30	30	0	29	51	15	5	86	51	8	46	4	3	67	51	13	49	37
98	C₁₀H₁₅NO₃ *N-methyl-epinephrine		0	0	0	0	4	0	0	8	0	0	35	4	2	0	3	3	11	13	0	3	0
99	C₁₀H₂₆N₄ *spermine		62	79	36	18	21	0	15	48	7	0	87	45	1	14	0	1	64	25	4	36	25

No.	Formula	Compound																					
100	$C_{11}H_{13}N_3O$	tryptophanamide	25	31	6	3	3	0	2	6	1	0	3	4	0	2	0	1	14	0	0	4	1
101	$C_{11}H_{14}N_2$	*N-methyl-tryptamine	71	82	60	47	34	13	49	48	38	26	71	53	7	64	23	9	64	30	31	34	44
102	$C_{11}H_{14}N_2O$	*5-methoxy-tryptamine	65	82	54	39	25		38	41	20	11	46	30		54	13	4	47	12	12	32	21
103	$C_{11}H_{17}NO_3$	*isoproterenol (N-isopropyl-norepinephrine)	65	76	45	34	41	3	47	58	20	14	90	64	11	49	6	5	72	52	17	57	50
104	$C_{11}H_{17}NO_3$	*N-methyl-metanephrine	1	0	0	0	3	0	0	6	0	0	29	2	2	0	0	0	4	7	0	1	0
105	$C_{11}H_{17}NO_3$	2,3,4-trimethoxy-β-phenyl-ethylamine	67	77	51	45	58	7	47	71	25	20	91	52	18	65	15	13	62	59	18	50	43
106	$C_{11}H_{17}NO_3$	*2,4,5-trimethoxy-β-phenyl-ethylamine	61	70	39	30	40	3	41	61	23	16	88	47	10	44	6	7	53	44	16	41	34
107	$C_{11}H_{17}NO_3$	*3,4,5-trimethoxy-β-phenyl-ethylamine (mescaline)	62	73	42	35	43	3	35	61	20	12	86	41	9	47	6	5	55	41	13	39	30
108	$C_{12}H_{14}N_2O_2$	*5-hydroxy-N-acetyl-tryptamine (N-acetyl-serotonin)	6	6	2	0	1	0	2	4	1	0	7	3	0	0	0	0	18	1	1	5	3
109	$C_{12}H_{16}N_2O$	*5-hydroxy-N-dimethyl-tryptamine (bufotenine)	0	0	0	0	2	0	0	5	0	0	13	0	0	0	0	0	1	4	0	0	0
110	$C_{12}H_{16}N_2O$	*5-methoxy-N-methyl-tryptamine	65	77	51	43	31	10	56	49	33	18	70	47	7	61	21	6	61	36	30	51	42
111	$C_{13}H_{16}N_2O_3$	5-methoxy-6-hydroxy-N-acetyl-tryptamine (6-hydroxy-melatonin)	5	6	1	0	2	8	2	4	0	0	11	2	0	0	0	0	18	1	0	5	2
112	$C_{18}H_{37}NO_2$	sphingosine	60	69	37	25	17	3	11	30	4	1	37	14	3	21	4	2	35	12	3	17	14

Chromatographic conditions: adsorbent-200μ Silica Gel G layer (E. Merck, Darmstadt); activated for 2 hours at 110°C; temp.: 20–22°C; 50% relative atmospheric humidity; solvent vapor saturated chromatographic tanks. (The tanks were lined with two filter paper sheets, and two plates were run simultaneously.) Distance from the starting point to the edge of the plate: 2.5 cm; distance from the solvent front to the start point: 15 cm. For the solvent composition see Table II.
* DANS-derivatives which have been separated simultaneously.

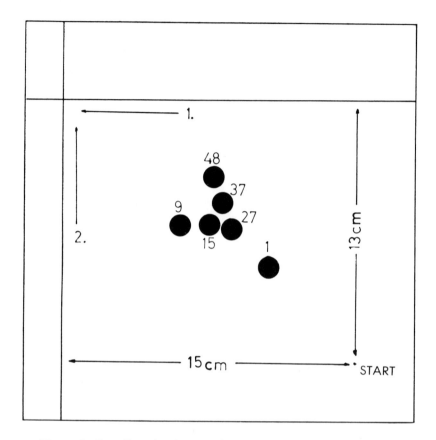

Figure 9. Two-dimensional separation of the DANS-derivatives of some aliphatic diamines. Adsorbent: 200μ Silica Gel G. First direction: tetrachloromethane–methanol (45:3), five times; second direction: chloroform–triethylamine (10:1); 1 = DANS-NH₂, 9 = DANS-ethylenediamine, 15 = DANS-trimethylenediamine, 27 = DANS-tetramethylenediamine, 37 = DANS-pentamethylenediamine, 48 = DANS-hexamethylenediamine (Seiler and Wiechmann).[132] Reproduced from Reference 132 by permission of Elsevier Publishing Co., Amsterdam.

acids. The present thin-layer chromatographic systems for the separation of DANS-amino sugars cannot be considered as fully satisfactory. Galoyan *et al.*[141] use 200μ layers prepared from 20 ml O.2M Na₂B₄O₇, 45 ml water, and 30 g Silica Gel G. The chromatograms are run in the first direction with solvent XXVIII. This separates DANS-glucosamine and DANS-galactosamine from most of the DANS-amino acids. The separation of these two DANS-hexosamines is then achieved with solvent XXIX (see Table II) in the second direction. The solvent (XXX) used for the separation of dansyl amino acids[142] is recommended also for the separation of DANS-alaninol from DANS-N-methyl-ethanolamine.[143]

Rf-Values of DANS-Derivatives

There are numerous parameters which may influence the mobility of spots on TLC-adsorbent surface, layer thickness, amount of substance to be separated, temperature, atmospheric humidity, saturation of the atmosphere with solvent vapor within the tank, and solvent demixing, among others. (For a more detailed consideration see References 144, 145.) These parameters cannot be held constant with appropriate accuracy in practice without the expenditure of considerable amounts of effort and time, so that the Rf-values determined at a different time or in different laboratories often differ considerably. One may question on grounds of good arguments whether it is suitable to determine Rf in TLC at all. The Rf-values given in Table III should be considered therefore only as an aid to select solvents for special separation problems.

Since the dansyl derivatives show some marked regularities concerning structure and mobility, as can be seen from Table III, their Rf-values may also help in some instances to decide certain structural problems, but the material available at present is not extensive enough to justify a detailed discussion of structure-mobility relationships.

QUANTITATIVE DETERMINATION OF DANS-DERIVATIVES

Fluorescence Characteristics of DANS-Derivatives

DANS-Amides appear under a suitable UV-lamp (365 nm Hg line) as intensely fluorescing yellow-green or yellow spots on TLC. They can easily be distinguished from the blue-green fluorescing DANS-OH. DANS-Imidazol derivatives exhibit a deep orange fluorescence, as is the case with DANS-phenol esters. This shift of the absorption and emission maxima to longer wavelength can be seen from Figure 10, where the activation and fluorescence spectra of DANS-β-phenylethylamine, of triDANS-epinephrine and of bisDANS-catechol are shown, as measured in equimolar solutions. Though the catechol derivatives possess two fluorophors and DANS-epinephrine even three, the quantum yield of these compounds is considerably lower than that of the β-phenylethylamine derivative. In aliphatic diamines, however, the quantum yield, as can be expected, is double that of DANS-β-phenylethylamine. This can be seen from Table IV, where the relative fluorescence intensities of some DANS-derivatives are summarized, together with the activation and fluorescence maxima.

The fluorescence characteristics of solutions of DANS-derivatives are dependent on the solvents used. With increasing dielectric constant of the solvent, the emission maximum is generally shifted to longer wave-

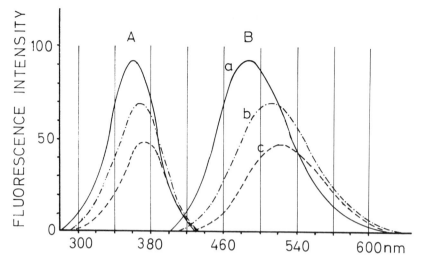

Figure 10. Activation (A) and fluorescence-spectra (B) of different DANS-derivatives. Solvent: benzene–triethylamine (19:1); concentration: 5 μM (a) ———————— DANS-β-phenylethylamine, (b) –.–.–.–. DANS-epinephrine, (c) -------- DANS-catechol (Seiler and Wiechmann).[114]

length, and the quantum yield, with few exceptions, decreases. This has been demonstrated by Chen[146] with DANS-tryptophan.

In the protonated form the fluorescence intensity of dansyl derivatives is very low, comparable with that of naphthalene.[114] In strong alkaline solution the amido group ionizes. This ionization causes a hypsochrome shift of the absorption maxima and of the emission maxima by about 10 nm. DANS-Derivatives of secondary amines and phenols, of course, do not exhibit this shift; therefore it can be used as a criterion for the distinction of the derivatives of primary and of secondary amines. For a more detailed discussion of the absorption and fluorescence characteristics of DANS-derivatives see Reference 114.

Elution Method

The principle of this method is well known and at present the most widely used quantitative evaluation technique in TLC.[147,148] For the quantitative assessment of DANS-derivatives the following procedure is recommended.[114,149] The samples should be spotted, if possible, on the chromatograms in a solvent, which is fairly nonpolar, *i.e.*, benzene. In this way chromatographic enlargement of the starting zone is kept to a minimum. Though two-dimensionally separated DANS-derivatives may be determined with the extraction method as well, experiences extend hitherto essentially to one-dimensional chromatograms. Samples are applied to 20 x 20-cm plates without damage of the layer 3 cm from

Table IV

Activation and fluorescence maxima and relative fluorescence intensities
of DANS-derivatives in different solvents

DANS-derivative	methanol λ_A (nm)	methanol λ_F (nm)	methanol I_F	methanol–aq. ammonia (sp. gr. 0.91) (95:5) λ_A (nm)	methanol–aq. ammonia (sp. gr. 0.91) (95:5) λ_F (nm)	methanol–aq. ammonia (sp. gr. 0.91) (95:5) I_F	benzene–triethylamine (95:5) λ_A (nm)	benzene–triethylamine (95:5) λ_F (nm)	benzene–triethylamine (95:5) I_F
ammonia	357	516	113	357	516	110	356	483	148
ethylamine	360	520	100	360	522	116	356	483	165
ethanolamine	361	522	103	360	521	109	359	485	163
cystamine	362	525	99	362	521	100	—	—	—
β-phenylethyl-amine	360	521	100	360	521	110	360	486	165
tyramine	362	525	58	364	525	60	366	507	232
epinephrine	361	530	40	365	530	40	365	510	131
piperidine	364	525	100	364	525	103	360	484	178
ethylenediamine	360	520	180	360	520	181	360	492	337
tetramethylene-diamine	360	518	204	360	518	205	360	489	352
hexamethylene-diamine	360	518	200	360	518	205	360	490	347
phenol	375	540	10	375	540	9	371	508	168
catechol	375	540	4	—	—	—	373	523	80

Fluorescence intensities are related to a $5.0 \cdot 10^{-6}$M solution of DANS-β-phenyl-ethylamine in methanol; wavelengths are uncorrected instrument readings; a Zeiss Spectrofluorometer with two monochromators M4QIII was used with a Xenon arc lamp LX 501 as a light source (Seiler and Wiechmann).[114] Courtesy of *Z. Anal. Chem.*
λ_A activation maximum; λ_F fluorescence maximum; I_F relative fluorescence intensity.

the edge of the plates. The distance of the spots along the origin line should be 1.5–2 cm. Each sample should be vicinal to a reference mixture, which contains amounts of the dansyl derivatives similar to that in the unknown sample.

After chromatography has been completed, the fluorescent zones are quickly marked with the aid of a suitable UV-light source. Then the plates are dried *in vacuo* in a desiccator containing P_2O_5 for 60 minutes. Since dansyl derivatives are sensitive to light, especially the phenol- and aminophenol-derivatives, the plates should be protected from direct sunlight. The zones containing the dansyl derivatives are scraped off, most conveniently with one of the commercially available zone extractors, or with a simple zone extractor,[113] that collects the adsorbent in a 10-ml centrifuge tube. For further techniques see Reference 147. Five ml of solvent is added to the centrifuge tube, which is then vigorously shaken for two minutes, followed by centrifugation for ten minutes in a conventional laboratory centrifuge. The clear solution is ready for fluorometry. Blank zones from the same plate are extracted in the same manner. These extracts are used to determine the zero point.

DANS-amides are normally extracted quantitatively from the Silica Gel G layer with solvents of relatively low polarity. Benzene–triethylamine (95:5) and benzene–acetic acid (99:1) proved to be especially suitable solvents,[114] since the quantum yield in these solvents is higher than in more polar solvents (see Table IV), and triethylamine and acetic acid respectively neutralize the influence of solvent traces, especially acids and bases extracted from the adsorbent layer. DANS-Amino acids are not extracted quantitatively by benzene or ethyl acetate; even with methanol–aq. ammonia (sp. gr. 0.91) (95:5), the recovery of DANS-glycine was only 85%.[114]

Fluorometry of the extracts is achieved with one of the commercial instruments. Normally an Hg-lamp can be used for excitation of the fluorescence, since the activation maxima of DANS-amides are near 365 nm (see Table IV).

DANS-derivatives show a marked fading of the fluorescence intensity, if they are adsorbed on silica gel. Though this fading process is partially irreversible, the reproducibility of the extraction method is ± 3.0–3.5% of the mean value, as can be seen from Table VI, if certain precautions are observed, especially if the whole procedure is properly timed. This reproducibility is in agreement with the findings of other investigators with the extraction technique on other analytical problems.[148] The mean error does not refer to standard solutions of DANS-derivatives, but to known amounts of the different amines, which have been dansylated in the manner described earlier. After extraction of the reaction product of the dansylation reaction with ethyl acetate, aliquots of the extract were applied to TLC. The standard deviation listed in Table V, therefore, includes all errors which are made throughout the procedure, that is, during pipetting, sample'application, extraction, and fluorescence intensity measurement.

With a Zeiss Spectrophotometer PMQ II and the fluorescence accessory ZFM 4, 0.1 nanomoles per 5 ml solvent of a DANS-amide can be determined. The sensitivity may be increased by lowering the solvent volume (*i.e.*, use of microcuvettes) and by measuring the fluorescence intensity in nonpolar solvents.

The fluorescence intensity of dansyl derivatives is directly proportional to the concentration in a very wide range, though in practice measurements are achieved in the range of $1 \cdot 10^{-8}$–$1 \cdot 10^{-10}$ moles per 5 ml solvent. As shown in Figure 11.

Table V

Reproducibility of amine determination by dansylation and extraction of the chromatographically separated DANS-derivative. (Each determination is from a different reaction mixture. Seiler and Wiechmann.[114])

Substance	Number of determinations	Amount of substance moles/spot	Solvent for extraction	Reproducibilitys (% of the average)
methylamine	16	$1.25 \cdot 10^{-9}$	methanol—aq. ammonia (sp. gr. 0.91) (95:5)	±3.5
β-phenylethylamine	20	$1.25 \cdot 10^{-9}$	methanol—aq. ammonia (sp. gr. 0.91) (95:5)	±3.0
3,4,5-trimethoxy-β-phenylethylamine (mescaline)	16	$1.0 \cdot 10^{-9}$	methanol—aq. ammonia (sp. gr. 0.91) (95:5)	±3.3
tyramine	16	$1.25 \cdot 10^{-9}$	methanol—aq. ammonia (sp. gr. 0.91) (95:5)	±10.2
tyramine	24	$1.25 \cdot 10^{-9}$	benzene—triethylamine (95:5)	±2.5
epinephrine	8	$1.25 \cdot 10^{-9}$	benzene—triethylamine (95:5)	±1.8
tryptamine	8	$1.25 \cdot 10^{-9}$	methanol—aq. ammonia (sp. gr. 0.91) (95:5)	±2.5

Table–courtesy of *Z. Anal. Chem.*

Direct Fluorometric Evaluation

The direct measurement of fluorescing substances on TLC is one of the most efficient scanning techniques available at present, since this method is simple in practice as well as on theoretical grounds, and very sensitive and reliable if certain precautions are observed.[89, 90, 150] For several spectrofluorometers accessories, which are more or less suitable for the *in situ* measurement on TLC, are commercially available at present. Our own experiments have been carried out with an accessory that has been constructed in our laboratory.[151]

Though the fading phenomenon of the dansyl derivatives adsorbed on silica gel seemed to prevent the direct quantitative assessment of these substances on TLC, it could be shown later on that a reproducible determination (± 3.5–5%) is achievable if the chromatograms are dried under defined conditions.[75, 114] Reproducible drying conditions are of great importance because the fluorescence intensity of dansyl derivatives depends on the water content of the adsorbent, as is also the case for DANS-derivatives adsorbed on paper.[116] It is recommended

that the plates be dried *in vacuo* for 1 hour in a desiccator containing
P_2O_5 and then equilibrating them in the room, in which the fluorescence
measurements are carried out, for a further 30 minutes. Linear calibration curves have been obtained in the range $1 \cdot 10^{-8} - 1 \cdot 10^{-10}$ moles.
Larger amounts have not been determined.

A very considerable increase in sensitivity is obtained if the chromatograms are sprayed with a solution of triethanolamine in propanol-(2).[114]
Other bases or even some hydrocarbons may have similar effects on the
fluorescence characteristics of dansyl derivatives adsorbed on silica gel;

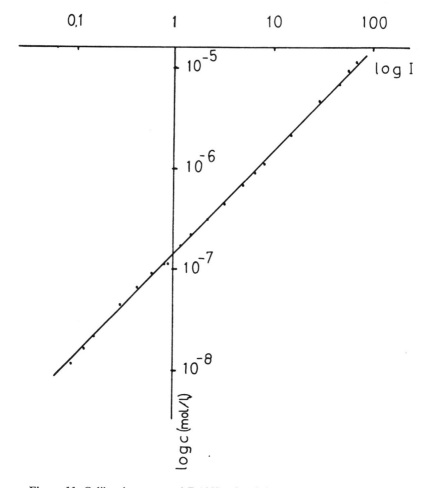

Figure 11. Calibration curve of DANS-epinephrine. Solvent: methanol. Ordinate: fluorescence intensity (log of the instrument readings). Abscissa: log of the
concentration in moles/l.

in practice it is necessary to use a reagent of low volatility. Figure 12 illustrates the enhancement of the fluorescence intensity after impregnation of a 20 x 20-cm plate with 10 ml of triethanolamine–propanol-(2) (1:4). Drying of the sprayed chromatogram causes a further increase in fluorescence quantum yield. In addition to the increased fluorescence intensity, a considerable stabilization of the DANS-derivatives is gained by the triethanolamine spray, so that after this treatment dansyl derivatives can be observed on TLC in very small amounts (0.001 nanomoles) under an UV-light source at least several days. Impregnation of the plates with triethanolamine is therefore also recommended for qualitative visualization of the spots of dansyl derivatives, if no further chromatographic separations are to be performed. It must be pointed out that from those dansyl derivatives, which are sensitive to alkaline hydrolysis, such as DANS-adenine or DANS-choline, DANS-OH may be formed, recognizable by its blue-green fluorescence. Actual changes of the fluorescence color after the triethanolamine impregnation of the plates can be accounted as a characteristic feature, being in some instances an aid in qualitative identifications of DANS-derivatives. It is obvious that triethanolamine reduces the adsorption of the dansyl derivatives to the polar and acidic silica gel, and thus increases the fluorescence quantum yield.

The plates, which are provided for quantitative assessments by direct fluorometry, have to be prepared very carefully, impurities being excluded as far as possible from the adsorbent layer and from the solvents. The samples are carefully applied to the plates, the distance between vicinal spots being 2 cm. As long as the whole spot area is scanned, shape and dimension of the spots is of little consequence in the quantitative assessment; of course, too large amounts of dansyl derivatives have to be avoided, since they can cause quenching of the fluorescence by absorption of light. It is advisable that similar spots be produced from both the unknown and the reference sample at the same time. With the solvents of Table II, normally symmetrical spots are obtained, so that the recorded curves approximate very closely to gaussian shape. Curve areas have been evaluated by planimetry, by cutting and weighing of the analog record chart and also by calculation from the height and the width at half height. The location of the base line is usually not difficult. The application of suitable mechanical or electronic integrators can considerably accelerate and improve the peak evaluation process.

Table VI shows reproducibilities as obtained from different DANS-derivatives by direct fluorometric analysis of TLC after spraying with triethanolamine. Amounts of 10^{-8}–$5 \cdot 10^{-12}$ moles can usually be accurately measured by this method.

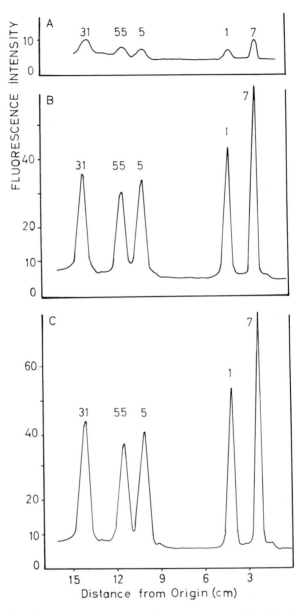

Figure 12. Influence of spraying the chromatograms with triethylamine–propanol-(2) (1:4) on the fluorescence intensity of DANS-derivatives, separated on Silica Gel G layers. 1 = DANS-NH₂, 5 = DANS-ethylamide, 7 = DANS-ethanolamide, 31 = DANS-piperidine, 55 = DANS-β-phenylethylamine. The separation of the DANS-derivatives was achieved by chromatography with benezene-triethylamine (5:1). A. Chromatogram dried for 2 hours *in vacuo*. B. Chromatogram A after spraying with 20 ml triethanolamine–propanol-(2) (1:4) and air dried for 2 hours. C. Chromatogram B dried *in vacuo* for 16 hours in a desiccator with silica gel. Chromatogram records A, B, and C were obtained under identical scanning conditions with the scanning attachment[149] (Seiler and Wiechmann[114]).

TABLE VI

Reproducibility of amine determination by dansylation followed by impregnation of the chromatograms with triethanolamine–propanol-(2) (1:4) and direct (*in situ*) fluorometry of the TLC

Substance	Solvent used for TLC	Standard deviation s* (% of the mean value) of	
		$1 \cdot 10^{-10}$ moles amine/spot	$5 \cdot 10^{-12}$ moles amine/spot
ethylamine	benzene–triethylamine (5:1)	±4.1	±6.9
ethanolamine		±3.6	±3.9
cysteamine		±1.4	±5.4
β-phenylethylamine		±2.3	±3.4
piperidine		±2.5	±2.5
spermine		±2.9	
dopamine		±4.7	±3.8
epinephrine		±3.5	±4.4
serotonin		±2.4	±3.4
spermidine	cyclohexane–ethyl acetate (1:1)	±2.9	
spermine		±4.2	
γ-aminobutyrate	cyclohexane–benzene–methanol (15:85:2)	±1.9	

* Standard deviation *s* was calculated from at least eight different determinations, each from a separate reaction mixture (Seiler and Wiechmann).[114,127,133]

Microdetection of Amines in Tissues

The microdetection and quantitative determination of amines in tissues with the dansyl methodology include some problems which should be discussed briefly. Tissues and body fluids contain complex mixtures of amines, and the concentrations of the amines usually vary in a wide range. For qualitative separations the dansyl derivatives from at most 100 mg of tissue can be applied to a TLC with normal (200–250μ) layer thickness. Tissue extracts in excess of 100 mg usually contain so much ammonia that badly streaked chromatograms are obtained. The solvents published for the thin-layer chromatographic separations of DANS-amides are really only suitable for microgram and lesser amounts. High lipid contents in tissues and sometimes other tissue constituents may also interfere with the chromatographic separations. In addition, the products of side reactions of DANS-Cl itself can cause (if present in large amounts) blue-green fluorescing streaks along the length of the plate, especially if alkaline solvents were used, so that quantitative evaluation in this case is poor. These disadvantages may be avoided if the chromatograms are first run with a neutral solvent of relatively low polarity, so that the hydrolyzable DANS-esters migrate near the solvent front. In a second run in the same dimension the desired separations can then be obtained with the appropriate solvent.

Since the standardization of quantitative measurements with reference samples on a different plate is not of the same reliability, one-dimensional separations are usually used for quantitative determinations, with the reference samples on the same plate. Microdetermination of substances with the dansyl methodology is therefore mainly a separation problem. Efforts have to be made in the future to find reliable and simple preseparation techniques for special applications of the dansyl methodology in tissue analysis.

However, several amines can be easily determined in different tissues without difficulties, as has been shown,[127,133] because suitable solvents have been found for their separation from the other fluorescing constituents of the dansylated tissue extract, and because their concentration in tissues was high enough ($0.1–1$ μmole/g) so that the extracts of small tissue samples could be applied to the chromatograms. The following procedure was applied. Weighed tissue samples were homogenized at dilution of 1:5 to 1:20 (depending on the amine concentration) in 0.2N $HClO_4$ at 0–5°. 0.1–0.5 ml-aliquots of these homogenates were then placed in glass-stoppered 10-ml centrifuge tubes. To 0.1 ml homogenate 0.3 ml of a solution of DANS-Cl (30 mg/ml) in acetone was added and the reaction mixture saturated with $Na_2CO_3 \cdot 10H_2O$ or with $NaHCO_3$, if easily dansylateable amines were determined. Reference samples with known amounts of the amines were run in parallel under the same conditions, the reference amounts being of the same order of magnitude as those in the unknown samples. Reaction was completed by storing the stoppered centrifuge tubes at room temperature overnight. To destroy the excess of DANS-Cl, 0.1 ml of a proline solution (150 mg/ml water) was added next morning and thoroughly mixed. One-half hour later the samples were shaken with 5 ml benzene, and then the layers were separated by centrifugation. (This procedure can also be performed without difficulty even in amounts 1/50 of that described above.) Aliquots of the benzene layer (generally 20 μl) are applied to TLC in the usual manner, but the entire benzene layer may be spotted as well. In the analysis of spermine and spermidine, solvent IV followed by solvent VI (see Table II) were used in the same direction,[133] if brain, nerve, liver or kidney tissue was analyzed. For tissues rich in epinephrine and norepinephrine (*i.e.*, adrenal gland) the polyamines and the catecholamines are separated using solvent XXVII (three times in the same direction) or solvent XII followed by diisopropylether.[133] In Figure 13 a scanning record is shown which was ob-

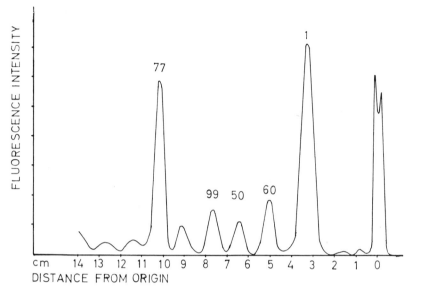

Figure 13. Record of the fluorescence intensity of a thin-layer chromatogram on which the dansylated homogenate of a mouse adrenal gland was separated on 200μ Silica Gel G in (a) cyclohexane–chloroform (1:19), three times in the same direction and (b) diisopropylether, also in the same direction. 1 = DANS-NH$_2$, 60 = DANS-norepinephrine, 50 = DANS-spermidine, 99 = DANS-spermine, 77 = DANS-epinephrine (Seiler and Wiechmann).[133]

tained by direct fluorometry of a TLC with the dansylated amines from a mouse adrenal gland, separated in the way described. Thus the catechinamines can be determined together with the polyamines.

Solvent XVIII proved useful for the separation of DANS-putrescine, DANS-spermidine, and DANS-spermine from the other fluorescent components of tumor cell cultures. Since the reaction product of γ-aminobutyrate, DANS-γ-butyrolactame, moves together with dansyl amides, it should be mentioned here that γ-aminobutyric acid can easily be determined in brain tissue after separation with solvent XXV (see Table II) of its reaction product with DANS-Cl.[127]

Amines (spermine, spermidine, γ-aminobutyric acid, etc.) added to the tissue samples were recovered quantitatively.[133, 127] Reproducibility of the amine determinations in tissue was the same as with marker mixtures, namely, ± 3–5% at amounts of 10^{-10}–$5 \cdot 10^{-12}$ moles.

Estimation of Enzyme Activities

As has been demonstrated, quantitative determination of various amines is quite simple if their concentration in tissue is relatively high (0.1–1 μmoles/g wet weight). Comparable and even higher substrate and reaction product concentrations are usual in enzyme reactions. Therefore it is near at hand to apply the dansyl methodology for the estimation of enzyme activities, the more so since a great variety of enzymes should be determinable in principle by this method specifically. Only the following presuppositions need to be fulfilled generally:

(1) The substrate or the reaction product of the enzymic reaction under consideration should have reactive groups (-NH$_2$; -NH; -OH) that will react quantitatively and without side reactions with dansyl chloride.

(2) The substrate should not be transformed into the reaction product (and vice versa) under the conditions of dansylation, as is the case, for example, with acetylcholine that is hydrolyzed to choline, the reaction product of the enzymatic reaction, so that acetylcholinesterase cannot be determined with the dansyl technique.

(3) A method must be available for the separation of the DANS-derivative of the reaction product, or, if the decrease of the substrate concentration is measured, for the separation of the DANS-derivative of the substrate from all other fluorescent substances present in the dansylated reaction mixture.

The determination of enzyme activities with the aid of the dansyl methodology was just applied hitherto for the determination of some esterases in different tissues,[118,134] but it can be assumed that this method can be of great value in the enzyme field because of its sensitivity, simplicity, reliability, and wide applicability.

CONCLUSION

1-Dimethylamino-naphthalene-5-sulfonyl chloride (dansyl chloride, DANS-Cl) reacts with primary and secondary amino groups, with phenolic and in some instances even with alcoholic hydroxyl groups quantitatively under favorable reaction conditions. Its derivatives are highly fluorescent substances that can be detected in very small amounts. Thus under favorable circumstances 0.005 nanomoles of a DANS-amide can be determined quantitatively by direct fluorometry, the sensitivity of this reagent being therefore comparable with methods that employ radioactive isotopes ^{14}C or ^{3}H as tracers.

Dansyl chloride has proved its value in several fields—in the physical investigation of size and shape of macromolecules, in immunochemistry, in enzyme chemistry, and as an end-group reagent in protein chemistry. Its most recent application in the microanalysis of amines and of other substances of low molecular weight that react with DANS-Cl has just started.

Dansyl chloride is a rather unspecific reagent, compared to its predecessor, 2,4-dinitrofluorobenzene. This lack of specifity dictates that it is only suitable in connection with appropriate separation methods. Paper electrophoresis, PC, and especially TLC proved to be valuable methods for the separation of different DANS-derivatives. An advantage of this lack of specifity is that a number of different substances with appropriate functional groups can be detected simultaneously.

If color reactions are compared, the identification of unknown compounds as their dansyl derivatives is superior in several respects: if color reactions are used for visualization, the substances are usually lost for further investigations, so that only single separating systems can be applied at once; dansyl derivatives on the contrary are easily extracted from the supporting media and can thus be identified by further separation techniques, by optical methods, or by mass spectrometry. The latter method should especially advance the application of the dansyl method in qualitative analysis.

Since GLC is restricted to volatile substances, dansylation combined with TLC fills a gap, at least in the microanalysis of amines. Dansyl chloride is not in every respect a satisfying reagent. One of its main handicaps is that its reaction with certain substances, for example with amino acids, is accompanied by fragmentations. But the superior sensitivity of the dansyl method, the simplicity of its application, the advantageous chromatographic qualities of the DANS-derivatives together with the wide applicability of the method open new possibilities in biochemistry, neurochemistry, pharmacology, pharmacy, and numerous other fields of analytical research.

REFERENCES

1. Guggenheim, M., *Die biogenen Amine* (New York and Basel: S. Karger-Verlag, 1951).
2. Elliott, K. A. C., I. H. Page, and J. H. Quastel, *Neurochemistry,* 2nd ed. (Springfield: Thomas, 1962).
3. Eichler, O., and A. Farah, *Handbook of Experimental Pharmacology,* Vol. 18, part 1 (Berlin, Heidelberg, New York: Springer-Verlag, 1966).
4. Holtz, P., and D. Palm, in *Reviews of Physiology, Biochemistry and Experimental Pharmacology,* Vol. 58 (Berlin, Heidelberg, New York: Springer-Verlag, 1966).
5. Himwich, H. E., and W. A. Himwich, *Progress in Brain Research,* Vol. 8 (Amsterdam, London, New York: Elsevier, 1964).

6. McIlwain, H., *Biochemistry and the Central Nervous System*, 3rd ed. (London: J. & A. Churchill Ltd., 1966).
7. Seiler, N., *Der Stoffwechsel im Zentralnervensystem* (Stuttgart: Georg Thieme-Verlag, 1966).
8. Lajtha, A., *Handbook of Neurochemistry*, Vol. 4 (New York: Plenum Press, in press).
9. Himwich, H. E., S. S. Kety, and J. R. Smythies, *Amines in Schizophrenia* (New York: Pergamon Press, 1967).
10. Weil-Malherbe, H., Advan. Enzymol. 29, 479 (1967).
11. Lajtha, A., *Handbook of Neurochemistry*, Vol. 7 (New York: Plenum Press, in press).
12. Hoffer, A., and H. Osmond, *The Hallucinogens* (New York, London: Academic Press, 1967).
13. Udenfriend, S., *Fluorescence Assay in Biology and Medicine* (New York, London: Academic Press, 1962).
14. Brodie, B. B., and S. Udenfriend, J. Biol. Chem. 158, 705 (1945).
15. Woods, L. A., J. Cochin, E. J. Fornefeld, F. G. McMahon, and M. H. Seevers, J. Pharmacol. Exp. Therap. 101, 188 (1951).
16. Axelrod, J., J. Pharmacol. Exp. Therap. 110, 315 (1954).
17. McIntire, F. C., L. W. Clements, and M. Sproull, Anal. Chem. 25, 1757 (1953).
18. Dubin, D. T., J. Biol. Chem. 235, 783 (1960).
19. Kolbezen, M. J., J. W. Eckert, and B. F. Bretschneider, Anal. Chem. 34, 583 (1962).
20. Satake, K., T. Okuyama, M. Ohashi, and T. Shinoda, J. Biochem. (Tokyo) 47, 654 (1960).
21. Mokrasch, L. C., Anal. Biochem. 18, 64 (1967).
22. Wilk, S., S. E. Gitlow, M. J. Franklin, and H. E. Carr, Clin. Chim. Acta 10, 193 (1964).
23. Heyns, K., R. Stute, and J. Winkler, J. Chromatog. 21, 302 (1966).
24. Tamura, Z., Chem. Pharm. Bull. (Japan) 16, 699 (1968).
25. Drawert, F., R. Felgenhauer, and G. Kupfer, Angew. Chem. 72, 555 (1960).
26. Völlmin, J. A., I. Omura, S. Seibl, K. Grob, and W. Simon, Helv. Chim. Acta 49, 1768 (1966).
27. Perry, T. L., and W. A. Schroeder, J. Chromatog. 12, 358 (1963).
28. Perry, T. L., S. Hansen, and L. C. Jenkons, J. Neurochem. 11, 49 (1964).
29. Perry, T. L., S. Hansen, J. G. Foulks, and G. M. Ling, J. Neurochem. 12, 397 (1965).
30. Perry, T. L., S. Hansen, M. Hestrin, and L. MacIntyre, Clin. Chim. Acta 11, 24 (1965).
31. Perry, T. L., M. Hestrin, L. MacDougall, and S. Hansen, Clin. Chim. Acta 14, 116 (1966).
32. Tabor, C. W., and S. M. Rosenthal, Methods Enzymol. 6, 615 (1963).

33. Unemoto, T., K. Ikeda, M. Hayashi, and K. Miyaki, Chem. Pharm. Bull. (Tokyo) 11, 148 (1963).
34. Shimizu, H., Seikagaku 36, 279 (1964).
35. Holder, S., and H. J. Bremer, J. Chromatog. 25, 48 (1966).
36. Gasparič, J., in *Handbuch der Papierchromatographie*, Vol. 1, Ed. by I. M. Hais and K. Macek (Jena: VEB Gustav Fisher-Verlag, 1958), p 392.
37. Stein von Kamienski, E., in *Papierchromatographie in der Botanik*, Ed. by H. F. Linskens (Berlin, Göttingen, Heidelberg: Springer-Verlag, 1959).
38. Herbst, E. J., D. L. Keister, and R. H. Weaver, Arch. Biochem. Biophys. 75, 178 (1958).
39. Teichert, K. H., E. Mutschler, and H. Rochelmeyer, Deut. Apotheker Ztg. 100, 283 (1960).
40. Grasshof, H., J. Chromatog. 20, 165 (1965).
41. Lüthi, U., and P. G. Waser, Nature 205, 1190 (1965).
42. Gnehm, R., H. U. Reich, and P. Guyer, Chimia (Aarau) 19, 585 (1965).
43. Parrish, J. R., J. Chromatog. 18, 535 (1965).
44. Eberhardt, H., and M. Debackere, Arzneimittel-Forsch. 15, 929 (1965).
45. Lynes, A., J. Chromatog. 23, 316 (1966).
46. Lauckner, J., E. Helm, and H. Fuerst, Chem. Tech. (Berlin) 18, 372 (1966).
47. Bassl, A., H. J. Heckemann, and E. Baumann, J. Prakt. Chem. 36, 265 (1967).
48. Hammond, J., and E. J. Herbst, Anal. Biochem. 22, 474 (1968).
49. Gerlach, H., Pharm. Zentralhalle 105, 93 (1966).
50. Bassl, A., H. J. Heckemann, and E. Baumann, J. Prakt. Chem. 36, 274 (1967).
51. Stahl, E., and P. J. Schorn, in *Dünnschichtchromatographie*, 2nd ed., Ed. by E. Stahl (Berlin, Heidelberg, New York: Springer-Verlag, 1967), p 470.
52. Seiler, N., and M. Wiechmann, Hoppe-Seylers Z. Physiol. Chem. 337, 229 (1964).
53. Choulis, N. H., J. Pharm. Sci. 56, 196 (1967).
54. Aures, S., R. Fleming, and R. Hakanson, J. Chromatog. 33, 480 (1968).
55. Genest, K., and D. W. Hughes, Analyst 93, 485 (1968).
56. Honegger, C. G., Helv. Chim. Acta 44, 173 (1961).
57. Kaltenbach, U., Dissertation, Saarbrücken, 1964.
58. Neurath, G., and E. Doerk, Chem. Ber. 97, 172 (1964).
59. Heyns, K., H. P. Harke, H. Scharmann, and H. S. Grützmacher, Z. Anal. Chem. 230, 118 (1967).
60. Jart, A., and A. J. Bigler, J. Chromatog. 29, 255 (1967).

61. Parihar, D. B., S. P. Sharma, and K. C. Tewari, J. Chromatog. **24**, 443 (1966).
62. Parihar, D. B., S. P. Sharma, and K. K. Verma, J. Chromatog. **29**, 258 (1967).
63. Dwivedy, A. K., D. B. Parihar, S. P. Sharma, and K. K. Verma, J. Chromatog. **29**, 120 (1967).
64. Asatoor, A. M., J. Chromatog. **4**, 144 (1960).
65. Lockhart, I. M., Nature **177**, 393 (1956).
66. Parihar, D. B., S. P. Sharma, and K. K. Verma, J. Chromatog. **26**, 292 (1967).
67. Smith, A. D., and J. B. Jepson, Anal. Biochem. **18**, 36 (1967).
68. Day, E. W., Jr., T. Golar, and J. R. Koons, Anal. Chem. **38**, 1053 (1966).
69. Crawhall, J. C., and D. F. Elliott, Biochem. J. **61**, 264 (1955).
70. Eisen, H. M., S. Belman, and M. E. Carsten, J. Am. Chem. Soc. **75**, 4583 (1953).
71. Möhrle, H., and R. Feil, J. Chromatog. **34**, 264 (1968).
72. Schwartz, D. P., R. Brewington, and O. W. Parks, Microchem. J. **8**, 402 (1964).
73. Tancredi, F., H. C. Curtius, Z. Klin. Chem. Biochem. **5**, 106 (1967).
74. Zahn, H., and A. Wurtz, Biochem. Z. **322**, 327 (1952).
75. Pataki, G., and E. Strasky, Chimia (Aarau) **20**, 361 (1966).
76. Ghosh, P. B., Biochem. J. **108**, 155 (1968).
77. Keston, A. S., S. Udenfriend, and M. Levy, J. Am. Chem. Soc. **69**, 3151 (1947).
78. Cole, M., and J. C. Fletcher, Biochem. J. **102**, 825 (1967).
79. Schayer, R. W., Y. Kobayashi, and R. L. Smiley, J. Biol. Chem. **212**, 593 (1955).
80. Seiler, N., G. Werner, and M. Wiechmann, Naturwiss. **50**, 643 (1963).
81. Connors, W. M., and W. K. Boak, J. Chromatog. **16**, 243 (1964).
82. Klaus, R., J. Chromatog. **16**, 311 (1964).
83. Sawicki, E., T. W. Stanley, and H. Johnson, Microchem. J. **8**, 257 (1964).
84. Gordon, H. T., J. Chromatog. **22**, 60 (1966).
85. DeGalan, L., J. Van Leeuwen, and K. Camstra, Anal. Chim. Acta **35**, 395 (1966).
86. Hamman, B. L., and M. M. Martin, Anal. Biochem. **25**, 305 (1966).
87. Jork, H., Z. Anal. Chem. **221**, 17 (1966).
88. Pataki, G., and A. Kunz, J. Chromatog. **23**, 465 (1966).
89. Jänchen, D., and G. Pataki, J. Chromatog. **33**, 391 (1968).
90. Pataki, G., Chromatographia **1**, 492 (1968).
91. Weber, G., Biochem. J. **51**, 155 (1952).
92. Clayton, R. M., Nature **174**, 1059 (1954).
93. Mayersbach, H., Acta Histochem. **5**, 351 (1958).
94. Redetzki, H. M., J. Biol. Med. **98**, 120 (1958).
95. Uehleke, H., Z. Naturforsch. **13b**, 722 (1958).

96. Ito, M., and K. Nishioka, Japan J. Microbiol. **3**, 71 (1959).
97. Wolochow, H., J. Bacteriol. **77**, 164 (1959).
98. Rinderknecht, H., Experientia **16**, 430 (1960).
99. Sokol, F., L. Hána, and P. Albrecht, Folia Microbiol. **6**, 145 (1961).
100. Hartley, B. S., and V. Massey, Biochim. Biophys. Acta **21**, 58 (1956).
101. Gundlach, G., C. Köhne, and F. Turba, Biochem. Z. **336**, 215 (1962).
102. Gold, A. M., Biochemistry **4**, 897 (1965).
103. Hill, R. D., and R. R. Laing, Nature **210**, 1160 (1966).
104. Hill,.R. D., and R. R. Laing, Biochim. Biophys. Acta **132**, 188 (1967).
105. Kasuya, M., and H. Takashina, Biochim. Biophys. Acta **99**, 452 (1965).
106. Kasuya, M., and H. Takashina, J. Biochem. (Tokyo) **60**, 459 (1966).
107. Schmidt, A., P. Christen, and F. Leuthardt, Helv. Chim. Acta **49**, 281 (1966).
108. Kasuya, M., and H. Takashina, J. Biochem. (Tokyo) **60**, 108 (1966).
109. Gray, W. R., and B. S. Hartley, Biochem. J. **89**, 59P (1963).
110. Gray, W. R., Methods Enzymol. **11**, 139 (1967).
111. Gray, W. R., Methods Enzymol. **11**, 469 (1967).
112. Beale, D., *Chromatographic Techniques*, Ed. by I. Smith (London: Wm. Heinemann Medical Books Ltd., 1969).
113. Seiler, N., *Methods of Biochemical Analysis*, Vol. 18, Ed. by D. Glick (New York: Interscience, in press).
114. Seiler, N., and M. Wiechmann, Z. Anal. Chem. **220**, 109 (1966).
115. Neadle, D. J., and R. J. Pollitt, Biochem. J. **97**, 607 (1965).
116. Boulton, A. A., *Methods of Biochemical Analysis* **16**, 327 (1968).
117. Seiler, N., Hoppe-Seylers Z. Physiol. Chem. **348**, 601 (1967).
118. Seiler, N., L. Kamenikova, and G. Werner, Collection Czech. Chem. Commun. **34**, 719 (1969).
119. Seiler, N., Unpublished work.
120. Boyle, R. E., J. Org. Chem. **31**, 3880 (1966).
121. Seiler, N., and M. Wiechmann, Experientia **21**, 203 (1965).
122. Fussgänger, V., Ber. **35**, 976 (1902).
123. Serebryany, S. B., and A. G. Terentyev, Ukr. Khim. Zh. **33**, 527 (1967).
124. Rieche, A., and H. Seeboth, Angew. Chem. **70**, 52 (1958).
125. Rieche, A., and H. Seeboth, Angew. Chem. **70**, 312 (1958).
126. Creveling, C. R., K. Kondo, and J. W. Daly, Clin. Chem. **14**, 302 (1968).
127. Seiler, N., and M. Wiechmann, Hoppe-Seylers Z. Physiol. Chem. **349**, 588 (1968).
128. Boulton, A. A., 2nd Intern. Neurochem. Conf., Oxford, 1965.
129. Legg, E. F., M.S. Thesis, University of Birmingham, 1967.
130. Durkó, I., and A. A. Boulton, 1st Intern. Meeting International Soc. Neurochem., Strasbourg, 1967.
131. Seiler, N., and J. Wiechmann, Experientia **20**, 559 (1964).
132. Seiler, N., and M. Wiechmann, J. Chromatog. **28**, 351 (1967).

133. Seiler, N., and M. Wiechmann, Hoppe-Seylers Z. Physiol. Chem. **348**, 1285 (1967).
134. Seiler, N., L. Kameniková, and G. Werner, Hoppe-Seylers Z. Physiol. Chem. **348**, 768 (1967).
135. Creveling, C. R., and J. W. Daly, Nature **216**, 190 (1967).
136. Stüttgen, G., S. Richter, and D. Wildberger, Arch. Klin. Exptl. Dermatol. **230**, 349 (1967).
137. Stüttgen, G., H.-J. Schön, and D. Ollig, Arch. Klin. Exptl. Dermatol. **233**, 33 (1968).
138. Seiler, N., Z. Anal. Chem. **243**, 489 (1968).
139. Möllmann, H., H. Alfes, and J. Reisch, Med. Welt. **20**, 1268 (1967).
140. Reisch, J., H. Alfes, N. Jantos, and H. Möllmann, Acta Pharm. Suecica **5**, 393 (1968).
141. Galoyan, A. A., B. K. Mesrob, and V. Holeysovsky, J. Chromatog. **24**, 440 (1966).
142. Deyl, Z., and J. Rosmus, J. Chromatog. **20**, 514 (1965).
143. Laneelle, G., Compt. Rend. Acad. Sci. [C] (Paris) **1966**, 502.
144. Geiss, F., J. Chromatog. **33**, 9 (1968).
145. Pataki, G., *Techniques of Thin-Layer Chromatography in Amino Acid and Peptide Chemistry* (Ann Arbor, Michigan: Ann Arbor Science Publishers, 1968).
146. Chen, R. F., Arch. Biochem. Biophys. **120**, 609 (1967).
147. Gänshirt, H., in *Dünnschichtchromatographie,* 2nd ed. Ed. by E. Stahl (Berlin, Heidelberg, New York: Springer-Verlag, 1967), p 144.
148. Seiler, N., and H. Möller, Chromatographia **2**, 273 (1969).
149. Seiler, N., Angew. Chem. **77**, 684 (1965).
150. Seiler, N., and H. Möller, Chromatographia In press.
151. Seiler, N., Hoppe-Seylers Z. Physiol. Chem. **348**, 765 (1967).
152. Sourkes, T. L., and B. D. Drujan, Can. J. Biochem. Physiol. **35**, 711 (1957).

Chapter 5

Identification of Circulating Iodoamino Acids by Thin-Layer Chromatography

by E. Zappi

Most of the thin-layer chromatographic (TLC) systems for separating phenolic iodoamino acid mixtures have been proposed for the identification of thyroid secretion products in biological media. Some of these systems exhibit favorable properties which permit the isolation of thyroxine and triiodothyronine—recognized as the thyroid hormones[1]—and of some other iodothyronines and monoiodo- and diiodotyrosine. With the presence of iodotyrosines in the blood now firmly established,[2-11] a real interest exists for methods which permit their easy demonstration. These substances do not display hormonal activity but their concentration in the blood, like that of the iodothyronines, appears to change significantly in different thyroideal and extrathyroideal pathologic conditions, giving characteristic iodoamino acid patterns for these diseases.[12-27]

The circulating phenolic iodoamino acids are present in biological fluids in quite low concentration and, at least partially, are bound to carrier proteins. For this reason, their detection and identification depend not only on the resolving properties of the chosen TLC system but also extensively on the effectiveness of the extractive procedure and on the sensitivity of the detection technique used for localizing the spots present on the chromatogram. Some aspects of these problems will be discussed later.

In 1962, Gänshirt reported a TLC system which permits the separation of several iodophenols from some thyreostatics.[28] The next year, papers and communications appeared which dealt directly with the thin-layer chromatographic separation of mixtures of iodothyronines and iodotyrosines. Since then other systems have been proposed, using new solvent mixtures, other sorption media, or different chromatographic techniques in order to improve the results. Table I shows the principal contributors in this field, both chronologically and alphabetically, and gives some of the more important characteristics of the described TLC systems. These can be tentatively divided into two main groups: those requiring silica gel and those requiring cellulose layers. Organic solvents having either acidic or basic reaction are used in the first case. Solvents used in combination with cellulose, on the other hand, are sometimes organic and

Table I

Thin-Layer Chromatographic Systems
for Identification of Phenolic Iodoamino Acids

Author and year	Layer material	Solvent charact.	reaction	Other characteristics	Tested substances
Gänshirt, 1962[28]	Silica Gel G	organic	basic		thyreostatics, DIT, T_2, T_3, T_4
Berger et al., 1963[29]	AgCl + Dowex	organic	basic	juxtaposed layers	I^-, MIT, DIT, T_4
Hollingsworth et al., 1963[30]	cellulose	organic	basic acid	ammonia atmosphere	Tyr, MIT, DIT, Thy, T_2, T_3, T_4
Schneider and Schneider, 1963[31]	activated Silica Gel G	organic	basic acid	ammonia atmosphere	MIT, DIT, T_2, T_3, T_4, TA_2, TA_3, TA_4
Frey, 1964[32]	Silica Gel G	organic	basic acid	one- and two-dimens.	I^-, MIT, DIT, T_3, T_4
Massaglia and Rosa, 1964[33]	activated Silica Gel G	organic	basic acid		I^-, Tyr, MIT, DIT
Patterson and Clements, 1964[34]	cellulose + starch	organic	basic	ammonia atmosphere	I^-, DIT, T_2, T_3, T_4
Stahl and Pfeifle, 1964[35]	activated Silica Gel G + starch	organic	basic acid	radiopaque media	I^-, MIT, DIT, T_2, T_3, T_4
Faircloth et al., 1965[36]	cellulose G	organic aqueous	basic acid	two-dimens.	I^-, MIT, DIT, T_2, T_3, T_4
Gries et al., 1965[37]	cellulose G	aqueous	acid		MIT, DIT, T_1, T_2, T_3, T_4
Heider and Ramsey Bronk, 1965[38]	Silica Gel + silicon dioxide	organic	basic acid	two-dimens.	I^-, T_3, T_4, TA_3, TA_4
Herberhold and Neumüller, 1965[39]	Silica Gel + silicon dioxide	organic	basic acid		I^-, MIT, DIT, T_3, T_4
Schorn and Winkler, 1965[40]	Silica Gel	organic	basic		I^-, MIT, DIT, T_3, T_4
Sakurada, 1965[41]	diatomaceous earth G	organic	basic		I^-, MIT, DIT, T_3, T_4
West et al., 1965[42]	Silica Gel	organic	basic acid	one- and two-dimens.	I^-, MIT, DIT, T_2, T_3, T_4, TA_3, TA_4, TG
Ouellette and Balcius, 1966[43]	cellulose + Silica Gel G	organic	basic		MIT, DIT, T_3, T_4
Shapiro and Gordon, 1966[44]	Silica Gel G	organic	basic	run twice in same direction	I^-, MIT, DIT, T_3, T_4, TA_3, TA_4
Sofianides et al., 1966[45]	cellulose	organic	basic acid	two-dimens.	I^-, MIT, DIT, T_3, T_4, TA_3, TA_4

Table I (continued)

Coenegracht and Postmes, 1967[46]	cellulose + solvitose	aqueous	acid	I⁻, MIT, DIT, T₃, T₄
Zappi, 1967[47]	cellulose G	aqueous	acid	I⁻, Tyr, MIT, DIT, Thy, T₁, T₂, T₃, T₄

When not otherwise indicated, chromatograms are one-dimensional. Runs in the one- and two-dimensional systems, as well as in the repeated one-dimensional system are ascending. The following abbreviations were used:

Tyr: tyrosine
MIT*: 3-monoiodotyrosine
DIT*: 3,5-diiodotyrosine
Thy: thyronine
T_1*: 3-monoiodothyronine
T_2*: 3,5-diiodothyronine
T_3*: 3,3′,5-triiodothyronine
*According to Harington et al.[48]

T_4*: 3,3′,5,5′-tetraiodothyronine (thyroxine)
TA_2: diiodothyroacetic acid
TA_3*: triiodothyroacetic acid
TA_4*: tetraiodothyroacetic acid
TG_4: thyroxine glucuronide
TP_4: tetraiodothyropropionic acid

Table II

Identification of Phenolic Iodoamino Acids by TLC

Code	Author Ref.	Solvent
1b/S	Gänshirt[28]	butanol–methanol–5N ammonia (60:20:20).
2b/S	Schneider and Schneider[31]	phenol–acetone–1N ammonia (20:70:10).
3b/S	Frey[32]	n-butanol sat. with 2N ammonia (acc. to Barker).
4b/S	Frey[32]	collidine sat. with water (acc. to Barker).
5b/S	Stahl and Pfeifle[35]	ethyl acetate–isopropanol–25% ammonia (55:35: 20).
6b/S	Heider and Ramsey Bronk[38]	chloroform–methanol–30% ammonia (20:10:1)
7b/S	Schorn and Winkler[40]	methyl ethyl ketone–ethanol–1N ammonia (80:10: 10).
1a/S	Massaglia and Rosa[33]	phenol–water (75:15).
2a/S	Massaglia and Rosa[33]	n-butanol–acetic acid–water (10:1:1).
1b/C	Hollingsworth et al.[30]	chloroform–t-butanol–2N ammonia (60:376:70).
2b/C	Patterson and Clements[34]	t-amyl alcohol sat. with ammonia (acc. to Barker).
1a/C	Hollingsworth et al.[30]	n-butyl ether–n-butanol–glacial acetic acid–water (130:70:60:140) (Schneider-Lewbart, modified).
2a/C	Faircloth et al.[36]	formic acid–water (10:50) (acc. to Björkstén).
3a/C	Gries et al.[37]	methanol–0.5N acetic acid (20:80).
4a/C	Coenegracht and Postmes[46]	methanol–1N HCl (30:70).
5a/C	Zappi[47]	acetone–0.5N acetic acid (20:80).
1b/D	Sakurada[41]	chloroform–n-butanol (70:40), sat. with ammonia.

The code in the left column indicates first, the order number of a solvent in a group; second, its reaction (a = acidic, b = basic); third, the layer material used (S = silica gel, C = cellulose, D = diatomaceous earth).

149

sometimes aqueous; the latter are always of weak acidic reaction (Table II).

CHROMATOGRAPHY ON SILICA GEL

Silica gel has been used extensively in column chromatography. This material retains considerable amounts of water, giving suitable stationary phases for partition chromatography systems.[49-50] Mutschler and Rochelmeyer[51] as well as Brenner and Niederwieser[52] obtained the first resolutions of amino acids mixtures on TLC with the help of silica gel layers. The use of this support medium was later extended to the thin-layer chromatographic identification of iodinated amino acids, and of thyroid hormones in particular.* However, as these compounds did not possess the characteristic hydrophylic properties which distinguish their unhalogenated antecedents, other solvents had to be found to provide more favorable partition coefficients between the system phases and hence sharper resolution of the tested mixtures.

The great versatility of TLC facilitated empirical trials that Schneider and Schneider[31] started in 1963. Their study of the resolving power of organic or aqueous solvents containing glacial acetic acid or phenol on silica gel did not identify a single mixture able to separate simultaneously all the tested compounds (iodothyronines, iodotyrosines, and some of their deaminated acid derivatives). For this reason Schneider and Schneider recommended one of the phenolic solvents (Table II) for the identification of the amino acids, and a solvent containing acetic acid for the separation of the mentioned derivatives. Table III shows some Rf-values obtained with one of these systems.

Frey,[32] in his turn, applied silica gel layers for the separation of iodinated products from hydrolysates of thyroid gland. For this purpose he used three organic solvents: butanol–ammonia and collidine–water— which had been described by Barker[53] for paper chromatography (PC) (Table II)—as well as phenol–water. The chromatographic behavior of the studied substances in both of Barker's mixtures differed strongly when run on paper sheets in contrast to silica gel layers. (Table IV). It follows that both the chemical nature and the physical structure of support medium are important factors in determining their chromatographic properties (Pataki[54, 54a]).

As Table IV also shows, the differences between Rf-values obtained for the same substances when run in the same solvent either on cellulose layers or on paper sheets are by no means as striking as those obtained when paper and an inorganic support film are employed. Frey's third sol-

---

*For reviews see also References 54 and 54a.

Table III

Distribution of Several Iodo Compounds and Iodide by TLC on Silica Gel

Rf	2b/S	3b/S	6b/S	7b/S	1a/S	2a/S
1.00						
—						
—						
—						
0.90						
—						
—						
—						
0.80			I^- 0.80			
—				DIT 0.77		
—						
—						
0.70						I^- 0.70
—						
—			TA$_3$ 0.65			
—						
0.60						
—						DIT 0.56
—			TA$_4$ 0.53		MIT 0.52	
—		TA$_4$ 0.49				
0.50						
—						
—	T$_2$ 0.44					
—		I$^-$ 0.42				MIT 0.41
0.40	T$_3$ 0.40			I$^-$ 0.40	Tyr 0.40	
—			T$_3$ 0.38			
—						
—		T$_2$ 0.33				
—	T$_4$ 0.32	T$_3$ 0.32				
0.30						
—			T$_4$ 0.27			
—		T$_4$ 0.25				
—						Tyr 0.23
0.20						
—	MIT 0.17					
—	DIT 0.15	MIT 0.14		T$_3$ 0.14	I$^-$ 0.14	
—		DIT 0.12				
0.10				T$_4$ 0.09		
—				MIT 0.07		
—		TG$_4$ 0.05				
—				DIT 0.03		
0.00						

For code explanation see Table II.
The same abbreviations as in Table I are used.

vent, of weak acidic character, does not show better resolving power than the basic ones. Even the combined use of the solvents in two-dimensional technique as proposed by Frey does not allow separation of the afore-mentioned iodophenols. In 1964, Massaglia and Rosa[33] also reported different TLC systems on silica gel, which they used for the identification of iodotyrosines after their synthesis from tyrosine and radioiodine. Some of the applied organic solvents, whose composition is shown in Table II, yielded a clear separation of 3-monoiodo- and 3,5-diiodotyrosine from the starting material. Although the chromatographic behavior of other iodinated compounds has not been studied (Table III), eventually these

Table IV

Rf-Values of Phenolic Iodoamino Acids Chromatographed
with the Same Solvent on Paper Sheets or on Thin-Layers

	n-*butanol sat. with* 2N *ammonia*		*collidine sat.* *with water*		*formic acid, water* *10:50*	
	paper	*silica gel*	*paper*	*silica gel*	*paper*	*cellulose powder*
	(*Barker*)	(*Frey*)	(*Barker*)	(*Frey*)	(*Björk-stén*)	(*Fair-cloth*)
I⁻	0.23	0.53*	0.74	0.69*	0.79	0.90
MIT	0.06	0.11*	—	0.26*	0.77	0.83
DIT	0.07	0.11*	0.24	0.24*	0.67	0.72
T₂	0.26	—	0.00**	—	0.68	0.48
T₃	0.47	0.33*	—	0.38*	0.54	0.34
T₄	0.29	0.23*	0.55	0.32*	0.35	0.14

The same abbreviations as in Table I are used.
*recalculated values
**values corresponding to 3,3'-diiodotyrosine

systems should be able to separate simultaneously iodotyrosines from iodothyronines. Related to their studies on the detection of iodinated compounds in TLC, Stahl and Pfeifle[35] published in 1964 a series of organic solvents for the separation of a number of radiopaque media and some iodophenols (Table II) on activated silica gel. However, as the last iodocompounds run closely together, these systems do not offer real advantages, at least for the separation of thyroid hormones. Heider and Ramsey Bronk,[38] who were concerned with the TLC separation of thy-roxine, triiodothyronine, and some of their acid derivatives, published in 1965 a two-dimensional system on silica gel with a hydrated silicon dioxide as binder. They used a mixture of methanol and chloroform containing some ammonia solution (Table II) for the first run and the same mixture but with glacial acetic acid instead of ammonia for the second run. They attained a good resolution of the tested compounds

(Table III), but the chromatographic mobilities of iodotyrosines in the system were not reported. For the separation of iodinated products in thyroid lymph, Herberhold and Neumüller[39] also used silica gel and two organic solvents, one of which had been employed by Gänshirt.[28] As the first authors reported, the reproducibility of the Rf-values of some iodoamino acids run by them and by Gänshirt in the same mixture is limited to diiodotyrosine; the other tested compounds in both cases migrate with different velocities or even in an inverted order. That same year, Schorn and Winkler[40] published a paper which studied the properties of a considerable number of organic solvents of basic reaction on silica gel. They also used magnesium silicate with some of the solvents, reporting the same resolving effects but longer running times than those observed on silica gel. The obtained Rf-values on silica gel are in general low, and the systems do not seem very appropriate for the separation of the tested compounds (thyroxine, triiodothyronine, diiodo- and monoiodotyrosine and iodide). Tables II and III show the composition and the migration rates, respectively, afforded by one of the systems used by these authors for the identification of the iodinated compounds present in a serum extract.

West *et al.*[42] were confronted with the problem of inconsistent separations of iodoamino acids through one-dimensional runs on silica gel. In 1965, they tried two-dimensional systems on this material by applying alternately a solvent of ethyl acetate–methanol containing either ammonia or acetic acid solution and also butanol saturated with 2N ammonia as proposed by Frey.[32] Although the authors report satisfactory results in some cases, the complicated performance of these analytical procedures makes their use not very profitable. Shapiro and Gordon,[44] who also could not attain satisfactory separations of iodinated products through one-dimensional systems on silica gel, proposed in 1966 the chromatographing of the samples twice in the same direction, using for both runs two different solvents consisting of *t*-amyl alcohol–acetone–ammonia solution. In this way the authors were able to resolve mixtures of different iodinated compounds; however, the long duration of the procedure (approximately 24 hours) constitutes a serious disadvantage for its application.

As can be seen from Table III, the migration of the iodoamino acids is quite low in all the systems using organic solvents of basic reaction on silica gel; Rf-values over 0.6 are seldom observed. This is not, perhaps, a great disadvantage in the PC due to the large dimension of the sheets, which permits the separation of spots even when their migration rates are not clearly different. However, for the resolution of mixtures in TLC it is highly desirable to obtain a better distribution of the components on the whole chromatogram. Small Rf differences lead in practice to uncertain results concerning the separation of substances and their identification. In addition, the flow rate of the organic solvents of Table III is, in general, slow; several hours are sometimes necessary to cover short distances. Consequently, this increases the possibility of chemical changes in the running iodoamino acids, as was reported by many authors for column and paper chromatographic systems.[55-61] Björkstén et al,[62] in their comprehensive paper, reviewed many of these observations and stressed the probability of obtaining artifacts when using acidic solvents. Hollingsworth et al.[30] and other authors[38, 44, 45] discussed the possibility that breakdown or oxidation of iodoamino acids during TCL occurs when using this type of solvents. Finally, a feature common to many of the silica gel systems studied is the poor reproducibility of the observed Rf-values.

CHROMATOGRAPHY ON CELLULOSE

After silica gel, cellulose powder constitutes the most widely used coating material for TLC separation of iodoamino acids.* The mechanism involved in its resolving properties is still unclear,[50] but it must be kept in mind that this effect depends largely on the employed solvent and, of course, on the chemical nature of the compounds to be separated.[63] Hollingsworth et al.,[30] in 1963, were the first to employ cellulose layers for the identification of thyroid hormones and related iodophenols in TLC. After numerous trials they chose two organic solvents with low water content (Table II), one of which had been used by Schneider and Lewbart[64] for the PC resolution of steroids. This one (1a/C in Table II) seemed to yield better separation of the tested iodinated compounds than did the other (1b/C in Table V), which in addition flowed very slowly. Nevertheless, the cumbersome preparation of the chromatographic jar with the Schneider-Lewbart mixture, as described by Hollingsworth in the aforementioned paper, constitutes a serious drawback for the practical application of this system.

In 1964, Patterson and Clements[34] devised another system on cellulose with starch as the binder for investigating iodophenols in some animal dietary supplements. They again used an organic solvent of basic reaction (Table II) already applied by Barker[53] in PC. The obtained results were good, as judged by the exposed chromatogram where the thyroxine, triiodothyronine, mono-, iodo-, and diiodotyrosine spots appear clearly separated, but the corresponding Rf-values were not reported. The running time was 3 to 4 hours for 10-cm.

In 1965, Faircloth et al.[36] proposed a two-dimensional system on cellulose powder with gypsum for the separation and quantitation of

---

*For reviews see also References 54 and 54a.

Table V

Distribution of Several Iodo Compounds and Iodide
by TLC on Cellulose Layers

Rf	$1b/C$	$2b/C$	$2a/C$	$3a/C$	$4a/C$	$5a/C$
1.00						I⁻ 0.99
—						
—						
—						
0.90			I⁻ 0.90			Tyr 0.90
—					I⁻ 0.86	Thy 0.85
—			MIT 0.83			
—						
0.80						MIT 0.79
—						
—						
—			DIT 0.72			
0.70						
—						
—					MIT 0.66	DIT 0.67
—	I⁻ 0.62			MIT 0.62		
0.60						
—	T₂ 0.58					
—					DIT 0.55	T₂ 0.56
—						
—						
0.50	T₃ 0.50			T₁ 0.50		
—			T₂ 0.48	DIT 0.48		
—		T₄ 0.45				
—						
0.40						
—				T₂ 0.38		
—						
—			T₃ 0.34			
0.30						
—						
—		I⁻ 0.25				T₃ 0.25
—						
0.20					T₃ 0.21	
—	T₄ 0.18					
—				T₃ 0.16	T₄ 0.17	
—			T₄ 0.14			
—						T₄ 0.12
0.10						
—	MIT 0.07					
—	DIT 0.04			T₄ 0.04		
—						
0.00						

For code explanation see Table II.
The same abbreviations as in Table I are used.

iodoamino acids from hydrolysates of thyroid gland. They applied a mixture of formic acid and water described by Björksten *et al.*[62] as the initial solvent (2a/C in Table II) and the above mentioned Hollingsworth's mixture chloroform–*t*-butyl alcohol–ammonia for the second run (Table V). The former weak acidic solvent had a definite aqueous character, thus differing from all other solvents employed up to now in the TLC separation of iodoamino acids. Good resolutions are observed when this solvent is used in PC (Table IV) and further improved on cellulose layers (2a/C in Table V). The different iodo compounds appear separated by wide intervals which facilitate their identification. Gries *et al.*[37] have described another solvent to be used on cellulose layers, composed merely of diluted acetic acid with a low proportion of methanol (Table II). The resolving properties of this mixture resemble those of the formic acid–water solvent (2a/C in Table V), although the migration rates of the tested compounds do not seem to be constant. Coenegracht and Postmes[46] have tried a similar solvent with diluted HCl instead of acetic acid (Tables II and V). Zappi,[47] through further modifications, has arrived at another solvent (Table II) of still better resolving properties, which permits the simultaneous separation of a number of iodothyronines and iodotyrosines, as well as their parent substances and iodide (5a/C in Table V). In systematic investigations,[65] constant Rf-values were obtained with this solvent for runs of 9- and 18-cm length, at temperatures going from 0 to 20°C. These values were still reproducible using cellulose powder, with or without gypsum, and layers of different thickness. The solvent can be prepared in liter batches and stored in plastic flasks without other precautions for many months. The storage of chromatoplates in a desiccator over blue silica gel before use has been found to be an important factor in insuring good results.

All the described aqueous solvents possess a number of favorable properties for the separation of the studied compounds. First, their rapid flow rate on the cellulose layer enables short running times of 1 to 2 hours. This factor minimizes the possibility of chemical changes of the iodophenols during the chromatographic runs. Second, the low volatility of these solvents makes unnecessary the use of procedures to ascertain the equilibrium condition of the tank atmosphere. The chromatographic behavior of the amino acids is similar when developed in the four different aqueous-weak acid solvents on cellulose (Table V). The iodotyrosines run faster than the iodothyronines. The components of both groups show migration rates which are inversely proportional to the iodine content of their respective molecules; this ratio applies also to the parent compounds of both series. Accordingly, the substances distribute themselves along the whole separation distance, with the iodide spot showing in each case the highest Rf-value. For these reasons, it can be affirmed that these aqueous mixtures constitute almost ideal chromatographic solvents, according to Ivor Smith's definition.[66]

OTHER TECHNIQUES

Diatomaceous earth in conjunction with organic—usually basic—solvents also has been employed by Sakurada[41] for the one-dimensional separation of iodophenols. Sakurada obtained results similar to those observed when this type of solvents was applied on silica gel or cellulose powder; *i.e.*, the iodotyrosines remain near the origin whereas the iodothyronines migrate farther (Tables II and V). Aluminum oxide, which was also tried for the resolution of iodoamino acid mixtures,[67] does not present favorable properties combined either with organic or with aqueous solvent mixtures.

The use of juxtaposed layers of different materials on the same carrier plate, or the mixture of different adsorbents in variable proportions, was proposed by Berger *et al.*[29] and Ouellette and Balcius,[43] respectively, for the identification of iodophenols. A series of papers, exemplifying the application of TLC to the study of different aspects of thyroid physiopathology,[68-74] have appeared in recent years.

DETECTION

Iodoamino acid spots can be located on the chromatogram through the use of chemical reagents, application of UV light, or detection of spot radioactivity, assuming that the substances present in the spots have been previously labeled or that they can be activated *in situ*.

Activation techniques through neutron bombardment are applied for the resolution of particular analytical problems but are not of common use in clinical investigations. The usual way for labeling thyroid hormones in the human consists of administering radioiodide, which is taken up by the gland and released combined in its secretion products. However, the administering of unstable iodide is not always possible or permissible. Moreover, as a consequence of pathological or therapeutical changes, the thyroid gland may be unable to take up the administered radioactive iodide from the blood or to incorporate it into the corresponding radicals. Besides these limitations, it has to be mentioned that the chromatographic pattern of circulating iodophenols as revealed through isotopic methods is quite different from that obtained from the same chromatograms by chemical iodine reagents. This is due mostly to the failure of labeling iodotyrosines through the common isotopic techniques. In addition, the use of isotopes may lead to irradiation artifacts, either through lesions of the gland parenchyma,[75-78] or during chromatography performed under unfavorable conditions.[79-81] These reasons explain the increasing interest in the use of chemical reagents for the detection of iodoamino acids in TLC, despite their disadvantages of lower sensitivity and unspecificity compared with the isotopic techniques.

The detection of radioiodine-labeled compounds in TLC can be accomplished in different ways. Mangold[82] describes a series of procedures, most of which can be adapted for this purpose. One of the simplest is radioautography.[34, 45, 71, 83] Radioautograms are obtained by exposing an X-ray film to the chromatogram. Since the reduced size of the chromatoplate enables the whole field to be covered with one film, good topographical relationships of radioactive spots are obtained; unexpected labeled compounds can also be detected easily. In addition, radioautography has the particular advantage of revealing the shape of the spots. This is especially useful for comparative purposes when a chemical reagent is simultaneously employed. Scanning techniques are currently employed in TLC of iodophenols.[21, 31, 33, 40] The applied devices usually integrate the detected radioactivity in curves. This facilitates the determination of Rf-values and also permits the resolution of partially overlapping areas which cannot otherwise be separated. The use of scintillation counters[32, 70, 73] is indicated when the radioactivity which is present is too low to be estimated within a useful time either with radioautography or scanning techniques. In this case, discontinuous measures are obtained after dividing the thin-layer into pieces of variable size and shape (*cf.* Snyder in this volume).

Before considering the possibility for chemical detection of thyroid hormones in TLC, it must be pointed out that these compounds and their related circulating substances do not have a common characteristic chemical function that gives a specific reaction for the whole group. As a consequence, nonspecific phenolic or amino acid reactions or even iodine reactions have to be employed. The latter are, by far, the most sensitive ones.

Bowden and Maclagan[84] discovered in 1954 that after a paper chromatographic separation, a number of iodinated organic compounds would be able to react *in situ* with the Kolthoff and Sandell reagent, giving white spots on a yellow background. Kolthoff and Sandell's reagent, which was originally proposed for the quantitation of iodine, is a mixture of ceric sulfate and arsenious acid (C-A) in a strong acid solution. In the presence of trace amounts of the halogen, a catalytic-induced reduction of the ceric ions by the arsenious acid occurs, and a destaining of the yellow solution takes place. Bowden *et al.*[85] studied further the particular reactivity of iodophenols to the Kolthoff and Sandell reagent, recommending it as a highly suitable test for the detection of iodoamino acid spots in paper chromatography. The reagent is prepared as follows:

Solution A: 10 g $Ce(SO_4)_2 \cdot 4 H_2O$ are added to 100 ml 1N H_2SO_4 previously cooled to 0°C. The solution is centrifuged.

Solution B: 5 g $NaAsO_2$ are dissolved under vigorous stirring in 100 ml 1N H_2SO_4 cooled at 0°C.

Both solutions have to be kept in the refrigerator and mixed in equal volumes immediately before use.

Despite the poor visual contrast yielded by this reagent and the technical difficulties of its application, it has been widely used since 1954 for the location of thyroxine-like spots. The visualization can be improved in different ways. The white spots, for example, fluoresce when exposed to UV light, while the background fluorescence is quenched by the non-reduced ceric ion. Several chemical modifications also have been proposed;[86-90] one of the most effective seems to be that of Mandl and Block.[90] This modification consists of an additional spraying of the chromatogram with a 0.05% aqueous solution of Methylene Blue, followed by the exposure of the plate to ammonia vapors in order to neutralize the sulfuric acid. The limit of detection of the reaction is around 0.1 μg of different iodophenols, and the spots obtained remain unaltered for many months.

The Kolthoff and Sandell reaction is not specific for iodide and iodine. As many authors[53,91-93] have pointed out, a number of substances exist which give false positive reactions. Thiouracil and propyl thiouracil, which are commonly used as reducing agents during the serum extraction of thyroxine, are among these. Chloride, the presence of which is essential for the catalytic effect of iodothyronines and iodotyrosines in the reduction of the ceric ion by arsenious acid, is also able, in high amounts or during long reacting time, to fade the color of the ceric sulfate. Because of their reducing properties, phenol and substances possessing phenolic structure, are known to destain ceric sulfate.

In 1959, Gmelin and Virtanen[94] described another reaction for the detection of thyroxine-like substances on PC, based on the ability of organic iodide to catalize the reduction of ferric ions by arsenious acid. In this case, a simultaneous oxido-reduction occurs and an insoluble pigment of Prussian Blue precipitates. The reagent ferric–ferricyanide–arsenious acid (FFCA) is composed as follows:

Solution A: 2.7 g $FeCl_3 \cdot 6 H_2O$ dissolved in 100 ml 2N HCl.

Solution B: 3.5 g $K_3Fe(CN)_6$ dissolved in 100 ml distilled water.

Solution C: 5.0 g $NaAsO_2$ dissolved in 30 ml 1N NaOH at 0°C and mixed under vigorous stirring with 65 ml 2N HCl.

Immediately before use, 5 parts of solution A and 5 parts of solution B are mixed with 1 part of solution C.

After spraying the mixture, bright blue spots appear on the chromatogram, indicating the presence of iodoamino acids. The excess of reagent is removed by rinsing the paper sheet in water. In this way further oxidation as well as the destruction of the paper by the strong acid solution is prevented. In order to adapt the FFCA reagent to TLC, Patterson and Clements[34] have added starch to the cellulose used as a supporting medium in their system, obtaining a more resistant layer, that can be washed after spraying. To avoid the inconvenience of rinsing the chromatoplate, Zappi[95] has proposed diluting of the freshly prepared FFCA solution with an equal volume of distilled water. The sprayed solution is then easily neutralized by exposing the layer to diluted ammonia vapors. Then the chromatogram is treated with an emulsion of polyvinyliden chloride, which forms an impermeable film on the surface. Further oxidations are so prevented. The detection limit of FFCA reagent according to this modification is around 0.05 μg of different iodothyronines and iodotyrosines.

Because the mechanisms of the Kolthoff-Sandell and the Gmelin-Virtanen reaction are similar, the substances able to give false positive reactions with the latter should also give false positive reactions with the former. Gmelin and Virtanen stated in their original communication[94] that phenols, vitamin C, and other reducing substances react positively with the FFCA solution. That tyrosine also reacts positively was attributed to the reducing properties of the phenolic hydroxyl. Thyronine, which possesses a phenolic group, too, should also give a reaction of similar intensity in the presence of FFCA solution. A stoichiometric comparison[96] shows, however, that the color response of the thyronine molecule is much stronger than that of tyrosine; the reaction exceeds even those of the monoiodo- and diiodo- derivatives of tyrosine. Comparison of the structure of both molecules tends to indicate that the ether bond of thyronine is responsible for its stronger reaction when in contact with the FFCA solution. It is interesting to note that thyronine does not react in this way with C-A solution (Figure 1).

Since arsenite is an indispensable element in the cyclic reduction and further activity of iodine in the FFCA reaction, it can be expected that the elimination of this component in the reacting solution will weaken considerably—or even eliminate—the response of iodinated compounds in contact with it. This fact, already observed by Patterson and Clements,[34] was used by Postmes[97] in an attempt to eliminate the interference of false positive reactions in the FFCA test. Postmes showed that noniodinated substances which react with FFCA solution through their reducing properties also reduce FFC solution (without arsenite), whereas the iodinated compounds which react with FFCA solution through the cyclic oxido-reduction of iodide–iodine do not reduce ferric-ferricyanide

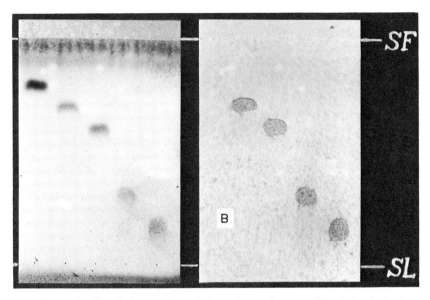

Figure 1. Chemical detection of thyronine and some of its iodo derivatives by means of FFCA or C-A reagent. On chromatogram (A) were spotted, from left to right, 0.05 μg from each of thyronine, monoiodo-, diiodo-, triiodo-, and tetraiodothyronine. On chromatogram (B) the same substances were applied in the same order and in 0.5 μg amounts. After spraying with FFCA reagent, five spots became visible on (A) (from top to bottom: thyronine, monoiodo-, diiodo-, triiodo-, and tetraiodothyronine). On (B), which was sprayed with C-A reagent,[50] the spots corresponding only to the iodothyronines appear. SL = starting line; SF = solvent front. Cellulose TLC plates and solvent acetone–1N acetic acid (2:8, v/v). In obtaining the chromatograms, the author is deeply indebted to Dr. I. Radichevich of Columbia University, New York, N. Y. 10032, and to Mr. E. Krikun of New York Medical College, New York, N. Y. 10029.

in the absence of arsenite. By comparing the results obtained in duplicated chromatograms sprayed separately with FFCA or with FFC solution, it can be determined whether a spot is due to a true catalytical reaction or to a false reaction. Row *et al.*,[98] who agree with this statement, find, however, that spraying with ceric sulfate solution—without natrium arsenite—yields better results for the identification of false positive iodine spots than does FFC solution.

QUANTITATIVE DETERMINATION

Because reproducible color responses were obtained with C-A as well as with FFCA solution in the detection of spots containing determined quantities of iodophenols, both reagents were proposed for the quantitation of thyroid hormones and iodo derivatives in PC and in TLC. Bowden *et al.*,[85] and Gmelin and Virtanen[94] affirmed that their respective reagents could be used for at least semiquantitative evaluation, through planimetry or measurement of the optical density of the obtained spots.* The quantitative determination of the iron present in a spot of Prussian Blue by alpha-alpha'-dipyridyl, which is a specific iron reagent, may give the amount of formed pigment proportional to the reacting iodophenols. This is the basis for Postmes' indirect quantitative determination of thyroid hormones in TLC.[100] If the sprayed solution contains radioactive instead of stable iron, the chemical quantitation can be transformed in an isotopic quantitative determination.

Two principal objections can be made to these quantitative techniques. First, since the sprayed solution comes in contact predominantly with the iodinated compounds located on the surface of the plate, an undetermined amount of substance does not react. Second, the color response of the iodophenols is not strictly proportional to the iodine content of the molecule for FFCA- or for C-A solution.[93, 96] In order to obtain reasonable results, a comparison with standards of known quantities of the same substances must be simultaneously performed. Milstien and Thomas[101] proposed the location of the spots on the plate with FFCA reagent. After removing the whole area from the carrier plate, the iodo compounds are eluted and quantitated by the use of the Kolthoff and Sandell reagent. As already demonstrated,[102] the destaining of C-A solution produced by different iodophenols dissolved in water—in the presence of chloride—is linear to their respective concentration. This fact makes unnecessary the tedious incineration and oxidation of iodide to iodate for the quantitative determination of this halogen.

The application of some general iodine reagents like PaCl or $AgNO_3$ does not offer real advantages for the location or quantitation of iodinated compounds.

Diazotized sulfanilic acid or ninhydrin are able to reveal thyroid hormones and derivatives through reactions involving their phenolic or amino acid groups, but only in quantities of several micrograms. For this reason and in view of their lack of specificity, the application of these compounds is not very useful in this respect. However, their combined use with some iodine reagent may afford valuable data in assessing the chemical identity of chromatographically isolated compounds, provided enough material is present.[103]

The application of UV light in the detection of iodoamino acids in TLC has been briefly mentioned. Another interesting application of UV light for revealing iodo compounds in TLC is found in a method pub-

---

* The direct scanning of spots should also be mentioned in this connection (*cf.* Reference 99).

lished by Stahl and Pfeifle.[35] These authors produce a photochemical deiodination of the substances by exposing the chromatogram to UV radiation. The liberated iodine reacts with starch present in the layer, and blue spots appear in the corresponding areas.

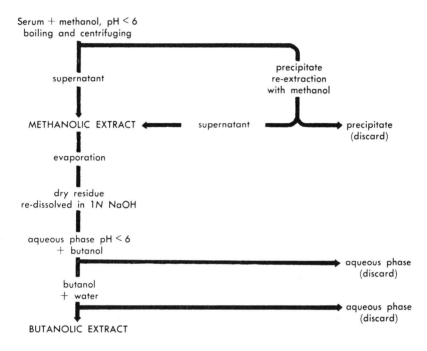

Figure 2. Combined methanolic–butanolic extraction of phenolic iodoamino acids from the plasma.

EXTRACTION PROCEDURES

In 1932, Leland and Foster proposed the extraction of thyroxine from hydrolysates of thyroid gland by butanol.[104] This method still remains widely used for the preparation of circulating thyroid hormones before their chromatographic identification.[105] However, it presents two main disadvantages. First, important losses of iodo compounds may occur, due to incomplete extraction according to their particular distribution coefficients.[47] Second, numerous impurities result in the crude extract, and they cannot be eliminated. These disturb the chromatographic runs[53] or interfere with the identification reactions, as already discussed. In order to avoid all of these inconveniences a preliminary hot methanolic extraction can be performed.[11] This procedure (Figure 2) is highly effective in the recovery of iodothyronines as well as iodotyrosines from the plasma.

The methanolic extract is evaporated and the dried residue is dissolved in water. Lipids are eliminated through a chloroform shaking, and after adjusting the pH to below 6, the iodoamino acids can be quantitatively transferred to a small volume of butanol. This butanol extract is further washed in order to eliminate remaining impurities—mostly in the form of salts. It is then concentrated and spotted on the chromatographic layer. Performed controls[106] show the high extraction rate of the outlined procedure.

REFERENCES

1. Pitt-Rivers, R., and J. R. Tata, *The Chemistry of Thyroid Diseases* (Springfield, Illinois: Charles Thomas Publ., 1960).
2. Werner, S. C., and R. J. Block, Nature (London) **183**, 406 (1959).
3. Beale, D., and J. K. Whitehead, Clin. Chim. Acta **5**, 150 (1960).
4. Block, R. J., S. C. Werner, R. H. Mandl, V. V. Row, and I. Radichevich, Arch. Biochem. **88**, 98 (1960).
5. Werner, S. C., and I. Radichevich, Nature (London) **197**, 887 (1963).
6. Dimitriadou, A., R. Fraser, and P. C. R. Turner, Nature (London) **201**, 575 (1964).
7. Dunn, J. T., and S. C. Werner, J. Clin. Endocrinol. **24**, 460 (1964).
8. Wiener, J. D., Acta Endocrinol. (Copenhagen) **48**, 199 (1965).
9. Rhodes, B. A., H. N. Wagner, Jr., Nature (London) **210**, 647 (1966).
10. Weinert, H., H. Masui, I. Radichevich, and S. C. Werner, J. Clin. Invest. **46**, 1264 (1967).
11. Zappi, E., G. Hoppe, M. Schmidt, and F. Prange, Z. Klin. Chem. **6**, 286 (1968).
12. Stanbury, J. B., A. A. H. Kassenaar, J. W. A. Meijer, and J. Terpstra, J. Clin. Endocrinol. **16**, 735. (1956).
13. Stanbury, J. B., J. W. A. Meijer, and A. A. H. Kassenaar, J. Clin. Endocrinol. **16**, 848 (1956).
14. Stanbury, J. B., and A. Querido, J. Clin. Endocrinol. **16**, 1522 (1956).
15. Arons, W., and J. D. Hydowitz, J. Clin. Endocrinol. **19**, 548 (1959).
16. Béraud, T., Schweiz. Med. J. **90**, 1340 (1960).
17. Klein, E., Klin. Wochschr. **40**, 3 (1962).
18. Wellby, M. L., and B. S. Hetzel, Nature (London) **193**, 752 (1962).
19. Lamberg, B. A., and G. Hintze, Deutsch Med. Wochschr. **88**, 434 (1963).
20. Means, J. H., L. J. De Groot, and J. B. Stanbury, *The Thyroid and its Diseases* (New York-Toronto-London: McGraw-Hill Book Co., 1963).
21. Wellby, M. L., B. Hetzel, and M. L. Isaachsen, Australian Ann. Med. **12**, 30 (1963).
22. Beierwaltes, W. H., in *The Thyroid*, Ed. by J. Beach Hazard and D. E. Smith (Baltimore: The Williams & Wilkins Co., 1964).
23. Kusakabe, T., and T. Miyake, J. Clin. Endocrinol. **24**, 456 (1964).

24. Shalom, E. S., J. Endocrinol. **36**, 1 (1966).
25. Földes, J., G. Gyertyánfy, G. Tamás, E. Gesztesi, and J. Takács, Nuclearmedizin **6**, 400 (1967).
26. Oberdisse, K., and E. Klein, *Die Krankheiten der Schilddrüse* (Stuttgart: Georg Thieme Verlag, 1967).
27. Schmidt, M., Inaugural Dissertation (Berlin: Freie Universität, to be published).
28. Gänshirt, H., in *Dünnschicht-Chromatographie*, Ed. by E. Stahl (Berlin-Göttingen-Heidelberg: Springer-Verlag, 1962).
29. Berger, J. A., G. Meyniel, P. Blanquet, and J. Petit, C. R. Acad. Sci. [D] (Paris) **257**, 1534 (1963).
30. Hollingsworth, D. R., M. Dillard, and P. K. Bondy, J. Lab. Clin. Med. **62**, 346 (1963).
31. Schneider, G., and C. Schneider, Hoppe-Seylers Z. Physiol. Chem. **332**, 316 (1963).
32. Frey, H., Scand. J. Clin. Lab. Invest. **16**, 470 (1964).
33. Massaglia, A., and U. Rosa, J. Chromatog. **14**, 516 (1964).
34. Patterson, S. J., and R. L. Clements, Analyst **89**, 328 (1964).
35. Stahl, E., and J. Pfeifle, Fresenius' Z. Anal. Chem. **200**, 377 (1964).
36. Faircloth, M. A., A. D. Williams, and W. H. Florsheim, Anal. Biochem. **12**, 437 (1965).
37. Gries, G., K. H. Pfeffer, and E. Zappi, Klin. Wochschr. **43**, 515 (1965).
38. Heider, J. G., and J. Ramsey Bronk, Biochim. Biophys. Acta **95**, 353 (1965).
39. Herberhold, C., and O. A. Neumüller, Klin. Wochschr. **43**, 717 (1965).
40. Schorn, H., and C. Winkler, J. Chromatog. **18**, 69 (1965).
41. Sakurada, T., Tohoku J. Exp. Med. **85**, 365 (1965).
42. West, C. D., A. W. Wayne, and V. J. Chavré, Anal. Biochem. **12**, 41 (1965).
43. Ouellette, R. P., and J. F. Balcius, J. Chromatog. **24**, 465 (1966).
44. Shapiro, O., and A. Gordon, Proc. Soc, Exp. Biol. Med. **121**, 577 (1966).
45. Sofianides, T., C. R. Meloni, E. Alger, and J. J. Canary, Proc. Soc. Exp. Biol. Med. **123**, 646 (1966).
46. Coenegracht, J., and T. Postmes, Clin. Chim. Acta **16**, 432 (1967).
47. Zappi, E., J. Chromatog. **30**, 611 (1967).
48. Harington, C. R., R. Pitt-Rivers, A. Querido, J. Roche, and A. Taurog, Nature (London) **179**, 218 (1957).
49. Waldi, D., in *Dünnschicht-Chromatographie*, Ed. by E. Stahl (Berlin-Göttingen-Heidelberg: Springer-Verlag, 1962).
50. Morris, C. J. O. R., and P. Morris, *Separation Methods in Biochemistry* (New York: Interscience, 1964).
51. Mutschler, E., and H. Rochelmeyer, Arch. Pharm. (Berlin) **292**, 449 (1959).
52. Brenner, M., and A. Niederwieser, Experientia **16**, 378 (1960).

53. Barker, S. B., in *Methods in Hormone Research*, Ed. by Ralph Dorfman (New York-London: Academic Press, 1962).

54. Pataki, G., *Dünnschichtchromatographie in der Aminosäure- und Peptid-Chemie* (Berlin: Walter de Gruyter & Co., 1966).

54a. Pataki, G., *Techniques of Thin-Layer Chromatography in Amino Acid and Peptide Chemistry*, 2nd ed. (Ann Arbor, Michigan: Ann Arbor Science Publishers, 1969).

55. Acland, D. J., Nature (London) 170, 32 (1952).

56. Dobyns Brown, M., and S. Barry, J. Biol. Chem. 204, 517 (1953).

57. Stanley, P. G., Nature (London) 171, 933 (1953).

58. Roche, J., R. Michel, and E. Volpért, C. R. Soc. Biol. (Paris) 148, 21 (1954).

59. Owen, C. A., B. F. McKenzie, and A. L. Orvin, J. Lab. Clin. Med. 47, 145 (1956).

60. Kennedy, T. H., Nature (London) 179, 50 (1957).

61. Wellby, M. L., Australian J. Exp. Biol. Med. Sci. 40, 405 (1962).

62. Björkstén, F., R. Gräsbeck, and B. A. Lamberg, Acta Chem. Scand. 15, 1165 (1961).

63. Randerath, K., *Thin-Layer Chromatography* (New York-London: Academic Press, 1965).

64. Schneider, J. N., and M. L. Lewbart, in *Recent Progress in Hormone Research*, Ed. by Gregory Pincus, (New York-London: Academic Press, 1959).

65. Prange, F., to be published.

66. Smith, I., *Chromatographic Techniques* (New York: Interscience, 1962).

67. Zappi, E., Inaugural Dissertation (Berlin: Freie Universität, 1967).

68. West, C. D., V. Chavré, and M. Wolfe, J. Clin. Endocrinol. 25, 1189 (1965).

69. Favino, A., D. Emrich, and A. von zur Mühlen, Acta Endocrinol. (Copenhagen) 54, 362 (1967).

70. Hoppe, G., E. Zappi, and G. Gries, Nuclearmedizin 6, 44 (1967).

71. Nauman, J. A., A. Nauman, and S. C. Werner, J. Clin. Invest. 46, 1346 (1967).

72. Volpért, E. M., M. Martínez, and J. H. Oppenheimer, J. Clin. Endocrinol. 27, 421 (1967).

73. Zappi, E., and G. Hoppe, Z. Klin. Chem. 5, 209 (1967).

74. Levis, G. M., D. A. Koutras, A. Vagenakis, G. Messaris, C. Miras, and B. Malamos, Clin. Chim. Acta 20, 127 (1968).

75. Benua, R. S., and M. Dobyns Brown, J. Clin. Endocrinol. 15, 118 (1955).

76. Emrich, D., in *Radio-Isotope in der Endokrinologie*, Ed. by G. Hoffmann (Stuttgart: F. K. Schattauer-Verlag, 1965).

77. Georgi, M., and K. E. Scheer, *Radio-Isotope in der Endokrinologie*, Ed. by G. Hoffmann, (Stuttgart: Schattauer Verlag, 1965).

78. Emrich, D., H. Reichenbach, G. Hoffmann, and W. Kleiderling, Nuclearmedizin 6, 149 (1967).
79. Pitt-Rivers, R., and I. Wolff, Endocrinology 64, 841 (1959).
80. Tata, J. R., Biochem. J. 72, 214 (1959).
81. Van Zyl, A., Clin. Chim. Acta 7, 20 (1962).
82. Mangold, H. K., in *Dünnschicht-Chromatographie,* Ed. by E. Stahl (Berlin-Göttingen-Heidelberg: Springer-Verlag, 1962).
83. Zappi, E., and G. Bublitz, J. Chromatog. 35, 441 (1968).
84. Bowden, C. H., and N. F. Maclagan, Biochem. J. 56, VII (1954).
85. Bowden, C. H., N. F. Maclagan, and J. H. Wilkinson, Biochem. J. 59, 93 (1955).
86. Fletcher, K., and P. G. Stanley, Nature (London) 175, 730 (1955).
87. Dragúnová, I., and P. Langer, Nature (London) 178, 537 (1956).
88. Gawienowski, A. M., Analyst 82, 452 (1957).
89. Stolc, V., Nature (London) 182, 52 (1958).
90. Mandl, R. H., and R. J. Block, Arch. Biochem. 81, 25 (1959).
91. Dimitriadou, A., F. T. Russell, J. D. H. Slater, and P. C. R. Turner, Nature (London) 187, 691 (1960).
92. Kono, T., L. Van Middlesworth, and E. B. Astwood, Endocrinology 66, 844 (1960).
93. Barker, S. B., Biochem. J. 90, 214 (1964).
94. Gmelin, R., and A. I. Virtanen, Acta Chem. Scand. 13, 1469 (1959).
95. Zappi, E., J. Chromatog. 31, 241 (1967).
96. Zappi, E., J. Chromatog. 42, 524 (1969).
97. Postmes, T., Clin. Chim. Acta 10, 581 (1964).
98. Row, V. V., R. Volpé, and C. Ezrin, Clin. Chim. Acta 13, 666 (1966).
99. Pataki, G., Chromatographia 1, 492 (1968).
100. Postmes, T., Acta Endocrinol. (Copenhagen) 42, 153 (1963).
101. Milstien, S., and D. W. Thomas, J. Lab. Clin. Med. 67, 495 (1966).
102. Morreale de Escobar, G., and E. Gutiérrez Ríos, Clin. Chim. Acta 3, 548 (1958).
103. Zappi, E., and G. Hoppe, Z. Klin. Chem. 6, 105 (1968).
104. Leland, J. P., and G. L. Foster, J. Biol. Chem. 95, 165 (1932).
105. Robbins, J., and J. E. Rall, in *Hormones in Blood,* Ed. by C. H. Gray and A. L. Bacharach (London-New York: Academic Press, 1967).
106. Zappi, E., and G. Hoppe, Nuclearmedizin 6, 420 (1967).

Chapter 6

Thin-Layer Chromatography in Studies of Carbohydrate Side Chains of Glycoproteins

by E. Moczar and M. Moczar

As the possibility of the separation of hydrophilic substances by TLC was recognized, the technique found a wide application, especially in the separation of monosaccharides. The advantages of the new chromatographic procedure, the sensitivity, the rapidity, and the simplicity have to be considered in connection with the necessity of structural elucidation of substances available only in small quantities. In this case, the disposable material imposes the choice of method for identification and separation.

In order to provide informations about the methods, the experimental data were selected on the basis of their sensitivity, which enables an adaptation to our special needs. In line with the definition given, the methodical aspects reported here will concern the thin-layer chromatographic separation of monosaccharides, their derivatives, oligosaccharides, and the determination of molar ratio of monosaccharides as well as the characterization of the type of linkage between the polypeptide and sugar chains.

According to Gottschalk's definition,[1] glycoproteins are conjugated proteins containing as prosthetic groups one or more heterosaccharides with a relatively low number of sugar residues without serially repeating units and bound covalently to the polypeptide chain. The carbohydrate content may vary between 0.5% for collagen and about 80% for blood group substances. Relatively few types of sugar occur in the glycoproteins and only six are commonly found: D-mannose, D-galactose, L-fucose, D-glucosamine, D-galactosamine and D-neuraminic acid. The collagen and other connective tissue glycoproteins may also contain D-glucose. Glycoproteins are widely distributed in the living organism. They are present in the body fluids, in the animal tissues and in several microorganisms. Some enzymes and hormones may be designated also as glycoproteins.

The presence of the amino acids in the polypeptide chains creates many difficulties in the investigation of the sugar contained in the glycoproteins. In consequence structural studies of the carbohydrate part require a proteolytic hydrolysis of the polypeptide, and the isolation of the glycopeptide possessing the intact carbohydrate chain attached to a peptide residue. The lack of repeating units in the sugar implies a complex structure. The methods of structural studies are similar to those used in the carbohydrate chemistry. Difficulties arise from the simultaneous presence of protein and carbohydrate in the material and from the eventually poor yield of glycopeptides prepared from some glycoproteins. Even in the latter case, the sensitivity of TLC enables the use of the classical methods.

ANALYSIS OF THE MONOSACCHARIDE COMPONENTS

The first step in the study of any heteropolysaccharide is the qualitative and quantitative analysis of their sugar components.

Neutral Sugars
Hydrolysis of the Glycoproteins

In order to liberate sugars from glycoproteins, acid hydrolysis is generally employed at present. Acid hydrolysis poses a major problem in the carbohydrate analysis of glycoproteins and other complex heteropolysaccharides associated with proteins. This problem has been studied by several authors,[2,3] most recently by Montreuil and Scheppler[4] and Montreuil and Spik.[5] The stability of the free monosaccharides to hot acid varies considerably. Additional difficulties arise from the interaction of sugars with certain amino acids. The published data indicate that no generalized conditions exist for acid hydrolysis. Each glycoprotein presents a different problem and the optimum conditions for hydrolysis must be ascertained by preliminary experiments.[2,5]

The hexoses are best released by 1N to 2.5N HCl at 100 °C for 1.5–6 hours. The sample was hydrolyzed in 0.3 ml 2N HCl in a vacuum-sealed tube for 2 hours (0.5–1 mg of glycoprotein or tissue extract containing 0.5–3% hexoses). The amino acids and the excess of mineral acid have to be removed by ion exchangers. In routine work 0.3 ml hydrolysate in 1.5–2N HCl is diluted with 0.4 ml of water in a hemolysis tube (12 x 70 mm) and is neutralized with 0.4 g of Amberlite IR-45 (OH⁻ form, 40–60 mesh). The pH of the solution is controlled and resin added, if necessary, to maintain pH 4–5. Using a capillary pipet, the liquid and the washings are transferred to the top of a column (5 x 120 mm) filled with Amberlite CG-120 (H⁺ form, 200–400 mesh) to a height of 40 mm. The effluents are evaporated to dryness in a dessicator over KOH pellets *in vacuo* (< 1 mm Hg).

Experiments carried out with the acetate and formiate form of a strongly basic resin (Amberlite IR 400) to eliminate the Cl⁻ ions[6] gave different retention rates for galactose, glucose and mannose. This could be avoided by a careful washing of the resin bed (30 ml water for 0.6 g resin). The use of Amberlite IR-45 (OH⁻ form) seems to be more advantageous because no selective retention was demonstrated for the three hexoses in the experimental conditions described above, when a washing liquid of 0.8–1 ml water was applied.

Hydrolysis of Glycopeptides

The glycopeptides isolated from the enzymatic hydrolysates may contain about 20–70% hexoses. In the author's experiments 0.05–0.2 mg glycopeptide were hydrolyzed in 0.1 ml 1.5N HCl for 2 hours at 100°C. The hydrolysate, diluted with water to 0.3 ml, is lyophilized in 10 x 100 mm test tubes. The resynthesis of oligosaccharides during the evaporation of HCl-containing hydrolysates at room temperature[2, 4, 5] presents difficulties in the quantitative analysis of sugars present in hydrolysates. Although formation of oligosaccharides can still be detected, no significant alteration of the proportion of hexoses was observed under this condition.[7] To avoid the formation of oligosaccharides, as far as possible, the Cl⁻ ions have to be eliminated before the lyophilization. The latter purification process can be realized by ion exchangers as described in the section above, but the treatment with acid ion exchanger resin may be omitted.

The outlined method of hydrolysis is applicable also to other types of carbohydrate-rich materials containing at least 15–20% hexoses.

Application of the Samples for TLC

The deposited quantity of sugar sample may vary in the range of 0.1–5 μg depending on the chromatographic layer and detection method employed. It should be noted that the determinations based on spectrophotometric evaluation may require 10–20 μg material as in paper chromatography. This problem will be discussed in the section on quantitative determination. For TLC the concentrated sample (aqueous solution of the purified, evaporated hydrolysate) is applied in several 0.2-μl portions on the starting line to assure the required concentration. A Hamilton microsyringe can be used. Application of larger volumes on the chromatographic layer should be avoided.

Chromatography on Inorganic Layers

The TLC of neutral sugars was described first by Stahl and Kaltenbach.[8] Partition chromatography was realized on Kieselguhr G (Merck) impregnated with sodium acetate. Ethyl acetate–isopropanol mixtures served as solvents. Within a short period of time many other chromatographic systems were introduced, as indicated in Tables Ia and Ib.

Table Ia

TLC Methods for the Separation of Sugars on Silica Gel or Kieselguhr

Author	Layer	Solvent
Bancher, Scherz and Kaindl[9]	Silica Gel G 0.1M sodium acetate	ethyl acetate-isopropanol –water (2:7:1)
Inglis[10]	Silica Gel G –dimethylformamide	ether; diisopropylether ether–diisopropylether (1:1)
Pastuska[11] Prey, Berbalk and Kausz[12]	Silica Gel G –0.1N boric acid	benzene–acetic acid– methanol (2:2:6) methyl ethyl ketone–acetic acid–methanol (6:2:2) n-butanol–acetone–water (4:5:1)
Ragazzi and Veronese[13]	Silica Gel G –phosphate buffer pH 8	n-butanol–dioxane–water (4:5:1) n-butanol–acetone–water (4:5:1)
Stahl and Kaltenbach[8]	Kieselguhr G–0.02M sodium acetate	ethyl acetate–isopropanol (65:35) ethyl acetate–isopropanol –water (90:5:5)
	Silica Gel G–0.1M phosphate pH 5.0	n-butanol–acetone–water (4:5:1)
	Silica Gel G –Alusil (1:1)	ethyl acetate–n-propanol –water–acetic acid (4:1:4:1) ethyl acetate–n-propanol –7% aq. ammonia (5:1:4)
Waldi[14]	silica gel–Alusil (1:1) activated at 110°C	n-butanol–acetic acid –water (6:3:1)
Brancher and Bauly[15]	Kieselguhr G	ethyl acetate–isopropanol –water (65:23:12)
Wassermann and Hanus[16]	Kieselguhr G –Silica Gel G (6:4)	ethyl acetate–isopropanol –water (27:3.5:1)

The inorganic supports have the advantage that drastic conditions— *e.g.*, sulfuric acid-containing reagents—may be used, allowing the detection of 0.5 μg sugars. The anisaldehyde–sulfuric acid reagent of Kägi-Miescher employed by Stahl and Kaltenbach[8] (0.5 ml anisaldehyde, 9 ml 95% ethanol and 5 ml sulfuric acid) permits, after heating at 100°C, the identification of sugars on the basis of polychromatic staining (Table II). The naphthoresorcine reagent of Pastuska[11] may also be used. Otherwise, the reagents used in paper chromatography can be employed,

Table Ib

TLC of Sugars on Other Type of Silicate

Author	Layer	Solvent
Grasshof[17]	magnesium silicate	n-propanol–water (1:1) n-propanol–water–propylamine (5:3:2) n-propanol–water–chloroform (6:2:1) n-propanol–water–methyl ethyl ketone (2:1:1)
Hesse and Alexander[18]	celite–Fe oxides (60:6)	
Tore[19]	calcium silicate Silene EF Silene EF–celite	n-butanol–water (100:14) n-butanol–butyl acetate (92:8)
Zhdanow, Dorofenko and Zelenskaya[20]	CaSO$_4$ (plaster of paris)	chloroform–methanol (19:2), (9:1), or (19:3)

but these are less sensitive than the sulfuric acid-containing reagents. A good differentiation is also possible using the aniline–diphenylamine reagent.*

Table II

Polychromatic Detection of Various Mono- and Disaccharides by the Anisaldehyde–Sulfuric Acid Reagent on Kieselguhr Layers Impregnated with Sodium Acetate as Described by Stahl and Kaltenbach[8]

Sugar	Coloration
D-(+)-digitoxose	blue
L-(+)-rhamnose	green
D-(−)-ribose	blue
L-(+)-arabinose	green-yellow
L-(−)-sorbose	violet
D-(−)-fructose	violet
D-(+)-mannose	green
D-(+)-glucose	blue-gray
D-(+)-galactose	green-gray
saccharose	violet
maltose	violet
lactose	green

---

* 20 ml of a solution of 1% aniline + 1% diphenylamine in acetone (stable for one week) is mixed immediately before use with 2 ml conc. H$_3$PO$_4$. After spraying, the plate is heated for 5–10 minutes at 110°C. Chromatograms made with pyridine-containing solvents must be dried 20 minutes at 110°C *before* spraying.

Table Ic

TLC of Sugars on Cellulose

Author	Layer	Solvent
Schweiger[21]	cellulose	ethyl acetate–pyridine–water (2:1:2)
Wolfrom, Patin and de Lederkremer[22]	microcrystalline cellulose Avirin	Solvents used in paper chromatography

Chromatography on Cellulose Layers

On thin-layers of cellulose (Schweiger,[21] and microcrystalline cellulose (Avirin, Table IC Wolfrom *et al.*[29]), the solvents applied in paper chromatography may be used. The time required for the separation varies from 30 minutes to 3 hours depending on the solvent used. The sugars can be detected by the same reagents used in paper chromatography. The Rf-values are comparable to those of paper chromatography. However the TLC technique achieves the result with about one-tenth of the quantity of the substance as needed in paper chromatography.

In experiments,[7] precoated microcrystalline cellulose layers (Schleicher and Schüll, 1440 plates) proved to be uniform and resistant to dipping in alcoholic solvents. The best results were obtained with the following systems:

(a) ethyl acetate–pyridine–acetic acid–water (5:5:1:3)
(b) *n*-butanol–pyridine–0.1N aq HCl (5:3:2, Bourrillon[3, 30])

For the detection of the spots, the plates are dipped in aniline oxalate reagent[25] (mixture of 2 vol of 2% aniline in ethanol and 3 vol of 2.5% oxalic acid in 50% ethanol). The silver nitrate reagent of Travelyan, Proctor and Harrison[26] gives very satisfactory results. The latter

Table Id

TLC of Sugars on Synthetic Polymers

Author	Layer	Solvent
Anderson and Stoddart[23]	Kodak Chromagram V 511 (polycarbonate) 0.2M phosphate pH 6.8	*n*-propanol–ethyl acetate–water (10:3:1) *n*-propanol–ethyl acetate–water (5:1:1)
Birkhofer, Kaiser Meyer-Stoll and Suppan[24]	polyacrylonitrile–polyamide Perlon (7:2)	*n*-amyl alcohol–*n*-propanol–acetic acid–water (3:2:2:1)

technique will be described in the section treating the separation of oligosaccharides.

Chromatography on Thin-Layers of Organic Polymers

Birkhofer *et al.*[24] separated sugars on a mixture of polyacrylonitrile and polyamide. Anderson and Stoddart[23] described the utilization of polycarbonate layers on plastic foils (Kodak Chromagram V 511 sheets Table Id). The latter sorbent does not contain reducing or furfural-forming groups which would interfere with the revelation of monosaccharides based on the reactivity of the reductive function. This property is of interest in the case of quantitative evaluation. In the following experimental conditions, the hexoses, galactose, glucose and mannose are well separated, and xylose, fucose, glucurolactone and N-acetyl-glucosamine may also be identified (Figure 1).

Hexosamines

Hydrolysis of Glycoproteins and of Glycopeptides

Hydrolysis conditions which liberate covalently bound hexosamines are described in several published works.[2,5] In general, the hexosamines need more energic hydrolysis than do the hexoses. In our experiments, the samples were treated in the following way: a glycoprotein or glycopeptide sample containing 2–10 μg amino sugars is hydrolyzed under nitrogen in 0.1–0.2 ml 4N HCl in a sealed tube and in a boiling water bath for 4–8 hours.[27] The hydrolysate is then evaporated to dryness *in vacuo* ($<$ 1 mm Hg) over KOH pellets. No appreciable decomposition of amino sugars could be demonstrated. The hydrolysates of the glycoproteins treated in analogous manner, *i.e.*, without purification of the acid hydrolysates gave in the most cases satisfactory results.

Separation by TLC

Stahl and Kaltenbach[28] first realized the separation of glucosamine and galactosamine on a 1:1 mixture of Silica Gel G and aluminum oxide, activated for 30 minutes at 110°C, in the solvent *n*-propanol–ethyl acetate–water–25% ammonia (5:5:1:3). The following solvents were used for the air-dried layer: *n*-propanol–ethyl acetate–water–25% ammonia (6:1:3:1) or *n*-butanol–acetic acid–water (6:3:1). Wolfrom *et al.*[29] preferred the microcrystalline cellulose (Avirin) layers for the separation of hexosamines with solvents used in paper chromatography. The authors obtained good results on microcrystalline cellulose (Schleicher & Schüll plates 1440) by using *n*-butanol–pyridine–0.1N aq HCl (5:3:1) according to Bourrillon[30,3] as well as by the system of Fischer and Nebel[31] who used pyridine–ethyl acetate–acetic acid–water (5:5:1:3).

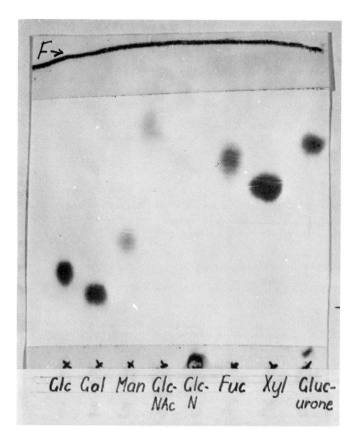

Figure 1. The distribution of the spots on a chromatogram of about 0.5 μg of different monosaccharides on Kodak Chromagram V 511 sheets. Solvent: ethyl acetate–*n*-propanol–water (1:5:1). The sugars were detected by dipping in AgNO₃-NaOH.[26, 52]

A routine separation of 0.1–1.5 μg glucosamine and galactosamine may be realized on precoated sheets (Kodak Chromagram V 511) impregnated with 0.2M phosphate buffer at pH 6.8 when ethanol–25% ammonia–water (80:2:18) is used as the solvent (Moczar *et al.*[27]).

QUANTITATIVE DETERMINATION OF NEUTRAL AND AMINO SUGARS BY TLC

The intensity of the color of a revealed spot may be measured by the procedures used in paper chromatography (Montreuil, Spik and Konarska[32]):

(1) visual estimation
(2) planimetry
(3) densitometry and fluorometry
(4) spectrophotometric or volumetric determination of the eluted chromophore.

The general details of these experimental techniques have been treated by Stahl[33] and will not be discussed here.

TLC may be suitable for the determination of the ratio of 0.1–2 μg of separated substances, using photodensitometry in transmittance and thin-layers of maximal uniformity (Privett, Blank and Lundberg,[34] Lugg[35]). However, the determination of the absolute values of 1 μg sugar cannot actually be achieved with acceptable accuracy at present.

The spectrophotometric determination of the eluted chromophore or chromogen would yield the desired precision for absolute determination, but, depending on the sensitivity of the spectrophotometric method, 10–20 μg substance are required. In this way, the concentration limits are the same as those in paper chromatography.

Densitometric Determination of Neutral Sugars and Osamines

Lamkin, Ward and Walborg[36] determined that galactose, glucose, mannose, rhamnose and fructose separated on cellulose (Macherey and Nagel MN 300) with an accuracy of s = ± 3.4–9.5%. The chromatogram run in the upper phase of ethyl acetate–pyridine–water (2:1:2) was sprayed with aniline phtalate reagent (0.05M in water-saturated *n*-butanol and treated during 10 minutes at 105°C. The spots were evaluated at 389 mμ with a sensitivity of 3 μg.

Moczar *et al.*[27] adopted Kodak Chromagram V 511 sheets (Anderson and Stoddart[23]) for the determination of the molar ratio of galactose, glucose, mannose, fucose, galactosamine, and glucosamine present in glycoproteins and in tissue hydrolysates.[37] As mentioned in this report, the absence of reducing groups in this type of thin-layer sheet increases the reproducibility of the sensible formazan method of Wallenfels.[38, 39] This fact permits the photodensitometric evaluation of 0.1–2 μg hexoses and 0.1–1.5 μg hexosamines.

Experimental Conditions

Samples containing about ten times the quantity necessary for one chromatogram—2–10 μg of each sugar component, are hydrolyzed in 0.2–0.4 ml of 2N or 4N HCl, as described above (pp. 170, 175). The hydrolysates treated by ion exchangers represent a volume of about 3 ml. This sample is evaporated *in vacuo* over KOH pellets in a conical centrifuge tube. The residue on the vessel wall is washed to the bottom of the tube with 3 x 5 μl of water.

The dried residue is dissolved in 20 μl of water. One to two μl of this solution are applied in 0.2-μl portions (spot diameter 5–6 mm). The starting line is about 15 mm from the lower edge of the sheet. Eastman Kodak Chromagram V 511 sheets (10 × 10 cm) impregnated with 0.2M phosphate buffer at pH 6.8 were used with solvents *n*-propanol–ethyl acetate–water (5:1:1) for the hexoses and ethanol–25% ammonia–water (85:0.5:14.5) for the hexosamines. The spots were detected by triphenyl-tetrazolium-chloride (TTC)[38,39] as follows: The air-dried sheets are dipped in a freshly prepared 1:1 mixture of 1% ethanolic TTC solution and of 1% methanolic sodium hydroxide and heated at 90°C in a water-saturated atmosphere for 15 minutes. The color intensity of the red spots is measured on the cut strips by a recording photodensitometer. The surface of the peak area is calculated by multiplying the height of the peak by its width at midheight.

Chromatograms and corresponding densitometric recordings of the hydrolysates of the glycopeptides derived from the enzymatic hydrolysis of structural glycoproteins,[40] from the stroma of the rabbit cornea,[41] from the media of porcine aorta[42,43] and a reference mixture of galactose, glucose and mannose are illustrated in Figure 2. The intensity of the coloration is proportional to the concentration applied in the range

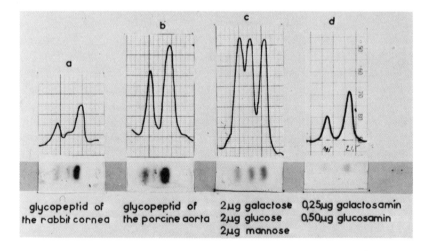

| glycopeptid of the rabbit cornea | glycopeptid of the porcine aorta | 2μg galactose 2μg glucose 2μg mannose | 0,25μg galactosamin 0,50μg glucosamin |

Figure 2. Chromatograms of hydrolysates of glycopeptides isolated from the structural glycoproteins of rabbit cornea (a), porcine aorta (b) and of standard mixtures of hexoses (2 μg galactose, 2 μg glucose, 2 μg mannose) (c), and hexosamines (0.25 μg of galactosamine, 0.50 μg of glucosamine) (d).[27] Reproduced from Reference 27 by permission of Elsevier Publishing Co., Amsterdam.

Table III

The Ratio of Galactose, Glucose, Mannose, and Fucose
in a Typical Run of Five Samples on the Same Sheet

Sample No.	Galactose	Glucose	Mannose	Fucose
1	1.00	1.08	0.95	0.82
2	1.02	1.10	1.02	0.67
3	0.95	1.02	0.95	0.61
4	1.06	1.07	1.06	0.82
5	1.03	1.08	0.97	0.74
Amount added (μg)	1.5	1.5	1.5	1.5
Standard error of the mean	± 1.4%	± 2.4%	± 1.7%	± 5.4%

of 0.2–2 μg of hexose (Figure 3). When a densitometer with a lower slit length is used, 0.05–0.1 μg hexose can be estimated. In this case the samples have to be applied as small spots and not as short lines. The color given by the fucose is less intense than that of the hexoses. Five samples composed of a 1:1:1:1 mixture of 1.5 μg galactose, glucose, mannose and fucose were analyzed and the results are shown in Table III. The standard error of the means is about ± 1.43–2.37% for the hexoses, and ± 5.4% for fucose. The hexose ratios were remarkably constant.

The glucosamine and the galactosamine are well-resolved with the solvent described (Figure 2d). The color yield of glucosamine is somewhat higher than that of galactosamine and galactose, ratios 1:0.9 and

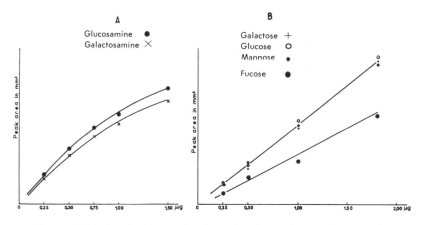

Figure 3. (a) Standard curve for the estimation of hexosamines, obtained as described in the text. Abscissa: μg of hexosamine applied. Ordinate: area of the densitometric recording in mm². (b) Standard curve for the estimation of hexoses.[27] Reproduced from Reference 27 by permission of Elsevier Publishing Co., Amsterdam.

1:0.8-0.7 respectively. The standard curve obtained with glucosamine and galactosamine in a typical experiment is represented in Figure 3. Although the correlation is not strictly linear, the method is suitable for quantitative determination up to 1.5 μg hexosamine. The standard error of the means of 5 repeated determinations was similar to that given for the hexoses ($\pm 2\%$).

GlcN   GalN

Hydrolysate of the entire exterior cornea of the whiting.

GlcN   GalN

Hydrolysate of the mucopolysaccharide-protein complex precipitated from the extract of the exterior cornea of the whiting.

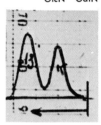

Figure 4. Densitometric recording of chromatograms of glucosamine and the galactosamine from a hydrolysate of the cornea of whiting, and the mucoprotein isolated thereof. Layer: Kodák Chromagram V 511, impregnated with 0.02M phosphate, pH 6.8; solvent: ethanol–water–25% ammonia (85:14:1), spots detected by TTC. Densitometry was carried out with a Photovolt recording densitometer.

For the estimation of the ratio of glucosamine and galactosamine, the crude hydrolysate of glycopeptides or glycoproteins, and in most cases even of tissues, can be used without further purification. Figure 4 illustrates, for example, the densitometric recordings of the chromatograms of the hydrolysate of the whiting cornea and of the purified mucoprotein fraction isolated from it.[37]

For the evaluation of molar proportion in unknown samples, standard sugar mixtures should always run on the same sheet. Amino acids and amino sugars in the amount that occur in the hydrolysate of glycopeptides did not interfere with the analysis of neutral sugars.

The application of this technique for structural considerations of the comparative determination of molar ratios of monosaccharides in the partial (see below) and total hydrolysate could be mentioned. The results may reveal the sequence analysis of the carbohydrate chains.

Spectrophotometric and Volumetric Determination after Elution

There are two different ways to perform spectrophotometry: (1) the color is developed on the plate, the localized zone is removed by scraping, and the chromophore determined by colorimetry after elution, and (2) the zone corresponding to the investigated substance is localized by the aid of a side strip. The nonrevealed sugar or its derivative is eluted and determined by spectrophotometry or volumetry.

Elution of the Spots

Wolfrom, de Lederkremer, and Schwab[44] separated the hexoses on microcrystalline cellulose layer pretreated with sodium borohydride in order to eliminate the interference of reducing groups present in the chromatographic support. The spots detected by aniline phthalate are scraped off and this material is retreated with 0.5 ml of the same reagent at 105–110°C for 1 hour in order to obtain a more intense coloration. Afterwards, the chromophore developed in these two steps is eluted by 4 ml acetone containing 4% HCl. After centrifugation, the color intensities are read at 360 mμ.

Bancher, Scherz and Kaindl[9] preferred silical gel layers and solvents described in the preceding sections. The sugars revealed by the benzidine reagent are eluted, and the eluate is heated with the same reagent. The absorption is measured at 350 mμ.

Elution of the Nondetected Sugars

On cellulose layers, Vomhoff, Truitt and Tucker[45] detected, separated and localized sugars in their eluate, free from cellulose fibers. The color was developed by the anthrone–sulfuric acid reagent. Tholey and Wurtz[46] described a similar procedure. Finally, Pastuska[11] applied the iodometry to the sugars eluted from Silica Gel G layers.

SEPARATION OF SUGARS AND THEIR DERIVATIVES FORMED BY PARTIAL HYDROLYSIS OF HETEROPOLYSACCHARIDES

A rapid and sensible method such as TLC to separate and identify the oligosaccharides present in partial hydrolysates seems to be of interest, but the potential and limit of this process have to be considered. The chromatographic pattern of the oligosaccharides can be related to the heteropolysaccharide structure, thus yielding useful information about glycoproteins with a complex carbohydrate chain. At present, oligosaccharides with a known structure are hardly available as reference substances, and their identification is possible by TLC in only a few cases.

There are three methods of partial hydrolysis for heteropolysaccharides: (1) application of diluted mineral acids; (2) use of strong acid ion exchanger; and (3) acetolysis by the mixture of acetic anhydride and acetic acid in the presence of mineral acids.

Partial Hydrolysis with Mineral Acids

According to experimental data,[47,5] the yield in oligosaccharide is very poor by this method. However, the process has practical application, e.g., the elucidation of the type of carbohydrate-peptide linkage in the glycoproteins. It is thus possible to obtain a relatively selective cleavage of glycopeptides with an aspartamido-glycosaminic linkage yielding the 2-acetamido-1-(L-β-aspartamido)-1,2-dideoxy-β-D-glucose.[48,49,50]

Detection of the Aspartamido-Glucosaminic Linkage

One to three mg of glycopeptide are hydrolyzed with 3 ml of 2N H_2SO_4 at 100°C for 20 minutes. The diluted hydrolysate is neutralized with saturated $Ba(OH)_2$ solution. Then 10% acetic acid is added to achieve pH 5. The slurry is centrifuged and the supernatant evaporated to dryness *in vacuo*. The residue is submitted to high voltage electrophoresis in pyridine–acetic acid–water (25:1:225) at pH 6.3 or in 0.25N acetic acid at pH 2.6. After localization of the fractions with ninhydrin on the side strips, the region corresponding to the asparagine and to the neutral amino acids is eluted. The eluted mixture of peptides is separated on microcrystalline cellulose (Schleicher and Schüll 1440 plates). The chromatograms are carried out in a continuous-flow-chamber[51] for 36 hours, using the following solvents: n-butanol–acetic acid–water (12:3:5) and n-butanol–pyridine–water (6:4:3).[48]

The $R_{asparagine}$ value of the 2-acetamido-1-(L-β-aspartamido)–1,2-dideoxy-β-D-glucose is 0.70 in the first solvent and 0.91 in the second one.[43]

The dried plates were dipped in dimethylamine–methyl ethyl ketone–ethanol (0.1:1:98) mixture and dried with hot air. The spots were then detected with ninhydrine (0.2% in ethanol) in the usual manner. The 2-acetamido-1-(L-β-aspartamido)–1,2-dideoxy-β-D-glucose appears as a characteristic orange-brown spot.[48,43]

Partial Hydrolysis by Ion-Exchanger Resin and Chromatography

Montreuil *et al.*[47] originally carried out the partial hydrolysis of heteropolysaccharides of ovomucoid by ion-exchanger resin. Systematic investigations in this field were also carried out by Montreuil *et al.*[5,32] The yields in oligosaccharides are better than those achieved by the use of mineral acids. The authors adapted this technique for 1–5 mg glyco-peptides.[52]

Hydrolysis

One to three mg of the sample are dissolved in 0.5–1 ml distilled water in 10 x 100-mm test tubes and 50–100 mg resin (Amberlite IR 120, 40–60 mesh in H$^+$ form) are added. The sealed tubes are shaken vigorously in a boiling water bath for one hour. The solution is drained off by a capillary pipet and dried over KOH pellets *in vacuo*. The residue is dissolved in 10 μl water, and 0.5–2 μl of this solution are applied on the plates for the two-dimensional separation.

Chromatography of Partial Hydrolysates

TLC is performed on microcrystalline cellulose (Schleicher and Schüll 1440 plates) and silica gel-coated glass plates in the following solvent systems:

(A) *n*-butanol–acetic acid–water (12:3:5)
(B) pyridine–ethyl acetate–acetic acid–water (5:5:1:3)
(C) pyridine–ethyl acetate–water (2:1:2, upper phase)
(D) *n*-propanol–ethyl acetate–water (7:2:1).

On cellulose layers solvent A is used in the first dimension in a con-tinuous horizontal flow chamber[51] for 24 hours. In the second dimension, solvent B or C is applied in an ordinary tank by the ascending method for 2 or 4 hours respectively. The silica gel layers are treated in the first dimension in the same manner as the cellulose layers. In the second dimension solvent D is used. Even by this method, the yields in oligo-saccharides are relatively poor. To obtain spots of oligosaccharides, the layer is overloaded with the monosaccharides present in the hydrolysate.

Detection of Oligosaccharides

The modified silver nitrate reagent of Trevelyan, Proctor and Harri-son[26] gives satisfactory results. The plates were dipped into a 1% silver nitrate solution (10 ml 10% AgNO$_3$ solution + 90 ml acetone). After-wards, the air-dried plates are dipped in a freshly prepared solution of 0.5% KOH in methanol. The background color can be partially elimi-nated by submerging the revealed plates for 30 seconds in ethanol–25% ammonia (9:1). An analogous treatment with 10% aq Na$_2$S$_2$O$_3$ solution–ethanol (1:1 v/v) also can be employed. The latter technique diminishes the background coloration better.

On silica gel layers, the separation of the oligosaccharides is not as sharp as on microcrystalline cellulose. The following spray-reagent may be used for the detection:

(1) 2N sulfuric acid followed by heating at 140°C for 15 minutes
(2) 3N sulfuric acid– 2% aq. orcinol (1:1 v/v) followed by heating at 110°C for 10–15 minutes. The sugars give different coloration.
(3) the anisaldehyde–sulfuric acid reagent.[8]

Scope and Limitations of the Method

The oligosaccharide mixtures derived from the partial hydrolysis of heteropolysaccharides give typical two-dimensional patterns on thin-layer chromatograms resembling the fingerprints of proteins. From the study of this pattern information concerning the identity of the oligo-saccharide units can be drawn on the structure of the polyosides. After-wards, the identification requires one-dimensional runs in at least three different solvents. The oligosaccharide patterns obtained in standardized conditions from different polysaccharides permit demonstration of the structural differences or similarities, even if most of the oligosaccharides cannot be identified. The complexity of the patterns may indicate the branching and heterogeneity of sugar chains.

The "fingerprints" of polysaccharides built up from repeating units are simple. The *Streptococcus A* polysaccharide,[53] composed of a poly-rhamnosic core attached to N-acetyl-glucosamine side chains (Figure 5) yielded only one important spot in the oligosaccharide region. In comparison, in the partial hydrolysate of an oligomannoside obtained from a glycoprotein of a calf corneal stroma, two different dimannosides were revealed. One of them was identified as a 1,6-dimannoside (Figure 6).[54] Examples of application from various glycoproteins such as ovomu-coid,[55] ovalbumin[48,49,50] and fibrinogen[56] are represented on Figures 7 and 8.

The acylated neuraminic acids (N-acetyl and N-glycoyl—appear as a well-separated spot above the virtual line connecting the galactose and the dimannoside spot.

Acetolysis of the Polysaccharides and TLC of the Products

Acetolysis, as a preparative method was applied at first to the poly-saccharide chains of cellulose.[57,58] However, this experimental technique was introduced only in the last decade for systematic structural studies on polysaccharides.[59,60,61]

Acetolysis

The experimental procedure used for yeast mannans by Stewart and Ballou[60] follows: 0.1 g substance is stirred at 40°C in a mixture of acetic anhydride–acetic acid–concentrated H_2SO_4 (10:10:1 v/v). The re-

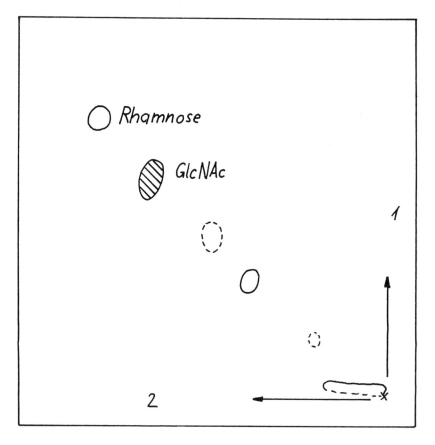

Figure 5. Two-dimensional thin-layer chromatogram of a partial hydrolysate of the *Streptococcus A* polysaccharide (repeating units built up from rhamnose and N-acetyl glucosamine). Layer: microcrystalline cellulose (Schleicher and Schüll 1440 plates). Solvents: (1) butanol–acetic acid–water (12:3:5) and (2) ethyl acetate–pyridine–acetic acid–water (5:5:1:3). The spots were detected by AgNO₃-NaOH.[26]

action is stopped after 13–70 hours by the addition of pyridine in cooling ice water. The acetylated oligosaccharides were extracted from the water-diluted solution with chloroform. The organic layer was washed with water and evaporated to dryness.

TLC of Acetylated Sugar Derivatives

The chromatography of the acetylated oligosaccharides formed by acetolysis of glycopeptides isolated from enzymatic hydrolysates of glycoproteins has not yet been studied. However, the separation of acetylated mono- and disaccharides were reported on magnesium silicate (Magnesol) with various solvent systems as reviewed in Table IV. The following methods are used for detection:

(1) 2–3N sulfuric acid spray followed by heating at 110–140°C for 10–30 minutes
(2) the mixture of 1% KMnO$_4$ and 1% Na$_2$CO$_3$ (1:1 v/v)
(3) the specific revelation method, based on the formation of hydroxamic acid by acetate esters, as described by Tate and

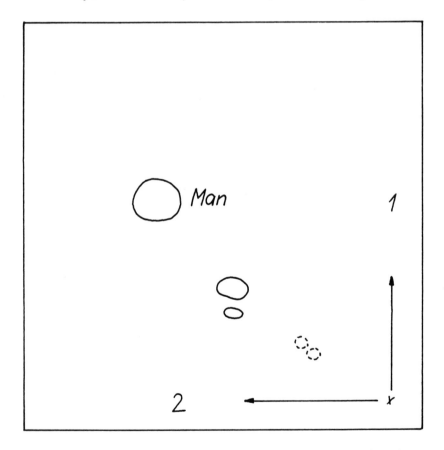

Figure 6. Two-dimensional thin-layer chromatogram of a partial hydrolysate of an oligomannoside, obtained from the glycoprotein fraction of a calf cornea. Experimental conditions: see Figure 5.[52]

Table IV

Separation of Acetylated Sugar Derivatives

Author	Layer	Solvent
Dumazert, Ghiglione and Pugnet[62]	Silica Gel G activated at 140°	benzene–ethyl acetate–ethanol (89:10:1) benzene–ethanol (95:5)
Micheel and Berender[63]	Silica Gel G	cyclohexene–diisopropyl-ether–pyridine (4:4:2)
Tate and Bishop[64]	silica gel	2–10% methanol in benzene
Wolfrom, Muchnik and de Lederkremer[65]	Magnesol (magnesium silicate)	ethyl acetate–pyridine (1:1)

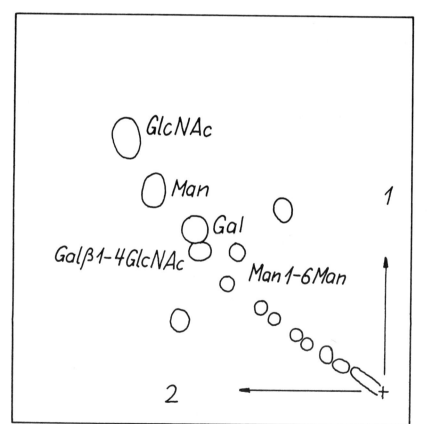

Figure 7. Two-dimensional thin-layer chromatogram of a partial hydrolysate of a crude ovomucoid preparation. Experimental conditions: see Figure 5.[52]

Bishop.[64] The plates are sprayed with a 10% aq. hydroxyl-amine hydrochloride solution and with 20% sodium hydroxide. After drying at 100°C, they are pulverized with 1% aq. ferric nitrate.

Dumazert, Ghiglione and Pugnet[62] revealed the acetyl derivatives by spraying with a 1:1 mixture of 12% hydroxylamine·HCl and 12.5% NaOH in 85% methanol and treating the dried plates with a solution prepared from 20 ml FeCl$_3$ solution, d = 1.26 (350 g/l) and 20 ml concentrated HCl completed to 100 ml with EtOH.

Separation of the Deacetylated Oligosaccharides

The deacetylation can be achieved by barium methylate.[60, 61] The sample is dissolved in dry methanol, and catalytic amounts of barium

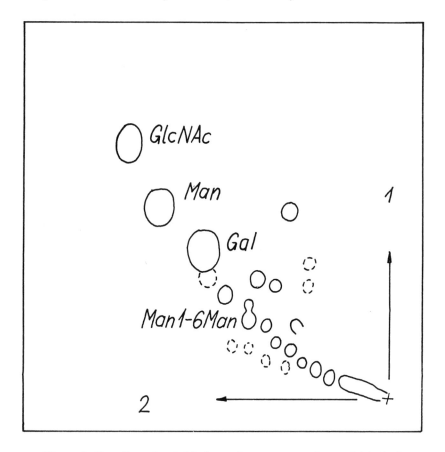

Figure 8. Two-dimensional thin-layer chromatogram of a partial hydrolysate of the glycopeptide mixture, obtained by pronase digestion of fibrinogen and freed from neuraminic acid. Experimental conditions: see Figure 5.[52]

methylate are added. After 15 minutes at room temperature, the Ba^{2+} is removed by the addition of solid carbon dioxide. The methanol is evaporated *in vacuo*. The residue is suspended in water and centrifuged to remove the $BaCO_3$.[60] The deacetylated oligosaccharides can be separated by two-dimensional TLC as described on page 183.

TLC OF METHYLATED SUGARS
Methylation

The classical method of Haworth[66] for structural studies of polysaccharides implies the methylation and identification of methylated monosaccharides. The experimental procedure is difficult and time-consuming. In recent years more advantageous operating conditions have been developed by Kuhn, Baer, and Gauhe,[67] Kuhn, Trischmann[68] and Srivastava *et al.*[69] By the method of Hakomori,[70] a complete methylation of the polysaccharide can be realized in a one-step operation using dimethyl sulfoxide (DMSO) as the solvent in the presence of dimethyl sulfinyl carbanions. Methyliodide serves as the methylating agent. From the reaction medium diluted with water the methylated polysaccharides are extracted with chloroform.

Frequently, certain polysaccharides and glycopeptides are barely soluble in DMSO or dimethylformamide (DMF). In order to achieve the methylation of these substances, the experiment may be carried out in suspension in DMSO or DMF according to Kuhn *et al.*[67,68] or Srivastava *et al.*[69] The partially methylated product is isolated from the water-diluted reaction mixture by chromatography on Sephadex G-25 columns. The substances separated are usually soluble in DMF or DMSO, and the methylation can be accomplished in the second step in a homogenous phase. This technique was reported for the methylation of bacterial polysaccharides[71] as well as the glycopeptides isolated from the different glycoproteins.[72,73]

Hydrolysis of Methylated Polysaccharides

Different mixtures of diluted acids[74,75,76,77] are recommended for hydrolysis in order to avoid the slight demethylating action of the diluted HCl. A two-step procedure gives good results: the sample is treated in a sealed tube with 90% formic acid at 100°C for one hour, and the cooled hydrolysate is diluted 1:4 with water or with 0.2N HCl. The hydrolysis is completed by heating the solution in the resealed tube in a boiling water bath for four hours. The samples are evaporated in a dessicator *in vacuo* ($<$ 1 mm Hg) over KOH pellets.

Chromatography of Partially Methylated Sugars

Inorganic layers are suitable for the separation of sugar methyl ethers in view of their considerably reduced hydrophilic character during methylation. Wolfrom, Muchnik, and de Lederkremer[65] report the use of magnesium silicate (Magnesol) layers. The following derivatives were separated in the solvent benzene–methanol (93:7):2,3,6-tri-O-methyl-mannose; 2,3,6-tri-O-methyl-D-glucose; 2,3,4,6-tetra-O-methyl-D-glucose; and 2,3,4,6-tetra-O-methyl-D-galactose. Wallenfels *et al.*[78] employed benzene–ethanol (200:40) on Silica Gel G.

The distinction of the α- and β-anomers of methylglycosides of methylated sugars is possible on activated silica gel according to Gee.[79] The monosaccharide derivatives are separated with diethyl ether–toluene (2:1) and the methylated disaccharides with methylethylketone–toluene (1:1).

Partially methylated monosaccharides prepared by the action of formic acid and diluted HCl on the methylated polysaccharides could be separated on Silica Gel G-coated plates in the following solvents (Moczar and Mester[71]):

(1) methylene chloride–methanol (9:1) for tri- and tetramethyl hexoses
(2) methylene chloride–methanol (8:2) for di- or monomethylated products
(3) methylene chloride–methanol–dimethylamine (75:25:0.2) for methylated hexosamines.

The $R_{\text{tetramethyl glucose}}$ values of some methylated hexose and hexosamine derivatives are reviewed in Table V. The methylated hexoses give sharp spots but the hexosamine methyl ethers give elongated ones.

Rf-Values are subject to considerable variations on silica layers depending on the activity of the layer and atmospheric humidity. The use

Table V

$R_{\text{tetramethyl glucose}}$ (R_{tg}) Values of Some
Methylated Hexose and Hexosamine Derivatives[71]

	Solvent	R_{tg}
2,3,4,6-Tetra-O-methyl-D-glucopyranose	1	1.00
2,3,4,6-Tetra-O-methyl-D-galactopyranose	1	0.93
1,3,4,6-Tetra-O-methyl-D-fructofuranose	1	1.12
2,3,6-Tri-O-methyl-D-glucopyranose	1	0.71
2,3,4-Tri-O-methyl-D-glucopyranose	1	0.60
2,3,4-Tri-O-methyl-D-galactopyranose	1	0.45
2,3-Di-O-methyl-D-glucopyranose	1	0.36
Mono-O-methyl-hexoses	1	0.2–0.1
3,4,6-Tri-O-methyl-D-glucosamine	3	0.82
3-O-Methyl-D-glucosamine	3	0.35

of reference substances is indispensable. The solvent has to be freshly prepared for each run.

The separation by TLC on silica gel of methyl glycosides of the partially methylated hexosamines was recently studied by Monsigny.[80] Benzene–ethanol–water–acetic acid (200:47:15:1) or benzene–ethanol–water–21% aq. ammonia (200:47:15:1) mixtures[81] are described as solvents. The conditions do not permit the separation of all the seven possible anomeric pairs of methylated methyl glucoside of glucosamine, but they do enable rapid orientation.

Detection of Partially Methylated Sugars

Visualization is carried out with the reagents used in paper chromatography: aniline oxalate, *p*-anisidine hydrochloride, or 2N H_2SO_4 at 110–120°C for 10–15 minutes.

Scope and Limitation of the Method

The identification of the partially separated methylated monosaccharides derived from the methylation process is widely applied to the structural investigation on polysaccharides. In this connection, the difficulties of preparation of the reference substances, the isomers of the O-methylated sugars have to be considered.

The tetra-O-methyl derivatives of the monosaccharide units, situated at the nonreducing end positions of the polysaccharide chains, are easily formed. In consequence, the methylation procedure in connection with TLC represents a tool for sugar "nonreducing end group" identification.

CONCLUSION

In this report, experiments were selected in view of their methodical aspect in demonstrating the application of TLC in glycoprotein chemistry. This experimental technique presents a tool for structural investigation on small quantities of oligo- and polysaccharides.

REFERENCES

1. Gottschalk, A., Perspectives Biol. Med. **5**, 327 (1962).
2. Neuberger, A., and R. D. Marschall, "Methods for the Qualitative and Quantitative Analysis of the Component Sugars" *Glycoproteins*, Ed. by A. Gottschalk (Amsterdam: Elsevier, 1966), p 190.
3. Bourrillon, R., and J. Michon, Bull. Soc. Chim. Biol. **41**, 267 (1959).
4. Montreuil, J., and N. Scheppler, Bull. Soc. Chim. Biol. **41**, 13 (1959).
5. Montreuil, J., and G. Spik, *Microdosage des Glucides*, Vol. 2 of *Methodes chromatographiques et électrophorétiques* (Lille: Monogra-

phies du laboratoire de Chimie Biologique de la Faculté des Sciences de Lille, 1968), pp 28–60.

6. Junqua, S., and E. Moczar, Unpublished results.

7. Moczar, E., and M. Moczar, Unpublished results.

8. Stahl, E., and U. Kaltenbach. J. Chromatog. **5**, 351 (1961).

9. Bancher, E., H. Scherz, and K. Kaindl, Mikrochim. Ichnoanal. Acta **1964**, 652 and 1043.

10. Inglis, G. R., J. Chromatog. **20**, 417 (1965).

11. Pastuska, G., Z. Anal. Chem. **179**, 427 (1961).

12. Prey, V., H. Berbalk, and M. Kausz, Microchim. Acta **6**, 968 (1961).

13. Ragazzi, E., and G. Veronese, El. Farmaco, Ed. Prat. **18**, 152 (1963).

14. Waldi, D., J. Chromatog. **18**, 417 (1965).

15. Bracher, C., and L. E. Bauly, Food Manuf. **40**, 38 (1965).

16. Wassermann, L., and H. Hanus, Naturwiss. **50**, 351 (1963). **17**, 488 (1965).

18. Hesse, G., and M. Alexander, Journées Intern. Etude Méthodes Séparation Chromatog. Paris **1961**, 229; and Chem. Abstr. **59**, 3295d (1963).

19. Tore, J. P., J. Chromatog. **12**, 413 (1963).

20. Zhdanow, Y. A., G. N. Dorofenko, and S. V. Zelenskaya, Dokl. Akad. Nauk. USSR **149**, 1332 (1963).

21. Schweiger, A., J. Chromatog. **9**, 374 (1962).

22. Wolfrom, M. L., D. L. Patin, and R. M. de Lederkremer, J. Chromatog. **17**, 488 (1965).

23. Anderson, D. H. W., and J. F. Stoddart, Carbohydrate Res. **1**, 417 (1966).

24. Birkhofer, L., C. Kaiser, H. A. Meyer-Stoll, and F. Suppan, Z. Naturforsch. **17B**, 352 (1962).

25. Partridge, S. M., Biochem. Soc. Symp. (Cambridge, Engl.) **3**, 52 (1949).

26. Travelyan, W. E., D. P. Proctor, and J. S. Harrison, Nature **166**, 444 (1950).

27. Moczar, E., M. Moczar, G. Schillinger, and L. Robert, J. Chromatog. **31**, 561 (1967).

28. Stahl, E., and U. Kaltenbach, "Zucker und Derivate" in Stahl, E., *Dünnschicht-Chromatographie* (Berlin: Springer-Verlag, 1962).

29. Wolfrom, M. L., D. L. Patin, G. Muchnik, and R. M. de Lederkremer, Chem. Ind. **1964**, 1065.

30. Bourrillon, R., Bull. Soc. Chim. France **1965**, 268.

31. Fischer, F. G., and H. G. Nebel, Z. Physiol. Chem. **302**, 10 (1955).

32. Montreuil, J., G. Spik, and A. Konarska, *Microdosage des glucides: Fasc.3. Méthodes chromatographiques de dosage des oses "neutres"* (Lille: Laboratoire de Chimie biologique de la Faculté des Sciences de Lille, 1967).

33. Stahl, E., *Dünnschicht-Chromatographie*, 2nd ed. (Berlin: Springer-Verlag, 1967).

34. Privett, O. S., M. L. Blank, and W. D. Lundberg, J. Am. Oil Chemists' Soc. **38**, 312 (1961).
35. Lugg, J. W. H., J. Chromatog. **10**, 272 (1963).
36. Lamkin, W. M., D. N. Ward, and E. F. Walborg, Anal. Biochem. **17**, 485 (1966).
37. Moczar, E., P. Payrau, and L. Robert, Comp. Biochem. Physiol. **30**, 73 (1969).
38. Wallenfels, K. W., Naturwiss. **37**, 491 (1950).
39. Wallenfels, K. W., E. Berndt, and G. Limberg, Angew. Chem. **65**, 581 (1953).
40. Robert, L., J. Parlebas, P. Oudea, A. Zweibaum, and B. Robert, "Structive and Function of Connective and Skeletal Tissue," in *Proceedings of the Advanced Study Institute*. Ed. by G. R. Tristram (London: Butterworth, 1964), p 406.
41. Moczar, E., and M. Moczar, Exposés Annuels de Biochimie Médicale Paris. In press, 1969.
42. Moczar, M., E. Moczar, and L. Robert, Biochem. Biophys. Res. Commun. **28**, 380 (1967).
43. Moczar, M., FEBS Letters **1**, 169 (1968).
44. Wolfrom, M. L., R. M. de Lederkremer, and G. Schwab, J. Chromatog. **22**, 478 (1966).
45. Vomhof, D. W., J. Truitt, and T. C. Tucker, J. Chromatog. **21**, 355 (1966).
46. Tholey, G., and B. Wurtz, Bull. Soc. Chim. Biol. **46**, 769 (1964).
47. Montreuil, J., A. Adam-Chosson, and G. Spik, Bull. Soc. Chim. Biol. **47**, 1867 (1965).
48. Bogdanov, V., E. Kaverzneva, and A. Andrejeva, Biochim. Biophys. Acta **65**, 168 (1962).
49. Yamashina, J., and J. Makino, J. Biochem. (Tokyo) **51**, 539 (1962).
50. Neuberger, A., and R. D. Marshall, "Linkage between heterosaccharides and peptide chains," in *Glycoproteins*, Ed. by A. Gottschalk (Amsterdam: Elsevier, 1966), p 275.
51. Brenner, M., and A. Niederwieser, Experientia **17**, 237 (1961).
52. Moczar, E., and M. Moczar, Bull. Soc. Chim. Biol. **49**, 1159 (1967).
53. Heymann, H., J. M. Mariello, and S. S. Barkulis, J. Biol. Chem. **238**, 502 (1963).
54. Moczar, E., Unpublished results.
55. Adam-Chosson, A., and J. Montreuil, Bull. Soc. Chim. Biol. **47**, 1880 (1965).
56. Mester, L., E. Moczar, and L. Szabados, C. R. Acad. Sci. (Paris) **265**, 877 (1967).
57. Franchimont, A. P. N., Chem. Ber. **12**, 1941 (1879).
58. Ost, W. Ann. **398**, 331 (1913).
59. Fujimoto, K., K. Matsuda, and K. Aso, Tohoku J. Agr. Res. **13**, 61 (1962).
60. Stewart, T. S., and C. E. Ballou, Biochemistry **7**, 1855 (1968).

61. Montreuil, J., "Colloque sur la biochimie du tissu conjonctif," Paris 1968; in Exposés annuels de biochimie médicale. In press, 1969. in Exposés annuels de biochimie médicale In press, 1969.
62. Dumazert, C., G. Ghiglione, and T. Pugnet, Bull. Soc. Chim. Biol. **1963**, 475.
63. Micheel, F., and O. Berender, Mikrochim. Ichnoanal. Acta **3**, 519 (1963).
64. Tate, M. E., and C. T. Bishop, Can. J. Chem. **41**, 1801 (1963).
65. Wolfrom, M. L., R. Muchnik, and R. M. de Lederkremer, Anal. Chem. **35**, 1357 (1963).
66. Haworth, W. N., J. Chem. Soc. **107**, 8 (1915).
67. Kuhn, R., H. Baer, and A. Gauhe, Chem. Ber. **89**, 2519 (1956).
68. Kuhn, R., and H. Trischmann, Chem. Ber. **96**, 284 (1963).
69. Srivastava, H. C., S. N. Harshe, and P. P. Singh, Indian J. Chem. **1**, 304 (1963).
70. Hakomori, S., J. Biochem. (Tokyo) **55**, 205 (1964).
71. Moczar, E., and L. Mester, Bull. Soc. Chim. Biol. **46**, 881 (1964).
72. Mester, L., E. Moczar, G. Vass, and L. Szabados, Pathol. Biol. Semaine Hop. **13**, 540 (1965).
73. Moczar, E., L. Robert, and M. Moczar, Life Sci. **8**, 757 (1969).
74. Bouveng, H. O., and B. Lindberg, Advan. Carbohydrate Chem. **15**, 53 (1960).
75. Egge, H., Bull. Soc. Chim. Biol. **42**, 1429 (1960).
76. Croon, I., G. Herrström, G. Kull, and B. Lindberg, Acta Chem. Scand. **14**, 1338 (1960).
77. Isbell, H. S., J. L. Frush, B. H. Bruckner, G. N. Kowkabany, and G. Wampler, Anal. Chem. **29**, 1523 (1957).
78. Wallenfels, K., G. Bechtler, R. Kuhn, H. Trischmann, and H. Egge, Angew. Chem. **75**, 1014 (1963).
79. Gee, M., Anal. Chem. **35**, 350 (1963).
80. Monsigny, M., Thèse Université de Lille, Faculté des Sciences, 1968.
81. Hay, G. W., B. A. Lewis, and F. Smith, J. Chromatog. **11**, 479 (1963).

Chapter 7

Layer-Chromatography of Oligonucleotides

by K. H. Scheit

The invention of paper chromatography by Consden, Martin and Gordon[1] was one of the great advances in analytical methods. The chemistry of nucleotides and polynucleotides is scarcely imaginable without this technique. In 1938 the Russian scientists Ismailow and Shraiber[2] reported the application of thin-layer chromatography. But only after Stahl[3,4,5] introduced more convenient techniques and adsorbents for preparations of thin-layers did this method start its triumphant advance. The advantages of this new separation technique—excellent, rapid separations together with high sensitivity—have caused its broad application. Furthermore thin-layer chromatography has the invaluable advantage of using the appropriate adsorbent separations which can be scaled up from analytical to preparative level (Halpaap).[6]

Chromatographical separations of nucleosides and nucleoside polyphosphates on cellulose thin-layers were first reported by Randerath.[7] Since that time a great number of authors described the thin-layer chromatography of this class of substances.[7a] However only a few reports appeared which dealt with the separation of oligonucleotides by means of thin-layer chromatography,[8,9,10]* although in the field of chemical synthesis of oligonucleotides the use of thin-layer chromatography, both for analytical and preparative separation, would mean an important improvement. A series of textbooks and monographs which deal with the theory and applications of thin-layer chromatography are already available.[11]

This article will give a synopsis of layer chromatography of oligonucleotides from the standpoint of an organic chemist working in the field of nucleotide and oligonucleotide chemistry. One of the reasons for writing this article was to make known to organic chemists working on the synthesis of nucleotides and oligonucleotides some new aspects and techniques in separation and isolation of the above mentioned materials. Since most of the discussed work is not yet published in

---

*Very recently the separation of oligonucleotides on PEI-Cellulose has been reported by Randerath.[10a,b]

197

detail, some principle examples together with experimental details will
be presented in this paper, thus allowing colleagues to make use of
silica gel layer chromatography instead of the sometimes more laborious
separation methods. Moreover, the separation of oligonucleotides on
cellulose is also described. The techniques using PEI-cellulose[29, 30] are
not included.

THIN-LAYER CHROMATOGRAPHY OF
OLIGONUCLEOTIDES ON CELLULOSE

Despite the evident advantages of thin-layer chromatography, only
few applications to oligonucleotides have been reported so far. First
Yardon and Sober[8] used ion-exchange electrophoresis on DEAE-cellu-
lose thin-layers for separations of polynucleotides. In model experiments
they were able to separate oligoadenylic acids up to the octanucleotide.
Bergquist[9] reported the characterization of an enzymatic hydrolysate of
E. coli tRNA by means of a two-dimensional thin-layer technique.
Combining electrophoresis and chromatography on a cellulose thin-layer,
he achieved excellent separations of ribooligonucleotides up to tetra-
nucleotides. Recently the same slightly modified method was applied by
Gassen[12] for the analysis of oligonucleotides derived from enzymatic
hydrolysis of phenylalanine tRNA from *E. coli*. Figure 1 gives an example for the two-dimensional separation of such a hydrolysate. Gassen
also discussed the limitations of this technique. The separation on and
the isolation from cellulose thin-layers seems to be possible up to ribo-
hexanucleotides. Above this critical chain length increasing difficulties
with respect to elution from the adsorbent and also immobility of oligonucleotides have been observed.

The above-mentioned applications of thin-layer chromatography are
analytical techniques, because maximal 10–20 optical density units of
oligonucleotides can be separated. Until now the preparative separation
of ribooligonucleotides by layer chromatography in connection with the
chemical synthesis of these substances was impossible since stable cellulose layers of 2-mm thickness could not be prepared. It should also be
noted that thin-layer chromatography of deoxyoligonucleotides on cellulose using solvent systems known from paper chromatography gave no
satisfactory results.[13]

SILICA GEL THIN-LAYER CHROMATOGRAPHY
OF DEOXYOLIGONUCLEOTIDETRIESTERS

The chemical synthesis of deoxyoligonucleotides by the so-called
triester method demands the condensation of a suitably blocked

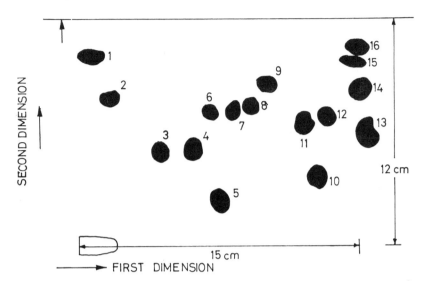

Figure 1. Two-dimensional separation of a ribonuclease digestion of 4 nmoles tRNA (containing 2.6 nmoles tRNAphe from *E. coli* B). First dimension, thin-layer electrophoresis: 0.1M HCOONH₄ (pH 2.50), 1300 V, 50 mA, 50 minutes; second dimension, thin-layer chromatography: isoamyl alcohol–*t*-butanol–0.5M HCOONH₄, pH 3.8 (1:49:50, v/v); 8 h, sheet: 20 x 16 cm, MN polygram 300 cellulose without binder and UV-indicator.

Spot	Composition
1	cytidine-3'-phosphate; Rf = 0.82, Re⁺ = 0
2	adenylyl-(3'-5')-cytidine-3'-phosphate; Rf = 0.62, Re⁺ = 0.01
3	7-methylguanylyl-(3'-5')-cytidine-3'-phosphate; Rf = 0.38, Re⁺ = 0.25
4	adenylyl-(3'-5')-guanylyl-(3'-5')-cytidine-3'-phosphate; Rf = 0.39, Re⁺ = 0.36
5	adenylyl-(3'-5')-guanylyl-(3'-5')-adenylyl-(3'-5')-guanylyl-(3'-5')-cytidine-3'-phosphate; Rf = 0.14, Re⁺ = 0.46
6	guanylyl-(3'-5')-cytidine-3'-phosphate; Rf = 0.55, Re⁺ = 0.44
7	adenylyl-(3'-5')-guanosine; Rf = 0.56, Re⁺ = 0.52
8	nonidentified; Rf = 0.58, Re⁺ = 0.60
9	adenylyl-(3'-5')-uridine-3'-phosphate; Rf = 0.68, Re⁺ = 0.65
10	adenylyl-(3'-5')-guanylyl-(3'-5')-adenylyl-(3'-5')-guanylyl-(3'-5')-uridine-3'-phosphate; Rf = 0.25, Re⁺ = 0.82
11	adenylyl-(3'-5')-guanylyl-(3'-5')-inosine-3'-phosphate; Rf = 0.50, Re⁺ = 0.79
12	5'-phosphorylguanylyl-(3'-5')-cytidine-3'-phosphate; Rf = 0.53, Re⁺ = 0.88
13	guanylyl-(3'-5')-guanylyl-(3'-5')-thymidine-3'-phosphate and guanylyl-(3'-5')-guanylyl-(3'-5')-inosine-3'-phosphate; Rf = 0.44, Re⁺ = 1.02
14	guanylyl-(3'-5')-uridine-3'-phosphate; Rf = 0.66, Re⁺ = 1.00
15	pseudouridine-3'-phosphate; Rf = 0.78, Re⁺ = 0.98
16	uridine-3'-phosphate; Rf = 0.86, Re⁺ = 1.00

Re⁺ distance moved relative to uridine-3'-phosphate (= 1.0).

deoxynucleoside-3'-phosphoric acid ester with the 5'-OH group of a deoxynucleoside. So far deoxynucleotide-(2,2,2)-trichloroethylester,[14] deoxynucleotide-(2)-cyanoethylester,[15] and deoxynucleotidephenylester[16]

Table I

Silica Gel Thin-Layer Chromatography of Deoxyoligonucleotide-(2,2,2)-trichloroethylesters

Composition	Rf-values in solvents		
	1	2	3
5'-O-trityldeoxythymidylyl-(3'-5')-3'-O-acetyldeoxythymidine-trichloroethylester[14]		0.73	
deoxythymidylyl-(3'-5')-3'-O-acetyldeoxythymidine-trichloroethylester[14]			0.40
5'-O-trityldeoxythymidylyl-(3'-5')-deoxythymidine-trichloroethylester[14]			0.43
deoxythymidylyl-(3'-5')-deoxythymidine-trichloroethylester[14]			0.14
5'-O-trityldeoxythymidylyl-(3'-5')-deoxythymidylyl-(3'-5')-deoxythymidine-(tris)-trichloroethylester[18]			0.48
deoxythymidylyl-(3'-5')-deoxythymidylyl-(3'-5')-3'-O-acetyl-deoxythymidine-(tris)-trichloroethylester[18]			0.38
deoxythymidylyl-(3'-5')-deoxythymidylyl-(3'-5')-3'-O-acetyldeoxythymidine-(bis)-trichloroethylester[18]			0.40
5'-O-dimethoxytrityl-N6-benzoyldeoxyadenylyl-(3'-5')-3'-O-methoxyacetyl-N6-benzoyldeoxy-adenosine-trichloroethylester[18]		0.44	
5'-O-dimethoxytrityl-N6-benzoyldeoxyadenylyl-(3'-5')-N6-benzoyldeoxyadenylyl-(3'-5')-N6-benzoyl-3'-O-methoxyacetyl-deoxyadenosine-(bis)-trichloroethylester[18]		0.32	
N6-benzoyldeoxyadenylyl-(3'-5')-N6-benzoyl-3'-O-methoxyacetyldeoxyadenosine-trichloroethylester[18]			0.53
5'-O-dimethoxytrityl-N6-benzoyldeoxyadenylyl-(3'-5')-N6-benzoyldeoxyadenosine-trichloroethylester			0.55

Compound	R_f
5'-0-dimethoxytrityldeoxydenylyl-(3'-5')-deoxyadenosine-trichloroethylester[18]	0.31
deoxyadenylyl-(3'-5')-deoxyadenosine-trichloroethylester[18]	0.20
5'-0-dimethoxytrityl-N[6]-benzoyldeoxyadenylyl-(3'-5')-3'-0-acetyldeoxythymidine-trichloroethylester[18]	0.48
5'-0-dimethoxytrityl-N[6]-benzoyldeoxycytidylyl-(3'-5')-3'-0-acetyldeoxythymidine-trichloroethylester[18]	0.49
5'-0-trityldeoxythymidylyl-(3'-5')-3'-0-acetyl-4-thiodeoxythymidine-trichloroethylester[17]	0.54
deoxythymidylyl-(3'-5')-3'-0-acetyl-4-thio-deoxythymidine-trichloroethylester[17]	0.40
5'-0-trityldeoxythymidylyl-(3'-5')-deoxythymidylyl-(3'-5')-3'-0-acetyl-4-thiodeoxythymidine-(bis)-trichloroethylester[17]	0.63
5'-0-trityl-4-thiodeoxythymidylyl-(3'-5')-deoxythymidylyl-(3'-5')-3'-0-acetyldeoxythymidine-(bis)-trichloroethylester[17]	0.48
5'-0-trityl-4-thiodeoxythymidylyl-(3'-5')-3'-0-acetyldeoxyinosine-trichloroethylester[17]	0.24
5'-0-dimethoxytrityldeoxythymidylyl-(3'-5')-3'-0-acetyldeoxyinosine-trichloroethylester[19]	0.20
4-thiodeoxythymidylyl-(3'-5')-4-thiodeoxythymidylyl-(3'-5')-3'-0-acetyl-4-thiodeoxythymidine-(bis)-trichloroethylester[17]	0.54
4-thiodeoxythymidylyl-(3'-5')-3'-0-acetyl-4-thiodeoxythymidine-trichloroethylester[17]	0.64
5'-0-(bis)-trichloroethylphosphoryldeoxythymidylyl-(3'-5')-3'-0-acetyl-4-thio-deoxythymidine-trichloroethylester[17]	0.56

Chromatography was performed on silica gel thin-layer plates F_{254} (Merck AG, Germany); distances between start and front average 10–15 cm average. Solvent 1: chloroform–methanol (98:2, v/v); solvent 2: chloroform–methanol (95:5, v/v); solvent 3: chloroform–methanol (93:7, v/v).

201

have been used for this purpose. The condensations lead to deoxyoligo-nucleotide triesters which in contrast to normal deoxyoligonucleotides bear no negative charges. It is therefore not astonishing that these substances can be nicely separated by thin-layer chromatography on silica gel using organic solvents.[14, 17] The best solvent system is chloroform–methanol. Increasing amounts of methanol enhance the mobility of these triesters on silica gel thin-layers. It was found convenient to vary the methanol content between 1 and 10%. More methanol often leads to tailing and broadening of the spots. Silica gel containing fluorescence indicator allows one to detect even small amounts of oligonucleotides under UV light. The phosphate reagent from Isherwood and Hanes could not be used to detect phosphate-containing substances on silica gel thin-layers, but oligonucleotide derivatives have been localized on silica gel by staining the thin-layer plates with iodine vapor. Oligonucleotides containing a trityl substituent were detected on silica gel thin-layers after spraying with diluted perchloric acid and warming the thin-layer plate for a short time. Trityl residues showed yellow, monomethoxytrityl residues orange, and dimethoxytrityl groups red colors. Table I gives Rf-values of oligonucleotide-trichloroethylesters in thin-layer chromatography on silica gel in various solvents. It should be emphasized, however, that these Rf-values allow correct identification only together with a chromatographical comparison of a known standard.

PREPARATIVE LAYER CHROMATOGRAPHY OF DEOXYOLIGONUCLEOTIDE TRIESTERS

The principles and advantages of this chromatographical method will be shown in two typical examples.

Synthesis of Deoxythymidylyl-(3'-5')-3'-0-acetyl-4-thiodeoxythymidine-trichloroethylester[17]

5'-0-Trityldesoxythymidine-3'-phosphoric acid trichloroethylester was condensed with 3'-0-acetyl-4-thio-deoxythymidine to the corresponding triester. After acid hydrolysis of the trityl residue, the reaction mixture was chromatographed on 2-mm silica gel layers in chloroform–methanol (95:5, v/v). Figure 2 shows the graphical representation of this separation. In the case of insufficient separations the chromatography was repeated after drying of the silica gel layer. Since one of the starting materials bears a charge, it did not move from the origin and was easily separated. The UV-positive bands were scraped off and the substances eluted with chloroform–methanol (1:1, v/v) from the silica gel. On a silica gel layer of the dimensions 2 x 200 x 1000 mm 1 to 1.5 g of reaction mixture were separated.

Figure 2. Isolation of deoxythymidylyl-(3′-5′)-3′-0-acetyl-4-thiodesoxythymi-dine-trichloroethylester by silica gel layer chromatography. Solvent: chloroform–methanol (95:5, v/v); layer: 2 mm silica gel PF_{254} (Merck AG., Germany)

1   deoxythymidine-3′-phosphate-trichloroethylester
2   deoxythymidylyl-(3′-5′)-3′-0-acetyl-4-thiodeoxythymidine-trichloroethylester
3   3′-0-acetyl-4-thiodeoxythymidine
4   triphenylcarbinol

Synthesis of 5′-0-trityldeoxythymidylyl-(3′-5′)-deoxythymidylyl-(3′-5′)-3′-0-acetyl-4-thiodeoxythymidine-(bis)-trichloroethylester[17]

The condensation of 5′-0-trityldeoxythymidine-phosphoric acid tri-chloroethylester with deoxythymidylyl-(3′-5′)-3′-0-acetyl-4-thiodeoxy-thymidine-trichloroethylester lead under chain elongation to a product which displayed greater mobility as the starting materials.

Figure 3 shows the silica gel layer chromatogram of the reaction mix-ture. The differences between starting material and product are more suitable for separation if preformed blocks are used in the synthesis of oligonucleotide triesters. In this way heptadeoxy-4-thiothymidylic acid-(hexa)-trichloroethylester[17] was synthesized and chromatographed on silica gel after removal of the trityl blocking group. The synthesis of

Figure 3. Isolation of 5′-0-trityldeoxythymidylyl-(3′-5′)-deoxythymidylyl-(3′-5′)-3′-0-acetyl-4-thiodeoxythymidine-(bis)-trichloroethylester by silica gel layer chromatography. Solvent: chloroform–methanol (95:5, v/v); layer: 2 mm silica gel PF$_{254}$ (Merck AG, Germany).

1   5′-0-trityldeoxythymidine-3′-phosphate-trichloroethylester
2   deoxythymidylyl-(3′-5′)-3′-0-acetyl-4-thio-deoxythymidine-trichloroethylester
3   5′-0-trityldeoxythymidylyl-(3′-5′)-deoxythymidylyl-(3′-5′)-
     3′-0-acetyl-4-thiodeoxythymidine-(bis)-trichloroethylester
4 and 5   side products

deoxynucleotides via corresponding triesters allows the rapid and exact separation of these intermediates by silica gel layer chromatography which seems to be superior to column chromatography.

SILICA GEL THIN-LAYER CHROMATOGRAPHY OF OLIGONUCLEOTIDES

Organic chemists working on the synthesis of nucleotides and oligonucleotides grievously missed the application of thin-layer chromatography for rapid identification of the reaction products in often very complex mixtures. Attempts to replace paper chromatography in oligonucleotides synthesis by cellulose thin-layer chromatography have failed.[13] In 1961 Struck and Randerath[7] reported separations of nucleotides and nucleosidpolyphosphates on silica gel thin-layers. But because of the instability of homemade silica gel layers against aqueous solvents, this technique was inferior to paper chromatography. Only when precoated silica gel thin-layer plates were available were sufficient separations of nucleosides, nucleotides, and oligonucleotides achieved using solvent systems known from paper chromatography. All of the advantages which thin-layer chromatography exhibits could be utilized in nucleotide and oligonucleotide chemistry:

(1) high capacity without tailing and broadening of spots
(2) separations can be achieved within 30 to 120 minutes
(3) high sensitivity due to fluorescence indicator
(4) a successful separation of analytical quantities on silica gel thin-layers in most cases means a possible separation in a preparative scale on 2-mm silica gel layers.

The following solvents have been used successfully in silica gel thin-layer chromatography of oligonucleotides and nucleotides:

solvent 1: isopropanol–$NH_4OH_{conc.}$–H_2O (6:3:1, v/v) nucleotides and derivatives, oligonucleotides and derivatives
solvent 2: isopropanol–$NH_4OH_{conc.}$–H_2O (8:1:1, v/v) nucleotideesters, oligonucleotide derivatives
solvent 3:[20] isopropanol–$NH_4OH_{conc.}$–H_2O (7:2.2:2.2, v/v) oligonucleotides
solvent 4:[21, 22, 23] isopropanol–0.5M triethylammonium bicarbonate (9:2, v/v) nucleotide derivatives, oligonucleotide derivatives
solvent 5:[24] isopropanol–0.5M triethylammonium bicarbonate (2:1, v/v) nucleotides, oligonucleotide derivatives
solvent 6:[24] *t*-butanol–0.5M triethylammonium bicarbonate (2:1, v/v) nucleotides and nucleotide derivatives, oligonucleotides
solvent 7:[24] *t*-butanol–0.5M triethylammonium bicarbonate (1:1, v/v) nucleotides and oligonucleotides.

The preceding list shows that all solvents are aqueous systems. So far no nonaqueous solvent mixture can be used to chromatograph the above-mentioned substances on silica gel thin-layers. All solvents, even the buffer-containing mixtures, consist of volatile components, thus allowing chromatography to be repeated after drying of the thin-layer plate. The separations of nucleotides and oligonucleotides obtained by silicia gel thin-layer are at least equivalent to those achieved by paper chromatog-

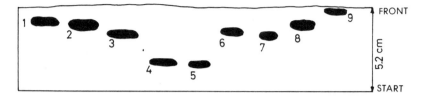

Figure 4. Separation of oligonucleotide and nucleotide derivatives on silica gel. Solvent: *t*-butanol–0.5M triethylammoniumbicarbonate (2:1, v/v); silica gel thin-layer plates F₂₅₄ (Merck AG, Germany).

1   5'-0-trityl-4-thiodeoxythymidylyl-(3'-5')-deoxythymidine
2   5'-0-trityl-4-thiodeoxythymidylyl-(3'-5')-4-thiodeoxythymidine
3   5'-0-trityl-4-thiodeoxythymidylyl-(3'-5')-4-thiodeoxythymidylyl-(3'-5')-4-thiodeoxythymidine
4   4-thiodeoxythymidine-5'-phosphate
5   4-thiouridine-5'-phosphate
6   4-thiodeoxythymidylyl-(3'-5')-deoxythymidine
7   4-thiodeoxythymidylyl-(3'-5')-4-thiodeoxythymidylyl-(3'-5')-4-thiodeoxythymidine
8   5'-0-trityldeoxythymidine-3'-phosphate
9   5'-0-trityldeoxythymidine-3'-phosphate-trichloroethylester

raphy using the same solvents. It seems likely that combination of different solvents in multi-dimensional silica gel thin-layer chromatography will lead to separations of even more complex mixtures of nucleotides and oligonucleotides.

After chromatography, nucleotides and oligonucleotides were eluted from silica gel by water or buffer. It was not determined in which yields the recovery of nucleotides and oligonucleotides took place. However, the characterization of these materials by spectroscopy and enzymatic reactions was not affected by simultaneously eluted traces of fluorescent indicator, binder and silica gel. The only exceptions have been observed with compounds traveling very fast, because most solvents wash colored and fluorescent admixtures into the solvent front.* In some cases it might be advisable to wash silica gel thin-layers of a previous chromatography in solvent 1, 2 or 3. It was mentioned above that thin-layer chromatography of oligonucleotides and nucleotides on silica gel was mostly done in the course of chemical synthesis of these materials. The chromatographic behavior of nucleotides, oligonucleotides and some of their protected intermediates are represented in the following tables and figures.

It is seen from Figure 6 that silica gel thin-layer chromatography was even used to separate reaction mixtures of chemical polymerizations of deoxythymidine-, deoxyadenosine-, and deoxycytidine mono-

---

*One has to remember in this context that silica gel usually contains traces of iron which move with the solvent front in most aqueous solvents.

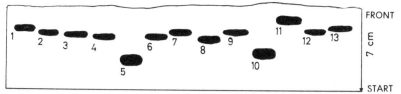

Figure 5. Separation of oligonucleotides on silica gel. Solvent: 2-propanol-NH₄OH$_{conc.}$-H₂O (6:3:1, v/v); silica gel thin-layer plates F$_{254}$ (Merck AG, Germany).

1 tetraadenylyl-(3'-5')-uridine
2 pentaadenylyl-(3'-5)-uridine
3 hexaadenylyl-(3'-5')-uridine
4 heptaadenylyl-(3'-5')-uridine
5 uridine-5'-phosphate
6 deoxythymidylyl-(3'-5')-deoxythymidylyl-(3'-5')-deoxythymidylyl-(3'-5')-deoxythymidine
7 deoxythymidylyl-(3'-5')-deoxycytidylyl-(3'-5')-deoxythymidylyl-(3'-5')-deoxycytidine
8 deoxythymidylyl-(3'-5')-deoxythymidylyl-(3'-5')-deoxyguanylyl-(3'-5')-deoxythymidine
9 deoxythymidylyl-(3'-5')-deoxythymidylyl-(3'-5')-deoxycytidylyl-(3'-5')-deoxythymidine
10 deoxythymidine-5'-phosphate
11 adenylyl-(3'-5')-uridine
12 guanylyl-(3'-5')-uridine
13 thymidylyl-(3'-5')-uridine

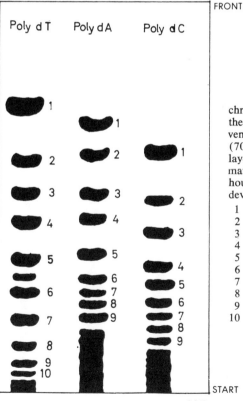

Figure 6. Silica gel thin-layer chromatography of chemically synthesized deoxypolynucleotides. Solvent: n-propanol–NH₄OH$_{conc.}$–H₂O (70:15:25, v/v); silica gel thin-layer plates F$_{254}$ (Merck AG, Germany); after chromatography of 15 hours the plate was dried and again developed for 15 hours.

1 cyclic dinucleotide
2 cyclic trinucleotide
3 dimer
4 trimer
5 tetramer
6 pentamer
7 hexamer
8 heptamer
9 octamer
10 nonamer

Table II

Silica Gel Thin-Layer Chromatography of Ribonucleotides and Oligonucleotides

Composition	Rf in solvent			
	1	2	6	7
uridine-5'-phosphate	0.29		0.22	0.58
4-thiouridine-5'-phosphate	0.32		0.32	
6-thioguanosine-5'-phosphate[25]	0.23			0.37
2-aminopurineriboside-5'-phosphate[25]	0.39			0.48
adenylyl-(3'-5')-uridine	0.65	0.27	0.71	
uridylyl-(3'-5')-guanosine	0.65			
uridylyl-(3'-5')-4-thiouridine[22]	0.55	0.09	0.78	
inosylyl-(3'-5')-4-thiouridine		0.18		
4-thiouridylyl-(3'-5')-4-thiouridine[22]	0.70			
uridylyl-(3'-5')-guanosine-2',3'-cyclophosphate	0.25			
guanylyl-(3'-5')-uridine	0.53	0.10	0.71	

thymidylyl-(3'-5')-uridine[26]	0.55	0.11	0.82
cytidylyl-(3'-5')-inosine	0.66	0.13	
uridylyl-(3'-5')-uridylyl-(3'-5')-adenosine	0.59		
uridylyl-(3'-5')-uridylyl-(3'-5')-uridine-3'-phosphate	0.11		
uridylyl-(3'-5')-1-methylinosine[26]	0.64		
uridylyl-(3'-5')-6-methoxypurineriboside[26]	0.69		
uridylyl-(3'-5')-uridylyl-(3'-5')-inosine-3'-phosphate[27]	0.13		
cytidylyl-(3'-5')-inosine-3'-phosphate[27]	0.30		
adenylyl-(3'-5')-adenylyl-(3'-5')-adenylyl-(3'-5')-uridine[27]	0.60		
tetraadenylyl-(3'-5')-uridine[27]	0.58	0.22	
pentaadenylyl-(3'-5')-uridine[27]	0.54	0.12	0.43
hexaadenylyl-(3'-5')-uridine[27]	0.52	0.05	
heptaadenylyl-(3'-5')-uridine[27]	0.50		

Chromatography was performed on silica gel thin-layer plates F_{254} (Merck AG, Germany); distances between start and front 5–8 cm; the number of solvents corresponds to the description of solvent systems in the text.

Table III

Silica Gel Thin-Layer Chromatography of Deoxynucleotides and Deoxyoligonucleotides

Composition	Rf in solvents						
	1	2	3	4	5	6	7
deoxythymidine-5'-phosphate	0.33				0.50	0.32	0.58
5'-trityldeoxythymidine-3'-phosphate						0.78	
4-thiodeoxythymidine-5'-phosphate[21]	0.33			0.27		0.34	0.66
5'-trityldeoxythymidylyl-(3'-5')-deoxyadenosine[24]		0.41		0.57			
4-thiodeoxythymidylyl-(3'-5')-4-thiodeoxythymidine[17]				0.47		0.68	
5'-0-trityl-4-thiodeoxythymidylyl-(3'-5')-4-thiodeoxythymidine[17]				0.62		0.78	
5'-0-trityl-4-thiodeoxythymidylyl-(3'-5')-4-thiodeoxythymidylyl-(3'-5')-4-thiodeoxythymidine[17]				0.37		0.68	
5'-0-phosphoryldeoxyguanylyl-(3'-5')-3'-0-acetyldeoxythymidine					0.40		
N6-benzoyldeoxyadenylyl-(3'-5')-deoxythymidine					0.96		
5'-0-trichlorethylphosphoryldeoxythymidylyl-(3'-5')-deoxythymidylyl-(3'-5')-deoxyguanosine[28]	0.64				0.68		
5'-0-trichlorethylphosphoryldeoxyadenylyl-(3'-5')-deoxycytidine[24]					0.63		
5'-0-trichlorethylphosphoryldeoxythymidylyl-(3'-5')-deoxythymidylyl-(3'-5')-deoxythymidine[28]	0.58						
5'-0-trichlorethylphosphoryldeoxythymidylyl-(3'-5')-deoxythymidylyl-(3'-5')-deoxyadenosine[28]	0.62						

Compound					
5'-0-trichlorethylphosphoryldeoxythymidylyl-(3'-5')-deoxyguanylyl-(3'-5')-deoxyguanosine[28]	0.53				
4-thiodeoxythymidylyl-(3'-5')-4-thiodeoxythymidylyl-(3'-5')-4-thio-deoxythymidine[17]				0.65	
deoxythymidylyl-(3'-5')-deoxythymidylyl-(3'-5')-deoxythymidylyl-(3'-5')-deoxythymidine	0.51	0.24	0.80	0.50	
deoxythymidylyl-(3'-5')-deoxycytidylyl-(3'-5')-deoxythymidylyl-(3'-5')-deoxycytidine	0.55				0.27
deoxythymidylyl-(3'-5')-deoxythymidylyl-(3'-5')-deoxycytidylyl-(3'-5')-deoxythymidine	0.52				0.45
5'-0-trichlorethylphosphoryl-N6-benzoyldeoxyadenylyl-(3'-5')-N6-benzoyldeoxyadenosine[24]		0.43			
5'-0-phosphoryl-N6-benzoyldeoxyadenylyl-(3'-5')-deoxythymidine		0.10			
5'-0-phosphoryl-N4-benzoyldeoxycytidylyl-(3'-5')-deoxythymidine		0.10			
5'-0-(bis)-trichlorethylphosphoryldeoxythymidylyl-(3'-5')-3'-acetyl-deoxythymidine[24]		0.67			
5'-methyldeoxycytidylyl-(3'-5')-5-methyldeoxythymidylyl-(3'-5')-5-methyldeoxycytidine[24]	0.70				
deoxythymidylyl-(3'-5')-deoxythymidylyl-(3'-5')-deoxyguanylyl-(3'-5')-deoxythymidine	0.47		0.68	0.48	

Chromatography was performed on silica gel thin-layer plates F$_{254}$ (Merck AG, Germany); distances between start and front 5–8 cm; the number of solvents corresponds to the description of solvent systems in the text.

phosphates.[20] Despite enhanced separation times (10–20 hours),* thin-layer chromatography, when compared with paper chromatography, led to sharper and faster resolution of the oligomers. The polymeric mixtures were fractionated up to octa- and nonanucleotides.

PREPARATIVE LAYER CHROMATOGRAPHY OF NUCLEOTIDES AND OLIGONUCLEOTIDES

An enumeration of nucleotides and nucleotide-derivatives which were isolated by preparative silica gel layer chromatography follows:

nucleotides: 5′-phosphates of 4-thiouridine, 4-thiothymidine, 4-thiodeoxythymidine and 5-methylcytidine.
nucleotide derivatives: nucleotide-morpholidates; nucleotide-imida-zolidates, nucleotide-(2)-cyanoethylesters; nucleotide-(2,2,2)-tri-chloroethylesters; nucleotides protected by acid or base labile block-ing groups (*e.g.*, trityl-, methoxytrityl-, ethoxymethylene-, ethoxy-ethylene-, tetrahydropyranyl-, acetyl- or benzoyl residues).

The solvents used in these separations are identical with those which were employed for analytical purposes. Silica gel layers of the dimensions 1000 x 200 x 2 mm were found capable of resolving 0.5–1.0 g nucleo-tide material. In general the isolated products are contaminated to some extent with silica gel, which was removed by filtration or centrifugation of concentrated aqueous or methanolic solutions. It was often observed that substances isolated by silica gel layer chromatography tended to crystallize more easily than those separated on cellulose.[17] The separation of chemically synthesized oligonucleotides by silica gel layer chromatog-raphy means an enormous facilitation in oligonucleotide chemistry. This new technique was first used to separate the reaction products of a large scale stepwise synthesis of oligo-4-thiodeoxythymidylates.[17] The separa-tions of these oligomers were excellent and furnished very pure materials, which started to crystallize up to the tetranucleotide. As mentioned in the preceding chapter, the reaction products of chemical polymerizations of deoxynucleotides have been chromatographed on silica gel thin-layers. Oligothymidylates derived from the chemical polymerization of deoxy-thymidine-5′-phosphate, even in a preparative scale, were separated on silica gel layers up to the decanucleotide.[20] The oligomers were eluted from silica gel with dilute ammonia and characterized by enzymatic hydrolysis.

---

*Editors' note: Other commercially available precoated silica gel layers, *e.g.*, from Macherey, Nagel & Co., Düren (W. Germany), do not show the most unfavorable effect of decreased flow rate of solvent.

ACKNOWLEDGMENT

It is a pleasant duty to thank my colleagues Drs. F. Eckstein, R. Helbig, J. R. Runyon, and Miss E. Gaertner for their generous support and Prof. F. Cramer for his kind interest.

REFERENCES

1. Consden, R., A. H. Gordon, and A. I. P. Martin, Biochem. J. **40**, 33 (1946).
2. Ismailow, N. A., and M. S. Shraiber, Farmatsiya (Sofia) **1938**, 1.
3. Stahl, E., Arch. Pharm. (Berlin) **292**, 411 (1959).
4. Stahl, E., Arch. Pharm. (Berlin) **293**, 531 (1960).
5. Stahl, E., Chemiker Ztg. **82**, 323 (1958).
6. Halpaap, H., Chem. Ingr.-Tech. **35**, 488 (1963).
7. Randerath, K., Biochem. Biophys. Res. Commun. **6**, 452 (1962).
7a. Pataki, G., Advan. Chromatogr. **7**, 47 (1968).
8. Yaron, A., and H. A. Sober, Anal. Biochem. **12**, 173 (1965).
9. Bergquist, P. L., J. Chromatog. **19**, 615 (1965).
10. Scheit, K. H., Biochim. Biophys. Acta **134**, 217 (1967).
10a. Randerath, E., and K. Randerath, J. Chromatog. **31**, 348 (1967).
10b. Randerath, K., and E. Randerath, J. Chromatog. **31**, 500 (1967).
11. Stahl, E., *Dünnschichtchromatographie* (Berlin: Springer-Verlag, 1962); Pataki, G., *Techniques of Thin-Layer Chromatography in Amino Acid and Peptide Chemistry* (Ann Arbor, Michigan: Ann Arbor Science Publishers, 1968); and Randerath, K., *Dünnschichtchromatographie* (Weinheim/Bergstr: Verlag Chemie, 1965).
12. Gassen, H. G., J. Chromatog. **39**, 147 (1969).
13. Scheit, K. H., Unpublished results.
14. Eckstein, F., and I. Rizk, Angew. Chem. **79**, 684 (1967); Angew. Chem. Intern. Ed. **6**, 695 (1967).
15. Letsinger, R. L., and K. V. Ogilvie, J. Am. Chem. Soc. **89**, 4801 (1967).
16. Reese, C. B., and R. Saffhill, Chem. Commun. **1968**, 767.
17. Scheit, K. H., and H. Petersen-Borstel, 5th Intern. Symp. Chem. Nat. Prod. Abstract **1968**, 458.
18. Eckstein, F., and I. Rizk, Chem. Ber. **102**, 2362 (1969).
19. Scheit, K. H., Unpublished results.
20. Hoffart, G., Thesis, Braunschweig, 1968.
21. Scheit, K. H., Chem. Ber. **101**, 1141 (1968).
22. Scheit, K. H., Biochim. Biophys. Acta **166**, 285 (1968).
23. Franke, A., K. H. Scheit, and F. Eckstein, Chem. Ber. **101**, 2998 (1968).
24. Scheit, K. H., Unpublished results.
25. Scheit, K. H., Manuscript in preparation, 1969.
26. Holy, A., and K. H. Scheit, Chem. Ber. **99**, 3778 (1966).

27. Gaertner, E., Max Planck Institute for Experimental Medicine, Göttingen. Substances provided, 1969.
28. Franke, A., F. Eckstein, K. H. Scheit, and F. Cramer, Chem. Ber. 101, 944 (1968).

Appendix

CONVERSION OF RF-VALUES TO R_M-VALUES

Rf-Values are directly measurable and are used widely for the documentation of the behavior of substances in TLC. However, the derived quantity, the R_M-value

$$R_M = \log \left(\frac{1}{Rf} - 1 \right)$$

is directly related to the distribution coefficient of the sample. On the basis of R_M-values it is sometimes possible to elucidate the structure of the chromatographed substance (see Chapter 1 in this volume) as well as to standardize adsorbents[1] and to compare chromatographic data from different laboratories or different separations (different plates).[1] For the latter purpose the $R_{M(1)}$-values from the one laboratory are plotted versus the $R_{M(2)}$-values of the other laboratory. Usually a straight line is obtained according to the equation

$$R_{M(1)} = a + b\, R_{M(2)}$$

where a and b are constants.

It should be emphasized that experimental Rf-values may differ from theoretical Rf-values for several reasons: the amount of mobile phase per gram adsorbent decreases in a characteristic way along the direction of solvent flow from immersion line to solvent front (solvent profile);[2,3] and the observed Rf-values are smaller than the theoretical values (which are related to a constant phase ratio):

$$Rf_{observed} \cdot \xi = Rf_{theoretical}$$

ξ is a correction factor[2] which is nearly independent of Rf. (However, for very quick moving substances ξ approaches the value 1.0.) In con-

Rf to R_M Conversion Table[9]

hRf	0	1	2	3	4	5	6	7	8	9
00	∞	3.000	2.698	2.522	2.396	2.299	2.219	2.152	2.093	2.042
01	1.996	1.954	1.916	1.881	1.848	1.817	1.789	1.762	1.737	1.713
02	1.690	1.669	1.648	1.628	1.609	1.591	1.574	1.557	1.540	1.525
03	1.510	1.495	1.481	1.467	1.453	1.440	1.428	1.415	1.403	1.392
04	1.380	1.369	1.358	1.347	1.337	1.327	1.317	1.307	1.297	1.288
05	1.279	1.270	1.261	1.252	1.243	1.235	1.227	1.219	1.211	1.203
06	1.195	1.187	1.180	1.172	1.165	1.158	1.151	1.144	1.137	1.130
07	1.123	1.117	1.110	1.104	1.097	1.091	1.085	1.079	1.073	1.067
08	1.061	1.055	1.049	1.043	1.038	1.032	1.026	1.021	1.015	1.010
09	1.005	1.000	0.994	.989	.984	.979	.974	.969	.964	.959
10	.954	.949	.945	.940	.935	.931	.926	.922	.917	.913
11	.908	.904	.899	.895	.891	.886	.882	.878	.874	.869
12	.865	.861	.857	.853	.849	.845	.841	.837	.833	.829
13	.826	.822	.818	.814	.810	.807	.803	.799	.796	.792
14	.788	.785	.781	.778	.774	.770	.767	.764	.760	.757
15	.753	.750	.747	.743	.740	.736	.733	.730	.727	.723
16	.720	.717	.714	.711	.707	.704	.701	.698	.695	.692
17	.689	.685	.682	.679	.676	.673	.670	.667	.665	.662
18	.659	.656	.653	.650	.647	.644	.641	.638	.635	.633
19	.630	.627	.624	.621	.619	.616	.613	.610	.607	.605
20	.602	.599	.597	.594	.591	.589	.586	.583	.580	.578
21	.575	.572	.570	.567	.565	.562	.560	.557	.555	.552
22	.550	.547	.545	.542	.540	.537	.535	.532	.530	.527
23	.525	.523	.520	.518	.515	.513	.511	.508	.506	.503
24	.501	.499	.496	.494	.491	.489	.487	.484	.482	.479
25	.477	.475	.472	.470	.468	.465	.463	.461	.459	.456
26	.454	.452	.450	.447	.445	.443	.441	.439	.436	.434
27	.432	.430	.428	.425	.423	.421	.419	.417	.414	.412
28	.410	.408	.406	.404	.402	.399	.397	.395	.393	.391
29	.389	.387	.385	.383	.381	.378	.376	.374	.372	.370
30	.368	.366	.364	.362	.360	.357	.355	.353	.351	.349
31	.347	.345	.343	.341	.339	.337	.335	.333	.331	.329
32	.327	.325	.323	.321	.319	.317	.316	.314	.312	.310
33	.308	.306	.304	.302	.300	.298	.296	.294	.292	.290
34	.288	.286	.284	.282	.280	.278	.277	.275	.273	.271
35	.269	.267	.265	.263	.261	.259	.258	.256	.254	.252
36	.250	.248	.246	.244	.242	.240	.239	.237	.235	.233
37	.231	.229	.227	.225	.224	.222	.220	.218	.217	.215
38	.213	.211	.209	.207	.205	.203	.202	.200	.198	.196
39	.194	.192	.190	.189	.187	.185	.183	.181	.180	.178
40	.176	.174	.172	.170	.169	.167	.165	.163	.162	.160
41	.158	.156	.154	.153	.151	.149	.147	.145	.144	.142
42	.140	.138	.136	.135	.133	.131	.129	.127	.126	.124
43	.122	.120	.119	.117	.115	.113	.112	.110	.108	.107
44	.105	.103	.101	.100	.098	.096	.094	.092	.090	.089
45	.087	.085	.084	.082	.080	.078	.077	.075	.073	.072
46	.070	.068	.066	.065	.063	.061	.059	.057	.056	.054
47	.052	.050	.049	.047	.045	.043	.042	.040	.038	.037
48	.035	.033	.031	.030	.028	.026	.024	.022	.020	.019
49	.017	.015	.014	.012	.010	.008	.007	.005	.003	.002
50	.000	−.002	−.003	−.005	−.007	−.008	−.010	−.012	−.014	−.015
51	−.017	−.019	−.020	−.022	−.024	−.026	−.028	−.030	−.031	−.033
52	−.035	−.037	−.038	−.040	−.042	−.043	−.045	−.047	−.049	−.050
53	−.052	−.054	−.056	−.057	−.059	−.061	−.063	−.065	−.066	−.068
54	−.070	−.072	−.073	−.075	−.077	−.078	−.080	−.082	−.084	−.085
55	−.087	−.089	−.090	−.092	−.094	−.096	−.098	−.100	−.101	−.103
56	−.105	−.107	−.108	−.110	−.112	−.113	−.115	−.117	−.119	−.120
57	−.122	−.124	−.126	−.127	−.129	−.131	−.133	−.135	−.136	−.138
58	−.140	−.142	−.144	−.145	−.147	−.149	−.151	−.153	−.154	−.156
59	−.158	−.160	−.162	−.163	−.165	−.167	−.169	−.170	−.172	−.174
60	−.176	−.178	−.180	−.181	−.183	−.185	−.187	−.189	−.190	−.192
61	−.194	−.196	−.198	−.200	−.202	−.203	−.205	−.207	−.209	−.211
62	−.213	−.215	−.217	−.218	−.220	−.222	−.224	−.225	−.227	−.229
63	−.231	−.233	−.235	−.237	−.239	−.240	−.242	−.244	−.246	−.248
64	−.250	−.252	−.254	−.256	−.258	−.259	−.261	−.263	−.265	−.267

Rf to R_M Conversion Table (continued)

hRf	0	1	2	3	4	5	6	7	8	9
65	−.269	−.271	−.273	−.275	−.277	−.278	−.280	−.282	−.284	−.286
66	−.288	−.290	−.292	−.294	−.296	−.298	−.300	−.302	−.304	−.306
67	−.308	−.310	−.312	−.314	−.316	−.317	−.319	−.321	−.323	−.325
68	−.327	−.329	−.331	−.333	−.335	−.337	−.339	−.341	−.343	−.345
69	−.347	−.349	−.351	−.353	−.355	−.357	−.360	−.362	−.364	−.366
70	−.368	−.370	−.372	−.374	−.376	−.378	−.381	−.383	−.385	−.387
71	−.389	−.391	−.393	−.395	−.397	−.399	−.402	−.404	−.406	−.408
72	−.410	−.412	−.414	−.417	−.419	−.421	−.423	−.425	−.428	−.430
73	−.432	−.434	−.436	−.439	−.441	−.443	−.445	−.447	−.450	−.452
74	−.454	−.456	−.459	−.461	−.463	−.465	−.468	−.470	−.472	−.475
75	−.477	−.479	−.482	−.484	−.487	−.489	−.491	−.494	−.496	−.499
76	−.501	−.503	−.506	−.508	−.511	−.513	−.515	−.518	−.520	−.523
77	−.525	−.527	−.530	−.532	−.535	−.537	−.540	−.542	−.545	−.547
78	−.550	−.552	−.555	−.557	−.560	−.562	−.565	−.567	−.570	−.572
79	−.575	−.578	−.580	−.583	−.586	−.589	−.591	−.594	−.597	−.599
80	−.602	−.605	−.607	−.610	−.613	−.616	−.619	−.621	−.624	−.627
81	−.630	−.633	−.635	−.638	−.641	−.644	−.647	−.650	−.653	−.656
82	−.659	−.662	−.665	−.667	−.670	−.673	−.676	−.679	−.682	−.685
83	−.689	−.692	−.695	−.698	−.701	−.704	−.707	−.711	−.714	−.717
84	−.720	−.723	−.727	−.730	−.733	−.736	−.740	−.743	−.747	−.750
85	−.753	−.757	−.760	−.764	−.767	−.770	−.774	−.778	−.781	−.785
86	−.788	−.792	−.796	−.799	−.803	−.807	−.810	−.814	−.818	−.822
87	−.826	−.829	−.833	−.837	−.841	−.845	−.849	−.853	−.857	−.861
88	−.865	−.869	−.874	−.878	−.882	−.886	−.891	−.895	−.899	−.904
89	−.908	−.913	−.917	−.922	−.926	−.931	−.935	−.940	−.945	−.949
90	−.954	−.959	−.964	−.969	−.974	−.979	−.984	−.989	−.994	−1.000
91	−1.005	−1.010	−1.015	−1.021	−1.026	−1.032	−1.038	−1.043	−1.049	−1.055
92	−1.061	−1.067	−1.073	−1.079	−1.085	−1.091	−1.097	−1.104	−1.110	−1.117
93	−1.123	−1.130	−1.137	−1.144	−1.151	−1.158	−1.165	−1.172	−1.180	−1.187
94	−1.195	−1.203	−1.211	−1.219	−1.227	−1.235	−1.243	−1.252	−1.261	−1.270
95	−1.279	−1.288	−1.297	−1.307	−1.317	−1.327	−1.337	−1.347	−1.358	−1.369
96	−1.380	−1.392	−1.403	−1.415	−1.428	−1.440	−1.453	−1.467	−1.481	−1.495
97	−1.510	−1.525	−1.540	−1.557	−1.574	−1.591	−1.609	−1.628	−1.648	−1.669
98	−1.690	−1.713	−1.737	−1.762	−1.789	−1.817	−1.848	−1.881	−1.916	−1.954
99	−1.996	−2.042	−2.093	−2.152	−2.219	−2.299	−2.396	−2.522	−2.698	−3.000

ventional TLC ξ amounts to about 1.1–1.2.[3] Impregnation of the dry adsorbent with solvent vapors (for technique see Reference 4) or with a liquid leads to an increase of ξ.[5] On the other hand, partial evaporation of the mobile phase during chromatography (for technique see Reference 6) leads to a decrease of ξ, to an extent being dependent on Rf.

Chromatographical solvent demixing—brought about by preferential adsorption of solvent components (frontal analysis)[7, 8]—can affect the chromatographic behavior so much that conventionally measured Rf-values may become meaningless. Therefore, if the purpose of investigation requires the calculation of R_M-values, chromatographic systems involving multicomponent solvents should be tested for suitability. This can be done by applying the same mixture of the substances involved several times on a diagonal starting line.[3, 8] The system is suitable without any correction if straight lines can be drawn which connect the corresponding substance spots and cross the solvent front and the diagonal starting line at the same point. A correction must be made if all straight lines connecting the substance spots cross the diagonal starting line at one point *behind* the solvent front. In this case a demixing line (α-, β-, . . or ω-front) is present, going through the mentioned crossing point and being parallel to the solvent front. Rf- and R_M-values must be related to this front (*e.g.*, β-front, giving $^\beta$Rf- and $^\beta R_M$-values). If the lines connecting the substance spots are not straight lines, the Rf-values determined in this chromatographic system usually cannot be used for the aforementioned purposes.

Therefore, before trying to calculate R_M-values the investigator is cautioned to check carefully the meaning of the observed Rf-values. If a critical examination shows that the observed values or their products with a constant factor ξ are true Rf-values (mean values of at least five determinations), then the above table[9] will be helpful in converting them to meaningful R_M-values.

REFERENCES

1. Snyder, L. R.   Advan. Chromatogr. **4**, 3 (1967).
2. Giddings, J. C., G. H. Stewart, A. L. Ruoff.   J. Chromatog. **3**, 239 (1960).
3. Brenner, M., A Niederwieser, G. Pataki, and R. Weber.   In *Dünnschichtchromatographie* (Berlin: Springer-Verlag, 1962), p 79–137.
4. Geiss, F., and H. Schlitt.   Chromatographia **1**, 392–402 (1968).
5. Snyder, L. R.   J. Chromatog. **28**, 432 (1967).
6. Niederwieser, A.   Chromatographia **2**, 362–375 (1969).
7. Niederwieser, A., and M. Brenner.   Experientia **21**, 50 and 150 (1965).
8. Niederwieser, A., and C. G. Honegger.   Advan. Chromatogr. **2**, 123 (1965).
9. Niederwieser, A.   Thesis, University of Basle, 1962.

Index

2-Acetamido-1-(L-β-aspartamido)-1,2-
  dideoxy-β-D-glucose, 182
Acetolysis of
  glycopeptides, 186
  phospholipids, 85
  polysaccharides, 184ff
N-Acetylamines DANS-, 115
Acetylceramides, 85
Acetyldiglycerides, 83
Acetylenic acids, 80
  hydroxy, 80
Acetylneuraminic acids, 184
Acetyloligosaccharides, 185ff
Acids (see also Fatty acids), 15, 16, 25,
  26, 40, 42
  dienoic, 81
  polyunsaturated, cis-, trans-, 79
  radioactive methylation, 66
Acyl phospholipids, 87
Alcohols, fatty-, 75
  radioactive acetylation, 66
Aldehydes
  fatty-, 75
  monoenoic, 82
Alkenyl phospholipids, 87
Amines, 94ff
  aliphatic diamines, 118
  DANS-derivatives, 94ff
  ion-exchange chromatography, 96
  gas chromatography, 96
  catecholamines, 96, 117ff
  charge-transfer complexes, 97
  3,5-dinitrobenzamides, 97
  2,4-dinitrophenyl derivatives, 97
  microdetection in tissues, 135
  ninhydrin reaction, 96
  4-nitroazobenzene-carbon-
    4-amides, 97
  4-phenylazobenzene sulfonamides, 97
  pipsyl derivatives 97
  p-toluene sulfonates, 97

Amino acids, 146, 150
  DANS-derivatives, 98, 99, 106, 109,
    130
  radio-TLC, 67
  131I-pipsyl derivatives, 97
  iodoamino acids, 146ff
γ-Aminobutyric acid, 110, 137
5-Amino-4-imidazole carboxamide, 110
1-Aminonaphthalene-5-sulfonic acid,
  109
Amino sugars (see Hexosamines)
Animal triglycerides, 83
Area scraping, radioassay, 53
Argentation-TLC, 74ff
  reversed-phase, 87
Aspartamido-glucosaminic linkage, 182
Aspirator tube, for elution, 54
Autoradiography, 53, 55, 57
Azelao glycerides, 83

Beta camera, 53, 60
Biogenic amines, 95ff
Boric acid, 18, 79
  complexes of steroids, 18
  impregnation with, 79

Carbohydrates (see also Mono-,
    Oligosaccharides)
  carbohydrate–peptide linkage, 182
  radio-TLC, 67
  side chains of glycoproteins, 168ff
Catecholamines
  GLC of trifluoroacetates, 96
  DANS-derivatives, 117ff
Ceramide acetates, 85
Chemical potential μ, 2
7-Chloro-4-nitrobenzo-2-oxa-1,3-diazole,
  97
Choline, 85
  phosphatidyl-, 85
  DANS-derivative, 99, 119, 133

Cis-, *trans*-polyunsaturated fatty acids, 79
Cleavage products of fatty acids, 77
Combustion analysis, radioassay, 53, 61
Combustion techniques, 67
Computer analysis system for TLC, 66
Computer monitoring, on-line, 66
Contamination, radioactive, 61
Conversion table Rf-R$_M$ (appendix), 215ff
Countercurrent distribution, 76, 77
Cyclopentenyl acids, 80
Cyclopropene acids, 80

DANS-Derivatives, 94ff
  amines, 94ff
  N-acetylamines, 115, 116
  aliphatic diamines, 99, 118
  amino acids, 98, 106, 109, 130
  amino acids, N-substituted, 99
  amino sugars, 110, 120
  catecholamines, 117ff
  fluorescence spectra, 127, 128
  quantitative determination, 127ff
Deacylation of oligosaccharides, 188
Decomposition by radiation, 62
Densitometric determination *in situ*
    (*see also* Quantitative determination, scanning)
  DANS-amines (fluorometry), 131–135, 137
  DNP-amines, 97
  neutral sugars, 177
  osamines, 177
Deoxynucleotides, 210
Deoxyoligonucleotides, 198, 207, 210
Deoxyoligonucleotide triesters, 198ff
  preparative, 202
Deoxypolynucleotides, 207
Detection by hydrogen flame on TLC, 61
Detection of
  2-acetamido-1-(L-β-aspartamido)-1,2-dideoxy-β-D-glucose, 182
  acetylated sugars, 186
  iodoamino acids, 157ff
  oligosaccharides, 183
  radioactivity (*see* Radioassay), 52ff
  sugars, 172–174, 178, 181, 182
Determination (*see* Quantitative determination)
Diacyl glycerophosphate, 86
Diacyl phospholipids, 87
Dialkenyl phosphatidyl ethanolamine, 85
Dienoic acids, 81

Diglycerides, 82–84
  aceto-, 83
  acetate, trityl derivatives, 85
  galactosyl-, 87
Dihydroxy fatty acids, threo-, erythro-, 79
1-Dimethylamino-naphthalene-5-sulfonyl chloride (*see also* DANS-), 98, 108
Dimethylphosphatidates, 83, 85, 86
3,5-Dinitrobenzamides, 97
2,4-Dinitrobenzene sulfonic acid, 97
2,4-Dinitrophenyl amines, 97
Disaccharides, 173
  acetyl-, 186

Electrophoresis
  amines, 96
  combination with TLC, 96, 198, 199
  ion-exchange of polynucleotides, 198, 199
  oligonucleotides, 198, 199
Elution analysis, 53, 128, 181
  radiometric procedures, 53ff
Enzyme activity estimation by dansylation, 137
Epoxy fatty acids, 76, 79
Esters
  fatty acid methyl, 76, 77
  sterol, 82
  wax, 82
Ethanolamine
  dialkenylphosphatidyl, 85
  phosphatidyl, 85, 86, 87
  plasmalogens, 85
Ethers, glyceryl, 82
Ethylenic acids, *trans*-, 79

Fatty acids (*see also* Acids), 75ff
  chemically altered, 80
  cyclopentenyl, 80
  cyclopropene, 80
  dihydroxy, 79
  epoxy, 76, 79
  furanoid, 80
  halohydroxy, 79
  hydrogenation of polyunsaturated-, 81
  hydroxy, 76, 79, 83
  methyl esters, 76, 77
  polyunsaturated, 79
  substituted, 79
  unsaturated, 78, 79
Fatty alcohols, 75
Fatty aldehydes, 75
Flame detector (hydrogen) for TLC, 61

Fluorescence
    DANS-amines, 127ff
    detection of iodoamino acids, 159
    quantum yield, 133
    scanning (DANS), 131, 134
    spectra of DANS-amines, 128
Fluoro-2,4-dinitrobenzene, 96
Fluorography, radioassay, 57
Fluorometry of amines, 96, 127ff
    after elution, 128
    in situ, 131–135, 137
Fundamental constant (R_M-function), 5, 13
Furanoid fatty acids, 80

Galactosamine (*see* Hexosamines)
Galactosyl diglycerides, 87
Gas-liquid chromatography, 53, 67
    of amines, 96
    of catecholamine trifluoroacetates, 96
Gas-liquid radiochromatography, 53, 67
Glucosamine (*see* Hexosamines)
Glycerides (*see also* Di-, Triglycerides)
    neutral, 64, 76, 82
    azelao, 83
Glycerophosphate, diacyl, 86
Glyceryl ethers, 82
Glycolipids, 82, 84, 85, 87
Glycolipid species, 87
Glycopeptides, 180
    hydrolysates, 178, 180
    hydrolysis, 171, 175
    partial hydrolysis, 182, 183
Glycoproteins, 180
    carbohydrate–peptide linkage, 182
    carbohydrate side chains, 168ff
    hydrolysis, 170, 175
    partial hydrolysis, 181ff
Gmelin & Virtanen reagent, detection of iodoamino acids, 159
G(−M)-value, 62
Ground constant (R_M-function), 5, 13
Group definition in Martin's relation, 10, 14

Herring lecithins, 83
Heteropolysaccharide (*see also* Glycoproteins), 170, 180–182
    partial hydrolysis, 181, 182
Hexosamines, 175–180
    aspartamido–glucosaminic linkage, 182
    DANS-derivatives, 110, 120
    methyl ethers, 190, 191
    quantitative determination, 176, 177, 180

Hexosamines (*cont'd*)
    molecular ratio, 179, 180
    separation, 175, 176, 179
Hexoses (*see also* Monosaccharides), 176–179, 181, 183
Hydrogenation of polyunsaturated fatty acids, 81
Hydrogenated vegetable oils, 81
Hydrogen flame detector for TLC, 61
Hydrolysis of glycopeptides, 171, 175
Hydrolysis of glycoproteins
    by ion-exchanger, 182, 183
    for hexosamines, 175
    for neutral sugars, 170
    partial, 181, 182, 184
Hydroxy fatty acids, 76, 79, 83
Hydroxy acetylenic acids, 80

Impregnated papers, 7
Impregnation, method of, 7, 76, 79
Iodoamino acids, 146ff
    aqueous solvents, 156
    detection by chemical reagents, 156
    detection by fluorescence, 159
    extraction from serum, 163, 164
    Gmelin & Virtanen reagent, 159
    Kolthoff & Sandell reagent, 158
    on cellulose, 154
    on silica gel, 150
    quantitative determination, 161, 162
[131]I-Iodobenzene-*p*-sulfonyl chloride (pipsyl reagent for amines, amino acids), 97
Iodotyrosines in blood, 147
Ion-exchange chromatography of amines, 96
Ion-exchange electrophoresis of poly-nucleotides, 198, 199
Isomers
    cis-, *trans-*, 76, 79, 80, 81
    positional, 81, 82
    threo-, *erythro-*, 79, 82
Isotopic fractionation, 63

Kolthoff & Sandell reagent for quantitation of iodoamino acids, 158

Labeled (radioactively)
    derivatives, 66
    internal standards, 63
    lipids, 64, 66
    substrates, 78
Lecithins, 85–87
    herring, 83
    liver, 86
Lipase, 64

Lipids, 74ff
  labeled, 64, 66
  quantitation by liquid scintillation
    quenching, 63
  radio-TLC, 67
  rat skin surface, 78
Liquid scintillation radioassay, 58
  quenching for quantitative determinations, 63

Martin's relation (*see* R_M-Function), 1ff
Mass measurements by radio labeling, 53
Mass spectrometry, 96
Methylated sugars, 189ff
Methylation of polysaccharides, 189
Methylglucosides, 189, 191
Monoenoic aldehydes, 82
Monosaccharides, 170ff
  acetylated, 186ff
  detection, 172ff, 181, 182
  methyl ethers, 189ff
  neutral monosaccharides, 170ff
    on cellulose layers, 171, 174, 183
    on silica gel layers, 172, 181, 183
    on layers of synthetic polymers, 174, 175
    quantitative determination, 176, 177, 180, 181
Mucopolysaccharide hydrolysate, 180
Mucoprotein hydrolysate, 180

Neuraminic acids, acetylated, 184
Neutral glycerides, 82
Neutral sugars (*see also* Monosaccharides), 170ff
Ninhydrin reaction of amines, 96
4'-Nitroazobenzene-carbon-4-amides, 97
Nomenclature used in this volume, xiii
Nucleic acids radio-TLC, 67
Nucleosides, 197ff
Nucleoside polyphosphates, 197
Nucleotides, 197ff, 205, 212
  derivatives, 198ff, 206, 212

Oils (*see also* Triglycerides)
  partially hydrogenated, 81
  seed, 78
  vegetable, 81
Oligonucleotides, 196ff
  derivatives, 198ff
  on cellulose layers, 198
  on silica gel layers, 204ff
  trityl-substituted, 200–202

Oligosaccharides, 181ff
  acetylated, 185
  deacylation of acetylated, 188
  detection, 183
  separation, 181, 183, 184
On-line computer monitoring, 66
Osamines, densitometric determination, 177

Partition chromatography, 2
Partition coefficient, 2, 4
PEI-Cellulose, 198
Peptides
  hydrolysis of glycopeptides, 171, 175
  peptide–carbohydrate linkage, 182
Phase ratio, 4, 7, 9
Phenols, structure and R_M-function, 28ff
4-Phenylazobenzene sulfonamides, 97
Phosphatidates, dimethyl-, 83, 85, 86
Phosphatidic acid, 86
Phosphatidyl choline, 85
Phosphatidyl ethanolamine, 85
  dialkenyl-, 85
Phospholipase C, 85
Phospholipase D, 86
Phospholipids 78, 82, 84–87
  acyl, 87
  alkenyl, 87
  diacyl, 87
  species, 86
Photodensitometry
  of autoradiograms, 57
  of sugars, 177
[131]I-Pipsyl derivatives, 97
Plasmalogens
  ethanolamine, 85
  species, 86
Polyamines, 96
Polynucleotides, 197, 198
  deoxy-, 207
Polysaccharides, 170, 184
  acetolysis, 184, 185
  methylation, 189
  partial hydrolysate, 182ff
Polyunsaturated acids
  cis-, trans-, 79
  hydrogenation, 81
Positional isomers, 81, 82
Prostaglandins, 79
Proteins, radio-TLC, 67

Quantitative determination (*see also* Densitometric determination)
  by liquid scintillation quenching, 63
  using labeled reagents, 65
  amino sugars, 176–180

Quantitative determination (*cont'd*)
  DANS-amines, 127ff
  DANS-amino acids, 130
  iodoamino acids, 161
  neutral sugars, 176–181

Radiation decomposition, 53, 61, 62
Radiation safety, 53, 61
Radioactive contamination, 61
Radioactively labeled substrates, 78
Radioassay, 52ff
  autoradiography, 53, 57
  beta camera, 53, 60
  combustion analysis, 53, 61, 67
  elution analysis, 53
  liquid scintillation, 58, 63
  noncombustion techniques, 68
  strip scanning, 53, 55, 58, 59, 64
Radiochromatography, 52ff
Radio gas-liquid chromatography, 53, 67
Radiometric procedures, 53, 54
Radio purity, 53, 62
Radio-TLC, 52ff
  amino acids, 67
  carbohydrates, 67
  lipids, 64, 67
  nucleic acids, 67
  proteins, 67
  steroids, 67
Raoult's law, 2
Reaction-gas chromatography, 96
Reversed-phase TLC, 8, 87
  argentation-TLC, 87
Rf-R_M conversion, 215ff
Ribonucleotides, 208
Ribooligonucleotides, 198, 207, 208
R_M, 5, 12, 215
  changes by chemical reaction, 43
  $R_{M(g)}$ definition, 12
  $R_{M(g)}$ determination, 12, 46
  $R_{M(r)}$, 12, 43
  $R_{M(s)}$, 12, 42, 43
  $R_{M(aromatic\ H)}$, 30
  $R_{M,branching)}$, 31
  $R_{(H-bonding)}$, 30, 41
  $R_{M(olefinic\ H)}$, 30
  $R_{M(ring\ attached\ CH_2)}$, 29
  R_M-Rf conversion table, 215ff
R_M-Function, 1ff
  branching parameter, 31
  for structural elucidations, 41
  ground constant, 5, 13
  "group" definition, 10, 14
  steric factors, 39

R_M-Values of
  amines, 37
  aniline derivatives, 38
  carboxylic acids, 15, 16, 25, 26, 40, 42
  17α-deoxy-keto steroids, 21
  dinitrobenzoates, 15
  dinitrophenyl hydrazides of fatty acids, 15
  dinitrophenyl hydrazones, 15
  fatty acids, 27
  hydroxy acids, 15, 25
  17α-hydroxy-keto steroids, 22
  nitrophenols, 16
  phenols, 16, 28ff, 36
  phenoxyacetic acids, 16
  progesterone derivatives, 18, 19, 23
  steroids, 17ff, 39
  t-RNA, hydrolysate of, 198, 199

Scanning (*see also* Densitometric determination) 53, 55, 56, 131–135, 177–180
  fluorometric, 131–135, 137
Scintillation
  liquid, radioassay, 58, 63
  photo, strip scanner, 56
Scraping devices, 59, 129
Seed oils, 78
Sialic acid (N-acetyl neuraminic acid), 184
Silver ion complexes, 76
Skin surface lipids, rats, 78
Species of
  glycolipids, 87
  phospholipids, 86
  plasmalogens, 86
  triglycerides, 83, 84
Sphingomyelins, 85
Steroids
  radio-TLC, 67
  R_M relation and structure, 17ff, 39
Sterols, 67, 76
  esters, 82
  radio-TLC, 67
Strip scanning, radiometry, 53, 55, 58, 59, 64
Structural analysis using R_M-function, 1, 41ff
Substituted fatty acids, 79
Sugars (*see* Monosaccharides)
System constant (R_M-function), 5, 13

Tankless chromatography, 7
threo-, *erythro*-Configuration, 79, 82
  dihydroxy fatty acids, 79

Thyroid hormones, 146ff
  extraction from serum, 163, 164
Thyroid secretion products, 147
trans-Ethylenic acids, 79
trans-Unsaturated fatty acids, 78
Trifluoroacetates of catecholamines,
  GLC, 96
Triglycerides, 76, 82, 83, 84
  animal, 83
  milk fat, 83
  species, 83, 84
  vegetable, 83
2,4,6-Trinitrobenzene sulfonic acid, 96
Triphenyltetrazolium chloride (TTC)
  for detection of sugars, 178, 180
Trityl derivatives of
  deoxyoligonucleotides, 200–202
  diglycerides, 85

Unsaturated fatty acids, *cis*-, *trans*-
  (*see also* Argentation-TLC), 78,
  79

Vegetable oils, partially hydrogenated,
  81
Vegetable triglycerides, 83

Wax esters, 82

Zonal profile scans, radioassay, 53, 58,
  64
Zonal scraper, 59
Zone analysis, radioassay, 53

*The text of this book was typeset at
SSPA Typesetting, Inc., Carmel, Indiana,
in 10-point Times Roman, with 2-point
leading. The chapter headings are in
14-point Craw Modern. The printing was done
by offset lithography by Braun-Brumfield, Inc.,
Ann Arbor, Michigan, and the paper is
60# Northville. The book is bound in
Columbia linen cloth.*